SIMPLE, DECENT
Cooking

PARTNERS IN THE KITCHEN
Habitat for Humanity

Edited, Designed and Manufactured by
Favorite Recipes® Press
an imprint of

FRP™

P.O. Box 305142, Nashville, Tennessee 37230
800-358-0560

Library of Congress Number: 97-72092
ISBN: 1-887921-29-X

Manufactured in the United States of America
First Printing: 1997   35,000 copies

Designer: Mark Földz
Project Manager: Debbie Van Mol

Cover Art by Sally Stockbridge
Photograph on Back Cover by Robert Baker

CONTENTS

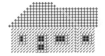

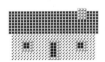

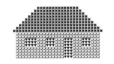

$\mathscr{F}$OREWORD

Linda Fuller
Co-Founder
Habitat for
Humanity
International

I am so pleased with the tremendous success of the Partners in the Kitchen cookbook series. Hundreds of copies of *From Our House To Yours* and *Home Sweet Habitat* are being sold every week. I expect *Simple, Decent Cooking* to be just as popular.

For many of us, the world's pace seems to hasten each day, shrinking the time we have for shopping and cooking, and making the hours we spend with family and friends even more precious. That is why I believe this cookbook, featuring simple and easy-to-prepare recipes, is so very timely.

The recipes come from Habitat homeowners, volunteers, board members and staff members, busy people themselves, who have taken the time to share recipes and their favorite Habitat stories. I know you will enjoy reading them as much as I have.

A heartwarming letter came with a recipe from a Habitat homeowner. "I really enjoy the cookbooks and selling them," she wrote in part, "because it's for a good cause, more new homes for families."

Yes, that is what it's all about...more homes for families desperately in need of simple, decent, affordable places to live. As we use these cookbooks in our kitchens, sell them to raise funds for Habitat's work and buy them as gifts for friends and relatives, let's be mindful of the tangible results...building decent houses and decent communities in which everyone can live and grow into all that God intended.

I want to express my deep appreciation to all of those who played a part in developing this third cookbook in the Partners in the Kitchen series. Sheilla Snell and Joy Highnote at Habitat for Humanity International have worked steadily by my side. Their skills and hard work have made this book possible. We are fortunate to have another beautiful cover by Sally Stockbridge, the artist who designed the first two cookbook covers. Favorite Recipes Press continues to amaze us with their personal service, ideas and cooperation in making this series of cookbooks true "works of art." Laurel Rummel, art director at Habitat Headquarters, also was instrumental in helping make this cookbook as beautiful as it is useful. Thanks, especially, to those who shared recipes. The book couldn't have happened without you.

To everyone using *Simple, Decent Cooking*, warm wishes for healthy, happy mealtimes with those you love. Enjoy!

Linda Fuller
Editor

Jesus has been found worthy of greater honor than Moses, just as the builder of a house has greater honor than the house itself.

Hebrews 3:3

5

NUTRITIONAL PROFILE GUIDELINES

The editors have attempted to present these family recipes in a form that allows approximate nutritional values to be computed. Persons with dietary or health problems or whose diets require close monitoring should not rely solely on the nutritional information provided. They should consult their physicians or a registered dietitian for specific information.

Abbreviations for Nutritional Profile

Cal — Calories
Prot — Protein
Carbo — Carbohydrates
Fiber — Dietary Fiber
T Fat — Total Fat

Chol — Cholesterol
Sod — Sodium
g — grams
mg — milligrams

Nutritional information for these recipes is computed from information derived from many sources, including materials supplied by the United States Department of Agriculture, computer databanks, and journals in which the information is assumed to be in the public domain. However, many specialty items, new products, and processed foods may not be available from these sources or may vary from the average values used in these profiles. More information on new and/or specific products may be obtained by reading the nutrient labels. Unless otherwise specified, the nutritional profile of these recipes is based on all measurements being level.

- Artificial sweeteners vary in use and strength so should be used "to taste," using the recipe ingredients as a guideline. Sweeteners using aspartame (NutraSweet and Equal) should not be used as a sweetener in recipes involving prolonged heating, which reduces the sweet taste. For further information on the use of these sweeteners, refer to the package.
- Alcoholic ingredients have been analyzed for the basic ingredients, although cooking causes the evaporation of alcohol, thus decreasing caloric content.
- Buttermilk, sour cream, and yogurt are the types available commercially.
- Cake mixes that are prepared using package directions include 3 eggs and $1/2$ cup oil.
- Chicken, cooked for boning and chopping, has been roasted; this method yields the lowest caloric values.
- Cottage cheese is cream-style with 4.2% creaming mixture. Dry curd cottage cheese has no creaming mixture.
- Eggs are all large. To avoid raw eggs that may carry salmonella, as in eggnog or 6-week muffin batter, use an equivalent amount of commercial egg substitute.
- Flour is unsifted all-purpose flour.
- Garnishes, serving suggestions, and other optional additions and variations are not included in the profile.
- Margarine and butter are regular, not whipped or presoftened.
- Milk is whole milk, 3.5% butterfat. Low-fat milk is 1% butterfat. Evaporated milk is whole milk with 60% of the water removed.
- Oil is any type of vegetable cooking oil. Shortening is hydrogenated vegetable shortening.
- Salt and other ingredients to taste as noted in the ingredients have not been included in the nutritional profile.
- If a choice of ingredients has been given, the nutritional profile reflects the first option. If a choice of amounts has been given, the nutritional profile reflects the greater amount.

Photograph at right by Robert Baker

APPETIZERS

The Lord declares to you that the Lord himself
will establish a house for you.

2 Samuel 7:11b

APPETIZERS

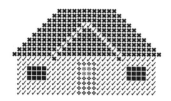

HFH RECIPE FOR A HOME

YIELD: 1 HFH HOUSE

A large dream
Lots of faith
Much excitement
Bunch of volunteers and friends

Joyful hearts
Many hands
Loads of materials
God's love

Combine dream, faith and excitement with volunteers and mix well. Add joyful hearts and many hands, stirring constantly until friendships develop. Stir in loads of materials to produce a Habitat for Humanity House, to be taken care of by a grateful partner family. Top with the amazing grace of God's love.

Annabelle Woods, Hamilton County HFH, Noblesville, IN

GLOWING FRUIT PUNCH

YIELD: 1 GALLON

1	quart apple juice	2	quarts ginger ale
1	(6-ounce) can frozen orange juice concentrate	1	pint lemon or orange sherbet
1	(6-ounce) can frozen lemonade concentrate		

Mix apple juice, orange juice concentrate and lemonade concentrate in punch bowl. Stir in ginger ale. Add sherbet and mix gently. Ladle into punch cups and serve immediately.

Approx Per Serving: Cal 140; Prot 1 g; Carbo 34 g; T Fat 1 g; 4% Calories from Fat; Chol 1 mg; Fiber <1 g; Sod 22 mg

Denise C. Otradovec, Spokane HFH, Veradale, WA

FRUIT SHAKE

YIELD: 2 SERVINGS

1	large banana, sliced	1/4	cup cold water
1	cup sliced strawberries, chilled		

Process banana, strawberries and cold water in blender until almost smooth. Add additional water if desired for thinner consistency. Pour over ice in glass. May substitute berries, peaches, melons, kiwifruit or apples for strawberries.

Approx Per Serving: Cal 77; Prot 1 g; Carbo 19 g; T Fat 1 g; 6% Calories from Fat; Chol 0 mg; Fiber 2 g; Sod 1 mg

Ellen Patton, Lebanon Area HFH, Waynesville, OH

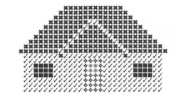

FRUIT SLUSH

YIELD: 20 SERVINGS

6	bananas, mashed	1	(12-ounce) can frozen orange juice concentrate
3	cups crushed pineapple		
3	cups sugar	1	orange juice can water
2	(8-ounce) cans mandarin oranges	30	ounces lemon-lime soda

Mix bananas, pineapple and sugar in bowl. Stir in undrained oranges and remaining ingredients. Freeze, covered, until firm. Let stand at room temperature for 1 to 2 hours before serving. Spoon into glasses.

Approx Per Serving: Cal 231; Prot 1 g; Carbo 59 g; T Fat <1 g; 1% Calories from Fat; Chol 0 mg; Fiber 1 g; Sod 4 mg

Rockford Area HFH, Rockford, IL

HOT ARTICHOKE DIP

YIELD: 12 SERVINGS

1	(14-ounce) can artichoke hearts, drained	1	cup mayonnaise
		1	teaspoon lemon juice
1	cup freshly grated Parmesan cheese	1/8	teaspoon garlic salt

Mash artichokes in bowl. Stir in cheese, mayonnaise, lemon juice and garlic salt. Spoon into shallow baking dish. Bake at 350 degrees for 10 minutes. Serve with wheat crackers.

Approx Per Serving: Cal 179; Prot 4 g; Carbo 3 g; T Fat 17 g; 85% Calories from Fat; Chol 17 mg; Fiber 0 g; Sod 389 mg

Bonnie Watson, HFHI and Former International Partner
Americus, GA

BACON AND TOMATO DIP

YIELD: 25 SERVINGS

1	pound bacon, crisp-fried, crumbled	1	cup mayonnaise-type salad dressing
1 1/2	cups sour cream	1	tomato, chopped

Combine all ingredients in bowl and mix well. Chill, covered, for 1 hour. Serve with fresh vegetables and/or bagel chips.

Approx Per Serving: Cal 116; Prot 1 g; Carbo 3 g; T Fat 11 g; 88% Calories from Fat; Chol 14 mg; Fiber <1 g; Sod 104 mg

Mary Paluso, Milwaukee HFH, Brookfield, WI

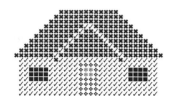

BLACK BEAN SALSA

YIELD: 32 SERVINGS

2	cups canned black beans, rinsed, drained	1/2	cup chopped fresh cilantro or mint
1/2	cup whole kernel corn, cooked, drained	1	(4-ounce) can green chiles, drained, chopped
1/2	cup chopped red bell pepper	3	to 4 tablespoons lime juice
1/2	cup chopped green bell pepper	2	to 3 tablespoons olive oil
1/2	cup chopped onion	1/2	teaspoon cumin
			Salt and pepper to taste

Combine beans, corn, red pepper, green pepper, onion, cilantro, chiles, lime juice, olive oil, cumin, salt and pepper in bowl and mix well. Adjust seasonings, adding additional lime juice if desired.

Approx Per Serving: Cal 29; Prot 1 g; Carbo 3 g; T Fat 1 g; 42% Calories from Fat; Chol 0 mg; Fiber 1 g; Sod 100 mg

Janice Drinan, Greater Portland HFH, Portland, ME

BLACK BEAN CORN DIP

YIELD: 16 SERVINGS

1	(15-ounce) can baby corn, drained, rinsed	1/2	cup coarsely chopped onion
1	(15-ounce) can black beans, drained, rinsed	1/2	cup balsamic vinegar
		1/3	cup olive oil

Cut corn into 1/2- to 3/4-inch pieces. Combine corn, black beans, onion, balsamic vinegar and olive oil in bowl and mix well. Chill, covered, for 4 hours or longer. Serve with tortilla chips. The more expensive brands of balsamic vinegar and olive oil will have a better flavor and thus produce a more flavorful dip.

Approx Per Serving: Cal 90; Prot 2 g; Carbo 11 g; T Fat 5 g; 47% Calories from Fat; Chol 0 mg; Fiber 2 g; Sod 170 mg

Margy Davey, Oshkosh HFH, Oshkosh, WI

Photo by Robert Baker

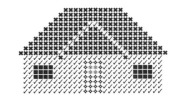

INSTANT SALSA

YIELD: 10 SERVINGS

1	(16-ounce) can Italian-style stewed tomatoes	1	medium jalapeño, chopped
1/2	onion, chopped	1	bunch cilantro, chopped
8	cloves of garlic, chopped		Juice of 1 lemon
		1/2	teaspoon salt

Combine undrained tomatoes, onion, garlic, jalapeño, cilantro, lemon juice and salt in bowl and mix well. Serve with corn chips.

Approx Per Serving: Cal 23; Prot 1 g; Carbo 5 g; T Fat <1 g; 2% Calories from Fat; Chol 0 mg; Fiber 1 g; Sod 204 mg

Patricia McCormick, North Kitsap County HFH, Poulsboro, WA

SASSY SALSA

YIELD: 24 SERVINGS

2	cups canned black beans, rinsed, drained	2	cups medium or hot salsa
2	cups Mexicorn, drained	1	large tomato, chopped
		1	teaspoon cayenne

Combine beans, Mexicorn, salsa, tomato and cayenne in saucepan and mix well. Simmer for 10 minutes, stirring occasionally. Serve hot or cold with corn chips.

Approx Per Serving: Cal 40; Prot 2 g; Carbo 8 g; T Fat <1 g; 7% Calories from Fat; Chol 0 mg; Fiber 2 g; Sod 377 mg

Pearl Van Hareren, Blue Spruce HFH, Evergreen, CO

BLEU CHEESE DIP

YIELD: 12 SERVINGS

2	cups sour cream	2	teaspoons fresh lemon juice
4	ounces bleu cheese, crumbled		

Combine sour cream, bleu cheese and lemon juice in bowl and mix well. Chill, covered, for 2 to 3 hours. Serve with corn chips or as a salad dressing or topping for baked potatoes.

Approx Per Serving: Cal 116; Prot 3 g; Carbo 2 g; T Fat 11 g; 82% Calories from Fat; Chol 24 mg; Fiber 0 g; Sod 152 mg

Sheilla W. Snell, HFHI, Americus, GA

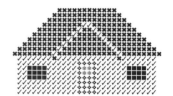

BROCCOLI DIP

YIELD: 15 SERVINGS

2	(10-ounce) packages frozen chopped broccoli	1	(4-ounce) can green chiles, drained, chopped
16	ounces Velveeta cheese, cubed	1/8	teaspoon garlic powder
1	(10-ounce) can cream of mushroom soup		

Cook broccoli using package directions; drain. Combine broccoli, cheese, soup, chiles and garlic in slow cooker and mix well. Cook until cheese melts and dip is heated through, stirring occasionally. Serve with tortilla chips or corn chips.

Approx Per Serving: Cal 141; Prot 8 g; Carbo 6 g; T Fat 9 g; 59% Calories from Fat; Chol 25 mg; Fiber 1 g; Sod 681 mg

Lois L. Gregory, Denton HFH, Sanger, TX

CRAB DIP

YIELD: 16 SERVINGS

1	(4-ounce) can crab meat, drained, flaked	1	tablespoon parsley flakes
1	cup mayonnaise	1	tablespoon sherry
1/2	cup sour cream	1	teaspoon lemon juice
1	onion, grated		Salt and pepper to taste

Mix crab meat, mayonnaise, sour cream, onion, parsley, sherry, lemon juice, salt and pepper in bowl. Chill, covered, for 5 hours or longer. Serve with fresh vegetables and/or chips.

Approx Per Serving: Cal 125; Prot 2 g; Carbo 1 g; T Fat 13 g; 89% Calories from Fat; Chol 18 mg; Fiber <1 g; Sod 106 mg

JoAnn Lyall, Fayetteville HFH, Fayetteville, AR

EMERGENCY HORS D'OEUVRE

YIELD: 8 SERVINGS

Quick and easy to prepare. Serve as an hors d'oeuvre or snack. It is spicy, nutritious and low in fat.

1	cup low-fat cottage cheese	2	tablespoons salsa

Mix cottage cheese and salsa in bowl. Serve with tortilla chips.

Approx Per Serving: Cal 27; Prot 4 g; Carbo 1 g; T Fat 1 g; 19% Calories from Fat; Chol 2 mg; Fiber <1 g; Sod 155 mg

F. R. Bliss, Greater New Bern HFH, New Bern, NC

FRUIT DIP

YIELD: 24 SERVINGS

1 (16-ounce) jar marshmallow creme

8 ounces cream cheese, softened
1 teaspoon ginger

Beat all ingredients in mixer bowl until smooth. Spoon into serving bowl. Serve with fresh fruit.

Approx Per Serving: Cal 96; Prot 1 g; Carbo 16 g; T Fat 3 g; 31% Calories from Fat; Chol 10 mg; Fiber 0 g; Sod 44 mg

Trish Snell, Sumter SC HFH, Sumter, SC

MOCHO NOCHO

YIELD: 15 SERVINGS

1 (16-ounce) can refried beans
2 (4-ounce) cans chopped green chiles, drained
1 cup salsa
8 ounces each Monterey Jack and Cheddar cheese, shredded

2 cups mashed avocados
Lime juice to taste
Salt and pepper to taste
1 cup sour cream
1 (4-ounce) can chopped black olives

Spread refried beans in 9x12-inch baking dish sprayed with nonstick cooking spray. Layer with chiles, salsa, Monterey Jack cheese and Cheddar cheese in order listed. Bake at 400 degrees until bubbly. Spread with mixture of avocados, lime juice, salt and pepper. Top with sour cream; sprinkle with olives. Serve with tortilla chips.

Approx Per Serving: Cal 250; Prot 11 g; Carbo 11 g; T Fat 19 g; 66% Calories from Fat; Chol 36 mg; Fiber 4 g; Sod 728 mg

Marianne Smith, Spokane HFH, Spokane, WA

PISTACHIO DIP

YIELD: 16 SERVINGS

1 (4-ounce) package pistachio instant pudding mix

2 cups plain yogurt

Mix pudding mix and yogurt in bowl. Chill for 4 hours or longer. Serve with sliced fresh fruit.

Approx Per Serving: Cal 47; Prot 1 g; Carbo 8 g; T Fat 1 g; 22% Calories from Fat; Chol 4 mg; Fiber 0 g; Sod 113 mg

Sandra L. Panchyshyn, Sullivan County HFH, Lake Huntington, NY

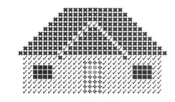

For a day in thy courts is better than a thousand. I had rather be a doorkeeper in the house of my God, than to dwell in the tents of wickedness.

Psalms 84:10

APPETIZERS

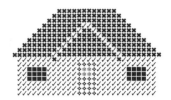

No way can HFH be beat. It provides a wonderful foundation for all the wonders it has brought people around the world.

Lucy S. Woodhouse, Georgetown County SC HFH

SHRIMP DIP

YIELD: 12 SERVINGS

Use fat-free products and decrease your fat grams as well as your guilt.

1   cup sour cream
1/3 cup cream cheese, softened
1   envelope Italian salad dressing mix

1   (4-ounce) can shrimp, drained
    Lemon juice to taste

Beat sour cream, cream cheese and dressing mix in mixer bowl until blended. Stir in shrimp and lemon juice. Chill, covered, for several hours. Serve with corn chips.

Approx Per Serving: Cal 79; Prot 3 g; Carbo 2 g; T Fat 6 g; 73% Calories from Fat; Chol 32 mg; Fiber <1 g; Sod 262 mg

Lucy S. Woodhouse, Georgetown County SC HFH, Georgetown, SC

SHRIMP MOLD

YIELD: 20 SERVINGS

2   teaspoons mayonnaise
1   envelope unflavored gelatin
1/3 cup water
1   (10-ounce) can tomato soup
2   (12-ounce) packages frozen cooked shrimp, thawed, cut into bite-size pieces

8   ounces cream cheese, cubed
1   cup mayonnaise
1/2 cup chopped celery
1/2 cup chopped green onions
1/4 teaspoon basil

Coat 6-cup mold with 2 teaspoons mayonnaise. Soften gelatin in water. Heat soup in saucepan. Stir in gelatin mixture, shrimp, cream cheese, 1 cup mayonnaise, celery, green onions and basil. Spoon into prepared mold. Chill for 8 to 10 hours. Invert onto serving platter. Serve with assorted party crackers.

Approx Per Serving: Cal 169; Prot 9 g; Carbo 3 g; T Fat 14 g; 73% Calories from Fat; Chol 86 mg; Fiber 0 g; Sod 285 mg

Polky Parrish, Lexington HFH, Lexington, KY

SARASOTA HOT WINGS

YIELD: 30 SERVINGS

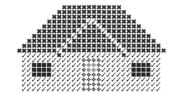

We know someone else got all the credit for coming up with the idea of "Buffalo Wings." That's o.k. by us, because once you try our version, you'll call them Sarasota Wings from now on.

5	pounds chicken wings	1	(5-ounce) bottle hot sauce
1½	cups butter or margarine		Vegetable oil for deep-frying

Rinse chicken wings and pat dry with paper towels. Joint, discarding tips. Combine butter and hot sauce in saucepan. Cook over medium heat until blended, stirring frequently. Place chicken wings in fry basket in batches of 10. Deep-fry in hot oil in 4-quart saucepan or fryer until they float to the top. Deep-fry for 2 minutes longer. Remove to warming tray with slotted spoon. Spoon approximately 1 tablespoon of the butter sauce over 5 chicken wings in covered bowl, shaking until coated. Repeat process until all chicken wings are coated with butter sauce. Serve with celery sticks, carrot sticks and bleu cheese salad dressing or ranch salad dressing for dipping. May substitute honey mustard sauce for hot sauce. Try these variations at your next Wing Ding, adding the following ingredients to the butter sauce.

Photo by Robert Baker

• **Cajun Wings:** Add cayenne, thyme, white pepper, black pepper and garlic powder to taste.

• **Curry Wings:** Add curry powder to taste and serve with cranberry-rhubarb chutney.

• **Mexican Wings:** Add cumin and oregano to taste and serve with tomato salsa.

• **Asian Wings:** Add dark sesame oil, soy sauce, garlic, ginger powder and finely chopped green onions to taste.

• **Italian Wings:** Substitute olive oil for butter or margarine and add minced fresh garlic and oregano to taste.

Approx Per Serving: Cal 247; Prot 15 g; Carbo <1 g; T Fat 20 g; 75% Calories from Fat; Chol 72 mg; Fiber <1 g; Sod 142 mg
Nutritional information does not include oil for frying.

Sandy Epps, Sarasota HFH, Sarasota, FL

APPETIZERS

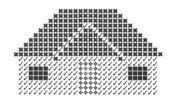

CHINESE CHICKEN WINGS

YIELD: 20 SERVINGS

20	chicken wings	2	tablespoons honey
1/4	cup dry sherry or white wine	1/4	teaspoon sesame oil
1/4	cup soy sauce	2	cloves of garlic
3	tablespoons oyster sauce	1	(1-inch) piece gingerroot, finely chopped
2	tablespoons sugar		

Rinse chicken wings and pat dry. Joint, discarding tips. Process sherry, soy sauce, oyster sauce, sugar, honey, sesame oil, garlic and gingerroot in blender until blended. Pour over chicken wings in shallow dish, turning to coat. Marinate, covered, in refrigerator for 2 hours or longer, turning occasionally. Arrange on baking sheet. Bake at 350 degrees for 45 minutes.

Approx Per Serving: Cal 118; Prot 10 g; Carbo 4 g; T Fat 7 g; 52% Calories from Fat; Chol 29 mg; Fiber <1 g; Sod 335 mg

Jennifer Weigel, Anchorage HFH, Eagle River, AK

GLACIER CHEESE BALLS

YIELD: 72 SERVINGS

32	ounces cream cheese, softened	1/8	teaspoon Worcestershire sauce
4	ounces bleu cheese, crumbled	6	small green onions, finely chopped
1/4	cup mayonnaise	3	ribs celery, chopped

Beat cream cheese, bleu cheese, mayonnaise and Worcestershire sauce in mixer bowl until blended. Stir in green onions and celery. Shape into 4 or 5 balls. Roll in crushed walnuts, pecans and/or chopped fresh parsley if desired. Chill, wrapped in plastic wrap, until serving time. Serve with assorted party crackers. May freeze for future use. Substitute low-fat products for a healthier appetizer.

Approx Per Serving: Cal 56; Prot 1 g; Carbo 1 g; T Fat 5 g; 87% Calories from Fat; Chol 16 mg; Fiber <1 g; Sod 65 mg

Debbie Adamson, Central Peninsula HFH, Kenai, AK

CRAB MEAT APPETIZERS

Yield: 10 servings

1   (4-ounce) can crab meat, drained
1   (8-ounce) jar Cheez Whiz
3   English muffins, split into halves

Cook crab meat and Cheez Whiz in saucepan until cheese melts, stirring constantly. Spread over cut side of muffins. Arrange on baking sheet. Broil until brown and bubbly. Cut into bite-size pieces.

Approx Per Serving: Cal 117; Prot 7 g; Carbo 10 g; T Fat 5 g; 41% Calories from Fat; Chol 23 mg; Fiber 1 g; Sod 422 mg

Nicole Jensen, Babson College HFH, Rumford, RI

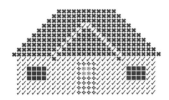

GREEN CHILE PIE

Yield: 12 servings

2   cups shredded Cheddar cheese
1   (4-ounce) can chopped green chiles, drained
6   eggs
    Salt and pepper to taste

Spread cheese in buttered baking dish. Sprinkle with chiles. Pour beaten mixture of eggs, salt and pepper over chiles. Bake at 300 degrees until set. Invert onto serving platter and slice.

Approx Per Serving: Cal 116; Prot 8 g; Carbo 1 g; T Fat 9 g; 69% Calories from Fat; Chol 126 mg; Fiber <1 g; Sod 259 mg

Jennie Borland, Gallatin Valley HFH, Bozeman, MT

PIZZA BREAD

Yield: 12 servings

1   loaf frozen French bread dough, thawed
1 1/2 to 2 cups pizza sauce
8   ounces sliced pepperoni
1 1/2 cups shredded mozzarella cheese
1   cup sliced mushrooms
1   cup chopped onion

Roll bread dough 1/2 inch thick on hard surface. Spread with pizza sauce. Top with pepperoni, cheese, mushrooms and onion. Roll as for jelly roll. Arrange seam side down on ungreased baking sheet. Cut diagonal slashes 1 inch apart in top. Bake at 350 degrees for 25 to 30 minutes or until golden brown; slice.

Approx Per Serving: Cal 256; Prot 10 g; Carbo 24 g; T Fat 13 g; 46% Calories from Fat; Chol 27 mg; Fiber 2 g; Sod 824 mg

Regina Hopkins, HFHI, Americus, GA

A Babson College HFH group, working on a house in Quincey, Massachusetts, faced the major task of transporting a pile of rocks to the basement area—a wheelbarrow-load at a time. The cement floor couldn't be poured until the rocks were in place, so one by one the volunteers hefted a shovelful of rocks into a wheelbarrow, then poured the load down the stairs through the bulkhead. After about two hours of backbreaking work, some curious backhoe operators working nearby offered us assistance. A pile with barely a dent quickly disappeared. I never thought a backhoe could look so nice.

Nicole Jensen
Babson College HFH

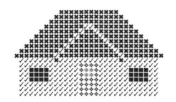

JANIE'S HAM BALLS

YIELD: 24 SERVINGS

Great recipe for making use of that leftover holiday ham.

16	ounces ground ham	1	cup packed brown sugar
1 1/2	pounds lean ground pork	1/2	cup wine vinegar
1	cup French bread crumbs	1/2	cup water
1	cup dry bread crumbs	1	teaspoon prepared
1	cup milk		mustard
2	eggs, beaten		

Combine ground ham, ground pork, bread crumbs, milk and eggs in bowl and mix well. Shape into 1 1/2- to 2-inch balls. Arrange in 9x13-inch baking pan. Combine brown sugar, wine vinegar, water and mustard in saucepan and mix well. Cook over low heat until brown sugar dissolves, stirring frequently. Pour over ham balls. Bake at 325 degrees for 1 hour, turning and basting every 20 minutes.

Approx Per Serving: Cal 163; Prot 12 g; Carbo 14 g; T Fat 7 g; 37% Calories from Fat; Chol 49 mg; Fiber <1 g; Sod 344 mg

Melanie G. Knier, Our Towns HFH, Mooresville, NC

STUFFED MUSHROOMS

YIELD: 40 SERVINGS

1/4	cup unsalted butter or margarine	3/4	cup dry bread crumbs
40	mushroom caps, rinsed, drained	1/4	cup minced fresh parsley
		6	green onions, thinly sliced
16	ounces backfin lump blue crab meat	1	teaspoon salt
		1	teaspoon cayenne
1 1/2	cups shredded Monterey Jack cheese	3/4	cup melted unsalted butter or margarine

Heat 1/4 cup butter in shallow baking dish until melted, tilting dish to coat bottom. Pat mushrooms dry with paper towel. Pick crab meat, discarding shell and cartilage. Combine crab meat, cheese, bread crumbs, parsley, green onions, salt and cayenne in bowl and mix well. Add 3/4 cup butter, stirring until mixed. Fill mushroom caps with crab meat mixture, mounding 1/2 inch above caps. Arrange stuffed side up in single layer in prepared baking dish. Bake at 350 degrees for 10 minutes or until light brown.

Approx Per Serving: Cal 80; Prot 3 g; Carbo 2 g; T Fat 7 g; 73% Calories from Fat; Chol 25 mg; Fiber <1 g; Sod 143 mg

Linda C. Parker, Union County HFH, Union, SC

Apple Pizza

Yield: 12 servings

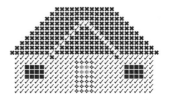

1   (8-count) can biscuits
1   (4-count) can biscuits
1   cup shredded mild Cheddar
     cheese
2   apples, peeled, sliced

$^1/_2$ cup packed brown sugar
2   tablespoons flour
$^1/_2$ teaspoon cinnamon
$^1/_4$ cup butter

Pat biscuits to flatten into 12 circles. Arrange on baking sheet. Sprinkle each circle with cheese; top with apples. Sprinkle with mixture of brown sugar, flour and cinnamon; dot with butter. Bake at 350 degrees for 20 to 30 minutes or until brown and bubbly. Let stand until cool.

Approx Per Serving: Cal 199; Prot 5 g; Carbo 24 g; T Fat 11 g; 50% Calories from Fat; Chol 20 mg; Fiber <1 g; Sod 401 mg

Sandra Israel, Kiski Valley HFH, Hyde Park, PA

Seafood Pizza

Yield: 16 servings

8   ounces cream cheese,
     softened
1   (8-ounce) jar seafood
     cocktail sauce

8   to 10 ounces crab meat,
     flaked
     Chopped fresh parsley to
     taste

Spread cream cheese on 8- to 10-inch plate. Spread cocktail sauce to within $^3/_4$ inch of the edge of cream cheese. Sprinkle with crab meat; top with parsley. Serve with assorted party crackers. May substitute fat-free cream cheese for cream cheese and popcorn shrimp or imitation crab meat for crab meat.

Approx Per Serving: Cal 81; Prot 5 g; Carbo 4 g; T Fat 5 g; 57% Calories from Fat; Chol 31 mg; Fiber <1 g; Sod 262 mg

Kathleen Miller, DeKalb County HFH, Auburn, IN

We put our application in on August 10, 1992, and waited for approval. Then June 24th, 1994, came, and we received a letter from Kiski Valley Habitat congratulating us on becoming a homeowner. My family is very grateful.

Sandra Israel
Kiski Valley HFH

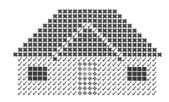

The day groundbreaking was started for my HFH home was my birthday. What a gift and a blessing of memories to treasure. Thanks, Habitat.

Cecilia Cartagena
Loveland HFH

VEGETABLE PIZZA

YIELD: 20 SERVINGS

2	(8-count) cans crescent rolls	1	cup finely chopped green bell pepper
16	ounces cream cheese, softened	1	cup finely chopped carrot
3/4	cup mayonnaise	1	cup broccoli florets, finely chopped
1	envelope ranch salad dressing mix	1	cup cauliflowerets, finely chopped
1	cup finely chopped red bell pepper	1	cup shredded Cheddar cheese

Unroll crescent roll dough. Press over bottom of 10x15-inch baking pan, pressing perforations and edges to seal. Bake using package directions. Let stand until cool. Beat cream cheese, mayonnaise and dressing mix in mixer bowl until blended. Spread over baked layer. Sprinkle with red pepper, green pepper, carrot, broccoli and cauliflower. Top with cheese. Slice into serving pieces. May use any fresh vegetables.

Approx Per Serving: Cal 252; Prot 5 g; Carbo 12 g; T Fat 21 g; 74% Calories from Fat; Chol 36 mg; Fiber 1 g; Sod 423 mg

Ann Meyer, Blount County HFH, Maryville, TN

CRUNCHY CHIPS

YIELD: 6 SERVINGS

12	corn tortillas	3	tablespoons seasoned salt
2	cups vegetable oil		

Cut tortillas into triangles. Deep-fry triangles in batches in hot oil in deep fryer until brown and crisp; drain on paper towels. Sprinkle warm chips with seasoned salt. Serve with salsa or bean dip.

Approx Per Serving: Cal 780; Prot 3 g; Carbo 28 g; T Fat 75 g; 84% Calories from Fat; Chol 0 mg; Fiber 3 g; Sod 2047 mg
Nutritional information includes entire amount of oil.

Cecilia Cartagena, Loveland HFH, Loveland, CO

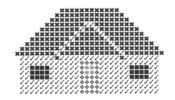

GRANOLA

YIELD: 12 SERVINGS

5	cups rolled oats	1/3	cup vegetable oil
1/2	cup wheat germ	1	teaspoon cinnamon
1/2	cup sliced almonds	1 1/2	cups raisins
1/2	cup honey		

Spread oats in ungreased 9x13-inch baking pan. Bake at 350 degrees for 10 minutes. Combine wheat germ, almonds, honey, oil and cinnamon in bowl and mix well. Stir in oats. Spoon into 9x13-inch baking pan. Bake for 30 minutes longer, stirring every 10 minutes. Let stand until cool. Stir in raisins. Store, loosely covered, in casserole in refrigerator. May add 1/2 cup packed brown sugar if desired.

Approx Per Serving: Cal 326; Prot 8 g; Carbo 54 g; T Fat 11 g; 28% Calories from Fat; Chol 0 mg; Fiber 5 g; Sod 5 mg

Peggy (Mrs. Tony) Campolo, Saint Davids, PA

PEANUTTY CARAMEL CORN

YIELD: 10 SERVINGS

5	cups air-popped popcorn	1/4	cup corn syrup
1	cup unsalted peanuts	1/4	teaspoon salt
1	cup packed brown sugar	1/2	teaspoon baking soda
1/2	cup butter		

Combine popcorn and peanuts in bowl and mix well. Spoon into 9x13-inch baking pan. Combine brown sugar, butter, corn syrup and salt in saucepan. Bring to a boil over low heat, stirring occasionally. Boil for 5 minutes; do not stir. Stir in baking soda. Pour over popcorn mixture, tossing to coat. Bake at 275 degrees for 30 minutes, stirring every 10 minutes. Spread on waxed paper. Let stand until cool. Break into bite-size pieces. Store in airtight container. May be frozen for future use. May omit peanuts if desired.

Approx Per Serving: Cal 271; Prot 4 g; Carbo 30 g; T Fat 16 g; 52% Calories from Fat; Chol 25 mg; Fiber 2 g; Sod 228 mg

Joyce Grimm, Franklin High School HFH, Murrysville, PA

$\mathscr{A}$PPETIZERS

CARAMEL CORN

YIELD: 32 SERVINGS

4	quarts air-popped popcorn	1/4	cup light corn syrup
1	cup packed brown sugar	1/2	teaspoon salt
1/2	cup butter or margarine, softened	1/2	teaspoon baking soda

Pour popcorn into large nonrecycled brown paper bag. Combine brown sugar, butter, corn syrup and salt in microwave-safe dish and mix well. Microwave until boiling. Boil for 3 minutes. Stir in baking soda. Pour over popcorn, shaking bag to coat. Place in microwave. Microwave for 3 minutes, shaking at 1-minute intervals. Spread caramel corn on waxed paper. Let stand until cool. Break into bite-size pieces.

Approx Per Serving: Cal 69; Prot 1 g; Carbo 11 g; T Fat 3 g; 38% Calories from Fat; Chol 8 mg; Fiber 1 g; Sod 88 mg

Diana Burny, Boise Valley HFH, Boise, ID

SPICED PECANS

YIELD: 24 SERVINGS

3/4	cup sugar	1/4	teaspoon allspice
2 1/2	tablespoons water	1	egg white, lightly beaten
1	teaspoon cinnamon	1 1/2	pounds pecans
3/4	teaspoon salt		

Combine sugar, water, cinnamon, salt, allspice and egg white in bowl and mix well. Add pecans, stirring until coated. Spread in single layer on ungreased baking sheet. Bake at 275 degrees for 45 minutes. Let stand until cool. Store in airtight container.

Approx Per Serving: Cal 214; Prot 2 g; Carbo 11 g; T Fat 19 g; 76% Calories from Fat; Chol 0 mg; Fiber 1 g; Sod 69 mg

Office Crew, Sarasota HFH, Sarasota, FL

Photograph at right by Robert Baker

$\mathscr{S}$OUPS & $\mathscr{S}$TEWS

John answered, "The man with two tunics
should share with him who has none,
and the one who has food should do the same."

Luke 3:11

*S*OUPS

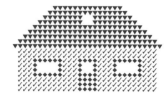

Habitat has made room for and welcomed men and women currently incarcerated in prisons. By allowing them to participate equally, as do other volunteers, Habitat provides a second chance. Praise God!

*Carol Freeland
HFHI Board of
Directors*

BEEF VEGETABLE SOUP

YIELD: 4 SERVINGS

Serve with corn bread or crusty French bread for a quick and easy meal.

1	pound lean ground beef	1 1/2	cups sliced carrots
1	large clove of garlic, minced	1	(15-ounce) can cannellini or Great Northern beans, rinsed, drained
1/2	teaspoon pepper		
1/2	teaspoon salt	1	medium zucchini, coarsely chopped
2	(14-ounce) cans beef broth		
1	(14-ounce) can stewed tomatoes	2	cups lightly packed torn fresh spinach

Brown ground beef with garlic in large saucepan over medium heat for 4 to 5 minutes, stirring until ground beef is crumbly; drain. Stir in pepper and salt. Add broth, undrained tomatoes and carrots and mix well. Simmer for 10 minutes, stirring occasionally. Stir in beans and zucchini. Cook for 4 to 5 minutes or until zucchini is tender-crisp, stirring occasionally. Stir in spinach. Ladle into soup bowls.

Approx Per Serving: Cal 443; Prot 40 g; Carbo 33 g; T Fat 17 g; 34% Calories from Fat; Chol 89 mg; Fiber 11 g; Sod 2490 mg

Carol Freeland, HFHI International Board of Directors, Richardson, TX

WHITE BEAN KALE SOUP

YIELD: 6 SERVINGS

This recipe was given to me by Ree Wilson, the Executive Chef at the Kentucky Governor's Mansion. This was one of our favorite recipes during our four years in the Governor's Mansion in Frankfort.

1	medium onion, chopped	1	cup cooked white beans
2	cloves of garlic, minced	1	medium chopped seeded tomato
2	tablespoons olive oil		
4	cups defatted chicken broth	1	medium potato, steamed, chopped
1/4	cup chopped celery	2	cups torn fresh kale
1/4	cup chopped carrot		

Sauté onion and garlic in olive oil in saucepan until tender. Add broth, celery and carrot and mix well. Stir in white beans, tomato and potato. Simmer for 20 minutes, stirring occasionally. Add kale and mix well. Simmer for 10 minutes longer, stirring occasionally. Ladle into soup bowls.

Approx Per Serving: Cal 142; Prot 8 g; Carbo 18 g; T Fat 5 g; 30% Calories from Fat; Chol 0 mg; Fiber 4 g; Sod 245 mg

Mrs. Brereton C. Jones, Kentucky HFH, Midway, KY

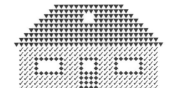

BROCCOLI SOUP

YIELD: 4 SERVINGS

1	large bunch broccoli, chopped
2	cups water
1	rib celery, chopped
3	green onions, chopped

2	chicken bouillon cubes
2	cups skim milk
3½	tablespoons flour
	Salt and pepper to taste

Combine broccoli, water, celery, green onions and bouillon cubes in saucepan. Cook until vegetables are tender. Process in blender until of the desired consistency. Add skim milk, flour, salt and pepper. Process until mixed. Return broccoli mixture to saucepan. Cook until thickened, stirring frequently. Ladle into soup bowls.

Approx Per Serving: Cal 108; Prot 9 g; Carbo 19 g; T Fat 1 g; 6% Calories from Fat; Chol 3 mg; Fiber 4 g; Sod 679 mg

Marlene Woodfield, Michigan City, Indiana HFH, LaPorte, IN

CREAMY BROCCOLI SOUP

YIELD: 4 SERVINGS

1	medium onion, chopped
1	clove of garlic, crushed
1	bay leaf
1	tablespoon sunflower oil or vegetable oil
16	ounces broccoli, chopped

2½	cups light vegetable stock
1	small potato, coarsely chopped
	Juice of ½ lemon
	Salt and pepper to taste
¼	cup low-fat plain yogurt

Sauté onion and garlic with bay leaf in sunflower oil in saucepan for 3 to 4 minutes. Add broccoli, stock and potato and mix well. Simmer, covered, for 10 minutes or until broccoli is tender-crisp and still bright green, stirring occasionally. Discard bay leaf. Cool slightly. Process in blender until almost smooth. Return to saucepan. Stir in lemon juice. Season with salt and pepper. Cook just until heated through, stirring frequently. Ladle into soup bowls. Top with yogurt. May sauté onion and garlic in saucepan sprayed with nonstick cooking spray. May substitute sour cream for yogurt.

Photo by Robert Baker

Approx Per Serving: Cal 113; Prot 6 g; Carbo 16 g; T Fat 5 g; 33% Calories from Fat; Chol 1 mg; Fiber 4 g; Sod 668 mg

Rosalynn Carter, The Carter Center, Atlanta, GA

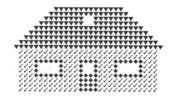

When we started work on our first Habitat house, we poured the cement but had no one who could finish it out by smoothing the surface. A man walking down the street approached the site and said he did that type work for a living. As he proceeded to apply the finishing touch, our prayers were answered.

Susie Bare
Crystal Coast HFH

BUFFALO VEGETABLE SOUP

YIELD: 12 SERVINGS

1	(2- to 3-pound) buffalo roast, trimmed, cut into chunks	1	(16-ounce) can stewed tomatoes
6	cups water	5	medium potatoes, peeled, chopped
1	large onion, chopped	3	carrots, chopped
1	teaspoon salt	4	ribs celery, chopped
1	teaspoon pepper		

Bring roast, water, onion, salt and pepper to a boil in a stockpot; reduce heat. Simmer for 1 hour. Add undrained tomatoes, potatoes, carrots and celery. Cook for 1 hour or until vegetables are tender. Ladle into soup bowls. Serve with crackers or fry bread and Wojopi (Indian Pudding) on page 170. May substitute beef roast for the buffalo roast.

Approx Per Serving: Cal 167; Prot 21 g; Carbo 17 g; T Fat 2 g; 10% Calories from Fat; Chol 55 mg; Fiber 2 g; Sod 333 mg

Karen Jeffries, Okiciyapi Tipi HFH, Eagle Butte, SD

CABBAGE PATCH SOUP

YIELD: 6 SERVINGS

1	pound ground beef	1½	cups water
3	slices bacon, chopped	1	onion, thinly sliced
1	(16-ounce) can tomatoes	½	cup chopped celery
1	(16-ounce) can red kidney beans, rinsed, drained	¼	cup margarine
2	cups shredded cabbage	1	teaspoon chili powder
			Salt and pepper to taste

Brown ground beef with bacon in saucepan, stirring until ground beef is crumbly; drain. Stir in undrained tomatoes, beans, cabbage, water, onion, celery, margarine, chili powder, salt and pepper. Simmer for 1½ hours, stirring occasionally. Ladle into soup bowls. May vary amounts of bacon, water and cabbage as desired.

Approx Per Serving: Cal 372; Prot 25 g; Carbo 23 g; T Fat 20 g; 49% Calories from Fat; Chol 59 mg; Fiber 8 g; Sod 321 mg

Susie Bare, Crystal Coast HFH, Havelock, NC

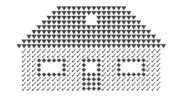
CHEESY CHOWDER

YIELD: 4 SERVINGS

1	vegetable bouillon cube	1	(17-ounce) can cream-style corn
1½	cups boiling water		
2	cups chopped potatoes	1	(10-ounce) can Cheddar cheese soup
1	(10-ounce) package frozen mixed vegetables	½	cup milk

Dissolve bouillon cube in boiling water in saucepan and mix well. Cook, covered, for 5 minutes. Stir in potatoes and mixed vegetables. Simmer, covered, for 10 minutes or until vegetables are tender. Add corn, soup and milk and mix well. Cook over low heat for 10 minutes or until heated through, stirring occasionally. Ladle into soup bowls.

Approx Per Serving: Cal 317; Prot 10 g; Carbo 53 g; T Fat 8 g; 23% Calories from Fat; Chol 22 mg; Fiber 7 g; Sod 1125 mg

Anita Bothun, LaCrosse Area HFH, LaCrosse, WI

CHILI

YIELD: 6 SERVINGS

1½	pounds ground beef	½	cup catsup
2	(15-ounce) cans kidney beans, drained	1	or 2 onions, chopped
2	(10-ounce) cans tomato soup	1	to 2 tablespoons brown sugar
1	soup can water		Prepared mustard to taste
			Chili powder to taste

Brown ground beef in saucepan, stirring until crumbly; drain. Stir in beans, soup, water, catsup, onions, brown sugar, mustard and chili powder. Cook over low heat for 1 hour or until of the desired consistency, stirring occasionally. Ladle into chili bowls.

Approx Per Serving: Cal 531; Prot 38 g; Carbo 56 g; T Fat 18 g; 30% Calories from Fat; Chol 84 mg; Fiber 14 g; Sod 1011 mg

Philomena Novicky, Mercer County HFH, West Middlesex, PA

I love our affiliate "House of Hope" fund-raising project. Thousands of area citizens sign their names on two-by-four boards located at area churches and businesses, and donate a dollar or more. The boards are made into a "house" float for our Oktoberfest parades. Later the float is disassembled and used to build an actual HFH home!

Anita Bothun
LaCrosse Area HFH

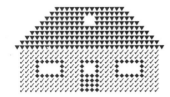

POOR MAN'S CHILI

YIELD: 15 SERVINGS

3	pounds ground beef	1/2	cup chopped onion
2	(46-ounce) cans tomato juice	1/2	cup chopped green bell pepper
2	(15-ounce) cans chili beans	3	envelopes chili seasoning mix
2	(15-ounce) cans whole or diced tomatoes		

Brown ground beef in skillet, stirring until crumbly; drain. Add 3 cups of the tomato juice, beans, undrained tomatoes, onion, green pepper and seasoning mix and mix well. Bring to a boil; reduce heat. Simmer for 15 to 20 minutes, stirring occasionally. Combine ground beef mixture and remaining tomato juice in large saucepan and mix well. Cook over low heat for 30 to 45 minutes or until of desired consistency, stirring 4 or 5 times. Ladle into chili bowls. May substitute ground turkey for ground beef.

Approx Per Serving: Cal 308; Prot 25 g; Carbo 18 g; T Fat 16 g; 45% Calories from Fat; Chol 77 mg; Fiber 4 g; Sod 1075 mg

The Pates Family, Knox County HFH, Galesburg, IL

WHITE CHILI

YIELD: 8 SERVINGS

16	ounces dried large white beans	1 1/2	teaspoons oregano
6	cups chicken broth	1/4	teaspoon ground cloves
2	medium onions, chopped	1/4	teaspoon cayenne
2	cloves of garlic, minced	4	cups chopped cooked chicken breast
1	tablespoon vegetable oil	3	cups shredded Monterey Jack cheese
2	(4-ounce) cans mild green chiles, drained, chopped	1/2	cup sour cream
2	teaspoons cumin	1/2	cup salsa

Sort and rinse beans. Combine beans, broth, 1 of the onions and garlic in stockpot. Bring to a boil; reduce heat. Simmer for 3 hours or until beans are tender, stirring occasionally and adding additional broth if needed. Sauté remaining onion in oil in skillet until tender. Add chiles, cumin, oregano, cloves and cayenne and mix well. Stir into bean mixture. Add chicken and mix gently. Simmer for 1 hour or until of the desired consistency. Ladle into chili bowls. Top with cheese, sour cream and salsa.

Approx Per Serving: Cal 560; Prot 50 g; Carbo 41 g; T Fat 22 g; 35% Calories from Fat; Chol 104 mg; Fiber 10 g; Sod 1370 mg

Pat Evans, Nashville Area HFH, Nashville, TN

CORN CHOWDER

4	cups frozen corn	1/2	cup water
1	potato, chopped	1/4	cup flour
1/3	cup (about) chopped onion	1	egg, beaten
1	chicken bouillon cube	1/2	teaspoon salt
4	cups milk	1/4	teaspoon pepper

Combine corn, potato, onion and bouillon cube in saucepan. Add enough water to come just below the surface of the ingredients. Bring to a boil; reduce heat. Simmer for 10 minutes or until potato is tender-crisp, stirring occasionally. Stir in milk. Cook just until heated through, stirring occasionally. Stir in a mixture of 1/2 cup water and flour. Beat 1 cup of the hot soup (no solids) into egg; stir egg into hot soup. Season with salt and pepper. Ladle into soup bowls. May omit potato if desired and substitute skim milk for whole milk.

Approx Per Serving: Cal 337; Prot 15 g; Carbo 45 g; T Fat 11 g; 29% Calories from Fat; Chol 86 mg; Fiber 5 g; Sod 693 mg

Ed Bolles, Kentucky HFH, Lexington, KY

CREAMY CORN CHOWDER

This soup may take a little more effort, but the results will be well worth the energy expended. Serve with crusty French bread.

1 3/4	cups chopped onions	4	cups fresh or frozen corn
1	large red bell pepper, chopped	2	large russet potatoes, peeled, chopped
2	tablespoons butter	1 1/2	cups half-and-half
3	slices crisp-fried bacon, crumbled		Salt and pepper to taste
3	tablespoons flour	1/2	cup shredded Cheddar cheese
4 1/2	cups chicken stock or broth		

Sauté onions and red pepper in butter in skillet for 10 minutes or until tender. Stir in bacon. Add flour gradually, stirring constantly. Cook for 2 minutes, stirring constantly. Combine stock and corn in stockpot and mix well. Stir in bacon mixture and potatoes. Simmer for 20 minutes, stirring occasionally. Add half-and-half and mix well. Simmer for 40 minutes longer or until slightly thickened, stirring frequently. Season with salt and pepper. Ladle into soup bowls. Sprinkle with cheese.

Approx Per Serving: Cal 285; Prot 11 g; Carbo 33 g; T Fat 13 g; 41% Calories from Fat; Chol 34 mg; Fiber 4 g; Sod 581 mg

Sandra Avis, Hillsdale County HFH, Hillsdale, MI

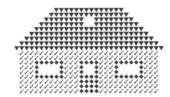

EGG DROP SOUP

YIELD: 6 SERVINGS

2	(14-ounce) cans chicken broth
1	broth can water
1	or 2 eggs, beaten

2	(5-ounce) cans chunk white meat chicken, drained
	Pepper to taste

Bring broth and water to a boil in saucepan. Add eggs. Cook for 1 minute, stirring constantly. Stir in chicken. Cook until heated through, stirring frequently. Season with pepper. Ladle into soup bowls. May substitute low-sodium chicken broth for chicken broth.

Approx Per Serving: Cal 135; Prot 17 g; Carbo 1 g; T Fat 6 g; 44% Calories from Fat; Chol 98 mg; Fiber <1 g; Sod 1059 mg

Pamela S. Chadbourne, Jefferson County HFH, Mt.Vernon, IL

FISH CHOWDER

YIELD: 4 SERVINGS

1	(8-ounce) fillet orange roughy, cut into 1/2-inch pieces
2	teaspoons vegetable oil
2	teaspoons Old Bay seasoning
2	cups water
2	carrots, chopped
1	rib celery, chopped

l	large potato, chopped
1	medium onion, chopped
1/4	cup chopped green bell pepper
1	vegetable bouillon cube
1	(8-ounce) bottle clam juice
1	(6-ounce) can vegetable juice cocktail
1/8	teaspoon Tabasco sauce

Sauté fish in oil in skillet for 2 to 3 minutes. Sprinkle with Old Bay seasoning. Combine water, carrots, celery, potato, onion, green pepper and bouillon cube in microwave-safe dish. Microwave on High for 5 minutes. Combine vegetable mixture with fish in skillet and mix well. Stir in clam juice, vegetable juice cocktail and Tabasco sauce. Simmer for 30 minutes, stirring occasionally. Ladle into soup bowls. May substitute any mild fish for the orange roughy.

Approx Per Serving: Cal 177; Prot 11 g; Carbo 18 g; T Fat 8 g; 37% Calories from Fat; Chol 14 mg; Fiber 3 g; Sod 676 mg

Frances L. Daily, Alliance Area HFH, Alliance, OH

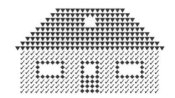

HEARTY PEA SOUP

YIELD: 6 SERVINGS

3	cups dried split peas	1/4	cup apple cider vinegar
9	cups water	5	cloves of garlic, sliced
2	carrots, sliced	3	bay leaves
2	ribs celery, sliced	2	teaspoons thyme
2	medium potatoes, cut into 1-inch pieces		Salt and pepper to taste
2	large onions, julienned	4	scallions, chopped
1/2	cup red wine	1/4	cup grated Parmesan cheese

Sort and rinse peas. Combine peas, water, carrots, celery, potatoes, onions, red wine, vinegar, garlic, bay leaves, thyme, salt and pepper in stockpot. Cook over low heat for 2 to 10 hours or until of the desired consistency, stirring occasionally. The longer cooking time leads to a more flavorful soup. Discard bay leaves. Process 1/2 to 3/4 of soup in a blender until puréed. Stir puréed soup into remaining soup in stockpot. Cook just until heated through, stirring frequently. Ladle into soup bowls. Top with scallions and cheese. May substitute sunflower kernels for scallions and/or cheese.

Approx Per Serving: Cal 446; Prot 28 g; Carbo 78 g; T Fat 3 g; 5% Calories from Fat; Chol 3 mg; Fiber 11 g; Sod 119 mg

Kristen Brennan and Michael Smith, Louisville Metro HFH
Louisville, KY

QUICK MINESTRONE

YIELD: 6 SERVINGS

4	carrots, sliced	1	to 2 cups water
4	small squash, chopped	1	cup potato flakes
	Salt to taste	2	tablespoons olive oil
1	(26-ounce) jar spaghetti sauce	1/4	teaspoon salt
2	(16-ounce) cans cream-style corn		

Cook carrots, squash and salt to taste in enough water to cover in saucepan until tender-crisp; drain. Combine carrot mixture, spaghetti sauce, corn, 1 to 2 cups water, potato flakes, olive oil and 1/4 teaspoon salt in stockpot and mix well. Cook over low heat until heated through, stirring occasionally. Ladle into soup bowls. Serve with grated Parmesan cheese and Italian bread. May substitute butter, soy bean oil, corn oil or canola oil for olive oil.

Approx Per Serving: Cal 361; Prot 7 g; Carbo 61 g; T Fat 11 g; 27% Calories from Fat; Chol 0 mg; Fiber 10 g; Sod 1232 mg

Maxine Henderson, Springfield HFH, Springfield, MO

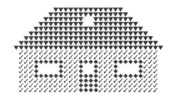

As a member of a new HFH group attempting to achieve affiliation, I became acquainted with a couple down the road and asked them to supper and cards. I invited them to join Silver Valley Habitat. They accepted and became our secretary and treasurer. They are talented individuals who are completely dedicated to HFH and have become regional represen-tatives, making it possible for our affiliate to build three homes in the Valley in the four years since our affiliation. Take a recipe from this book and invite your neighbors for dinner. You might be as lucky as we to inspire more Habitat volunteers.

Lois E. Shadle
Silver Valley HFH

SUSAN'S MUSHROOM SOUP

YIELD: 2 SERVINGS

12	to 16 ounces thinly sliced mixed white, cremini and shiitake mushrooms	2	cups low-sodium chicken broth
2	tablespoons margarine	1	to 1½ cups 1% milk
	Olive oil to taste		Salt and pepper to taste
		2	tablespoons sherry

Sauté mushrooms in margarine and olive oil in saucepan for 5 to 7 minutes or until tender and most of moisture has been absorbed; drain. Stir in broth. Cook over medium heat for 2 minutes; reduce heat. Simmer, covered, for 10 minutes, stirring occasionally. Remove from heat. Add milk, salt and pepper gradually, stirring until of the desired consistency. Ladle into soup bowls. Swirl in sherry. Omit sherry if desired. May substitute any combination of mushrooms. May substitute 2% milk, whole milk or light cream for the 1% milk and butter or water for the margarine.

Approx Per Serving: Cal 285; Prot 16 g; Carbo 21 g; T Fat 16 g; 48% Calories from Fat; Chol 7 mg; Fiber 3 g; Sod 876 mg

Kevin R. Sharp, Northeast Connecticut HFH, Putnam, CT

NORTH IDAHO SUPPER SOUP

YIELD: 8 SERVINGS

This soup is a hearty evening meal after a good day's work at the Habitat building site, especially on those winter days in North Idaho.

2	boneless skinless chicken breasts	½	cup chopped green bell pepper
2	(16-ounce) cans stewed tomatoes	2	chicken bouillon cubes
1	cup chopped celery	1	tablespoon Italian seasoning
1	cup chopped onion	½	teaspoon salt
1	cup chopped carrot	½	teaspoon pepper
1	cup chopped cabbage	½	cup small macaroni

Rinse chicken and chop. Combine chicken, undrained tomatoes, celery, onion, carrot, cabbage, green pepper, bouillon cubes, Italian seasoning, salt and pepper in 4-quart saucepan. Bring to a boil; reduce heat. Simmer for 2 hours, stirring occasionally. Add macaroni and mix well. Bring to a boil; reduce heat. Cook for 20 minutes, stirring occasionally. Ladle into soup bowls. Serve with hot French bread. May omit green bell pepper.

Approx Per Serving: Cal 133; Prot 14 g; Carbo 17 g; T Fat 2 g; 11% Calories from Fat; Chol 30 mg; Fiber 3 g; Sod 754 mg

Lois E. Shadle, Silver Valley HFH, Cataldo, ID

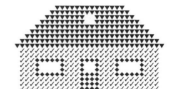
POTATO SOUP

YIELD: *4 SERVINGS*

12	ounces chicken broth	1	rib celery, finely chopped
1	cup water	1/2	cup nonfat dry milk powder
I	large baking potato, coarsely chopped		Shredded Cheddar cheese to taste
1	medium carrot, sliced	4	teaspoons bacon bits
1/2	medium onion, finely chopped		

Combine broth, water, potato, carrot, onion and celery in saucepan. Cook until vegetables are tender. Stir in milk powder and Cheddar cheese. Cook just until heated through, stirring frequently. Ladle into soup bowls. Sprinkle with bacon bits.

Approx Per Serving: Cal 101; Prot 6 g; Carbo 18 g; T Fat 1 g; 6% Calories from Fat; Chol 2 mg; Fiber 2 g; Sod 335 mg

Patricia Springer, West Chester-Mason HFH, West Chester, OH

SUPER PUMPKIN SOUP

YIELD: *4 SERVINGS*

1	(1 1/2-pound) pumpkin, peeled, chopped	1/2	teaspoon salt
3	cups chicken stock	1/4	teaspoon nutmeg
1	large leek, sliced	1/4	teaspoon coriander
2	teaspoons mixed herbs	2	tablespoons lemon juice
1/2	teaspoon coarsely ground pepper	2	tablespoons chopped fresh parsley

Combine pumpkin, stock, leek, mixed herbs, pepper, salt, nutmeg and coriander in saucepan. Bring to a boil; reduce heat. Simmer until pumpkin is tender, stirring occasionally. Process in blender until smooth. Stir in lemon juice and parsley. Add additional salt if desired. Ladle into soup bowls.

Approx Per Serving: Cal 78; Prot 5 g; Carbo 13 g; T Fat 1 g; 14% Calories from Fat; Chol 0 mg; Fiber 2 g; Sod 858 mg

Diana J. (Ian) Hay, HFHI Board of Directors, Auckland 4, New Zealand

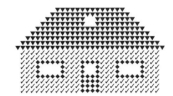

WILD RICE SOUP

YIELD: 6 SERVINGS

1	onion, chopped	1/2	teaspoon salt
1/4	cup olive oil	1/2	teaspoon curry powder
16	ounces fresh mushrooms, sliced	1/2	teaspoon dry mustard
		1/2	cup flour
1/2	cup chopped celery	1	cup chicken broth
5	cups chicken broth	2	cups 1% milk
1/2	cup cooked wild rice	3	tablespoons sherry

Sauté onion in olive oil in saucepan until tender. Add mushrooms and celery. Sauté for 2 minutes. Stir in 5 cups broth, wild rice, salt, curry powder and dry mustard. Simmer for 5 minutes, stirring occasionally. Stir flour into 1 cup broth in bowl. Add to mushroom mixture and mix well. Simmer for 10 minutes, stirring occasionally. Add milk and sherry and mix well. Simmer just until heated through, stirring constantly. Ladle into soup bowls.

Approx Per Serving: Cal 238; Prot 11 g; Carbo 21 g; T Fat 12 g; 44% Calories from Fat; Chol 3 mg; Fiber 2 g; Sod 1008 mg

Rockford Area HFH, Rockford, IL

WILD RICE CHEESE SOUP

YIELD: 60 SERVINGS

We served Millard Fuller Wild Rice Cheese Soup when he stopped for a quick visit at our regional center. He spoke so highly of the soup that I thought I would share the recipe.

1	to 2 pounds potatoes, peeled, coarsely chopped	8	pounds Cheddar cheese, shredded
3	pounds bacon, chopped	2	pounds Velveeta cheese, cubed
2	onions, chopped		
4	(10-ounce) cans cream of potato soup	4	soup cans water
		9	cups cooked wild rice

Combine potatoes with enough water to cover in saucepan. Cook until tender. Drain, reserving liquid. Sauté bacon and onions in large skillet, stirring until bacon is crisp and onions are tender; drain. Combine soup, Cheddar cheese, Velveeta cheese and water in stockpot. Cook until heated through, stirring frequently. Stir in bacon mixture and wild rice. Add potatoes and just enough of reserved liquid to make of desired consistency and mix well. Cook just until heated through, stirring frequently. Ladle into soup bowls.

Approx Per Serving: Cal 386; Prot 22 g; Carbo 12 g; T Fat 28 g; 65% Calories from Fat; Chol 83 mg; Fiber 1 g; Sod 858 mg

Gayle Waylander, Habitat Upper Midwest, Sioux Falls, SD

SANTA FE SOUP

YIELD: 6 SERVINGS

1 pound ground beef
2 (16-ounce) cans pinto beans
2 (16-ounce) cans whole kernel corn
1 (16-ounce) can kidney beans
1 (10-ounce) can tomatoes with green chiles
1 (16-ounce) can diced tomatoes
1 envelope ranch salad dressing mix
1 envelope taco seasoning mix

Brown ground beef in saucepan, stirring until crumbly; drain. Stir in undrained vegetables, salad dressing mix and taco seasoning mix. Cook until heated through and of the desired consistency. Ladle into soup bowls. Serve with tortilla chips and shredded cheese.

Approx Per Serving: Cal 491; Prot 32 g; Carbo 67 g; T Fat 12 g; 22% Calories from Fat; Chol 56 mg; Fiber 13 g; Sod 2203 mg

Larry Frank, Denton HFH, Denton, Texas

BIG SHRIMP BISQUE

YIELD: 6 SERVINGS

This recipe was a 1996 runner-up in the annual recipe contest sponsored by Newman's Own, Inc., and Good Housekeeping.

1½ pounds plum tomatoes, chopped
¼ cup olive oil
2 tablespoons butter
1 teaspoon salt
1 yellow onion, chopped
1 (16-ounce) jar medium Newman's Own Salsa
¼ cup chopped fresh cilantro
1 tablespoon dillweed
5 or 6 cloves of garlic, minced
2 pounds shrimp, peeled, deveined, rinsed
2½ cups milk

Sauté tomatoes in olive oil in saucepan for 2 to 3 minutes. Stir in butter and salt. Simmer, covered, for 10 minutes, stirring frequently. Add onion and mix well. Simmer, covered, for 5 minutes. Stir in salsa, cilantro, dillweed and garlic. Simmer, covered, for 5 minutes, stirring occasionally. Add shrimp and mix well. Simmer for 2 to 3 minutes or until the shrimp turn pink. Stir in milk. Bring to a simmer and cover. Remove from heat. Let stand for 10 minutes. Ladle into soup bowls. Garnish with cilantro leaves, tortilla chips, sour cream and additional Newman's Own Salsa.

Approx Per Serving: Cal 342; Prot 28 g; Carbo 17 g; T Fat 18 g; 47% Calories from Fat; Chol 239 mg; Fiber 1 g; Sod 1458 mg

Suzanne Probart, Albuquerque, NM

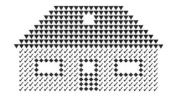

TACO SOUP

YIELD: *10 SERVINGS*

2	pounds ground chuck	3	(4-ounce) cans chopped green chiles, drained
1	small onion, chopped	1½	cups water
3	(15-ounce) cans stewed tomatoes	1	envelope ranch salad dressing mix
1	(16-ounce) can pinto beans, rinsed, drained	1	envelope taco seasoning mix
1	(16-ounce) can lima beans, rinsed, drained	1	teaspoon salt
1	(16-ounce) can red kidney beans, rinsed, drained	1	teaspoon pepper Shredded Cheddar cheese to taste
1	(15-ounce) can golden hominy, drained		

Brown ground chuck with onion in stockpot, stirring until ground chuck is crumbly; drain. Stir in undrained tomatoes, pinto beans, lima beans, kidney beans, hominy, chiles, water, dressing mix, seasoning mix, salt and pepper. Bring to a boil, stirring frequently; reduce heat. Simmer for 30 minutes or longer, stirring occasionally. May add additional water for desired consistency. Ladle into soup bowls; sprinkle with cheese. Serve with tortilla chips or corn chips. May substitute ground turkey for ground chuck.

Approx Per Serving: Cal 427; Prot 31 g; Carbo 45 g; T Fat 14 g; 29% Calories from Fat; Chol 67 mg; Fiber 12 g; Sod 1617 mg

Barbara Kirk, Knox County HFH, Monroe City, IN

TORTELLINI SOUP

YIELD: *6 SERVINGS*

1	medium to large onion, chopped	1	(14-ounce) can stewed tomatoes
1	clove of garlic, chopped	½	(10-ounce) package frozen chopped spinach, thawed, drained
3	tablespoons olive oil		
2	(15-ounce) cans chicken broth	½	cup grated Parmesan cheese
8	ounces frozen tortellini		

Sauté onion and garlic in olive oil in saucepan until tender. Add broth and mix well. Bring to a boil; reduce heat. Stir in tortellini. Simmer until tortellini are tender, stirring occasionally. Stir in undrained tomatoes and spinach. Cook for 10 minutes, stirring occasionally. Ladle into soup bowls. Sprinkle with cheese.

Approx Per Serving: Cal 292; Prot 17 g; Carbo 27 g; T Fat 14 g; 41% Calories from Fat; Chol 26 mg; Fiber 2 g; Sod 1369 mg

Grace Kent, Orleans County HFH, Albion, NY

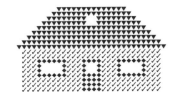

EFFORTLESS TORTELLINI SOUP *YIELD: 8 SERVINGS*

3	(15-ounce) cans chicken broth	1/2	cup picante sauce
1	(16-ounce) can stewed tomatoes	1	green bell pepper, chopped
7	ounces tortellini	1	large onion, chopped
		2	cloves of garlic, minced
		1	tablespoon basil

Combine broth, undrained tomatoes, tortellini, picante sauce, green pepper, onion, garlic and basil in saucepan and mix gently. Simmer for 25 minutes, stirring occasionally. Ladle into soup bowls. May cook in slow cooker.

Approx Per Serving: Cal 163; Prot 12 g; Carbo 20 g; T Fat 4 g; 21% Calories from Fat; Chol 11 mg; Fiber 2 g; Sod 1294 mg

Deanne Everton, HFH Northwest, Bend, OR

TWO-BY-FOUR SOUP   *YIELD: 10 SERVINGS*

2   pounds ground beef
1   onion, chopped
2   (16-ounce) cans pinto beans
2   (10-ounce) cans minestrone soup
2   (10-ounce) cans tomatoes with green chiles

Photo by Robert Baker

Brown ground beef with onion in saucepan, stirring until ground beef is crumbly; drain. Stir in undrained beans, soup and undrained tomatoes. Simmer over medium heat until of the desired consistency, stirring occasionally. Ladle into soup bowls. Serve with crackers or sliced buttered bread.

Approx Per Serving: Cal 329; Prot 28 g; Carbo 21 g; T Fat 15 g; 40% Calories from Fat; Chol 68 mg; Fiber 6 g; Sod 894 mg

Carrie Symonds, Fayetteville HFH, Springdale, AR

APPLE BEAN STEW

YIELD: 4 SERVINGS

1	pound pork sausage	1/2	cup packed brown sugar
1	(16-ounce) can red kidney beans, drained	1/2	cup tomato juice
2	medium tart apples, peeled, sliced	1/2	teaspoon chili powder
1	medium onion, sliced, separated into rings	1/8	teaspoon pepper

Brown sausage in skillet, stirring until crumbly; drain. Stir in beans, apples, onion, brown sugar, tomato juice, chili powder and pepper. Spoon into 1 1/2-quart baking dish. Bake, covered, at 350 degrees for 1 1/4 hours. Spoon into individual bowls.

Approx Per Serving: Cal 469; Prot 19 g; Carbo 60 g; T Fat 17 g; 33% Calories from Fat; Chol 44 mg; Fiber 12 g; Sod 813 mg

Etta Peabody, Northeast Kingdom HFH, Barton VT

ARNOCHI

YIELD: 4 SERVINGS

2	pounds lamb, cubed	1/2	teaspoon salt
4	cloves of garlic, minced	1/4	teaspoon pepper
1/4	cup olive oil	1	cup vegetable juice cocktail
3	onions, cut into thick slices	1	(8-ounce) can tomato sauce
2	pounds fresh green beans, sliced	1/4	teaspoon Tabasco sauce
4	medium red potatoes, cut into quarters	4	medium tomatoes, chopped

Brown lamb with garlic in olive oil in skillet. Remove lamb and garlic to bowl, reserving pan drippings. Sauté onions in reserved pan drippings until tender. Layer green beans and potatoes in slow cooker. Alternate layers of the lamb mixture and onions over prepared layers until all ingredients are used, sprinkling with salt and pepper between each layer. Pour vegetable juice cocktail, tomato sauce and Tabasco sauce over top. Cook, covered, on High for 1 hour; reduce heat. Cook, covered, on Low for 3 to 4 hours. Add tomatoes. Cook, covered, for 2 to 3 hours longer or until of the desired consistency.

Approx Per Serving: Cal 780; Prot 64 g; Carbo 63 g; T Fat 32 g; 36% Calories from Fat; Chol 170 mg; Fiber 14 g; Sod 1017 mg

Virginia Mattson, South Puget Sound HFH, Olympia, WA

Virginia's Lamb Stew

Yield: 8 servings

George and Virginia Works were instrumental in founding HFH of Montrose County in 1991. George has served as treasurer, president and finally director. Virginia died of cancer several months ago. She served as the affilate's first Family Selection and Nurture Chair.

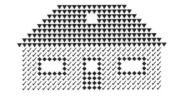

2	to 3 pounds lean lamb, cubed	1/4	teaspoon Worcestershire sauce
1/2	cup flour	1/8	teaspoon allspice
2	tablespoons butter	1	(6-ounce) can tomato paste
2	tablespoons olive oil	1	(750-ml) bottle red wine
1	cup sliced onion	8	to 10 small to medium carrots, cut into 1-inch slices
2	cloves of garlic, minced		
1	teaspoon salt		
1/2	teaspoon pepper	8	to 10 small red potatoes
1/2	teaspoon Tabasco sauce	1/2	cup minced fresh parsley

Coat lamb with flour. Heat butter and olive oil in heavy saucepan until butter melts. Brown lamb in hot butter mixture. Remove to a bowl with slotted spoon, reserving pan drippings. Sauté onion and garlic in reserved pan drippings until tender. Return lamb to saucepan. Stir in next 7 ingredients. Simmer for 2 to 3 hours or until lamb is tender, stirring occasionally. Adjust seasonings if needed. Add carrots. Cook for 20 minutes, stirring occasionally. Add potatoes. Cook for 20 to 45 minutes or just until potatoes are tender. Stir in parsley. Ladle into individual bowls.

Approx Per Serving: Cal 587; Prot 45 g; Carbo 41 g; T Fat 20 g; 31% Calories from Fat; Chol 135 mg; Fiber 5 g; Sod 624 mg

George Works, Montrose HFH, Montrose, CO

Slow-Cooking Beef Stew

Yield: 6 servings

1 1/2	pounds beef stew meat	2	large carrots, peeled, sliced
1	(16-ounce) can green beans	1	onion, sliced
1	(15-ounce) can Veg-All	1	(10-ounce) can cream of tomato soup
2	large potatoes, peeled, cut into quarters		

Combine stew meat, undrained beans, undrained Veg-All, potatoes, carrots and onion in 9x13-inch baking pan and mix gently. Pour soup over top. Bake, covered, at 275 degrees for 5 hours.

Approx Per Serving: Cal 318; Prot 26 g; Carbo 33 g; T Fat 9 g; 26% Calories from Fat; Chol 72 mg; Fiber 6 g; Sod 1054 mg

Yvette M. Carpentier, Knox County HFH, Galesburg, IL

STEWS

SLOW EASY BEEF STEW

YIELD: 12 SERVINGS

As a dietitian, my goal for good nutritional density is to include lots of extra "stuff" of phytochemicals in my recipes...hence the use of herbs and lots of vegetables.

4	pounds beef chuck roast, cubed	6	ribs celery, sliced
2	(16-ounce) cans tomatoes	2	tablespoons chopped fresh parsley
2	(16-ounce) cans Italian green beans	2	tablespoons Worcestershire sauce
2	cups vegetable juice cocktail	2	tablespoons tapioca
6	carrots, sliced	2	teaspoons oregano
2	large onions, chopped	2	teaspoons thyme
6	small potatoes, peeled, chopped	1/8	teaspoon cayenne
		1	teaspoon black pepper
4	cloves of garlic, minced	2	bay leaves

Combine all ingredients in roasting pan and mix gently. Cover with foil; top with roaster lid. Bake at 250 degrees for 4 to 5 hours or until beef and vegetables are tender. Discard bay leaves. Spoon into individual bowls.

Approx Per Serving: Cal 360; Prot 35 g; Carbo 24 g; T Fat 14 g; 35% Calories from Fat; Chol 109 mg; Fiber 4 g; Sod 682 mg

Sandra L. Struve-Seberger, Black Hills HFH, Rapid City, SD

FIVE-HOUR BEEF STEW

YIELD: 6 SERVINGS

2	pounds lean beef chuck roast, cut into bite-size pieces	2 1/2	cups tomato juice
		2	tablespoons minute tapioca
2	cups (1-inch) slices celery	2	tablespoons sugar
2	cups (1-inch) slices carrots	1/2	teaspoon salt
1	medium onion, cut into chunks	1/4	teaspoon pepper
		1/4	teaspoon minced garlic
2	medium potatoes, cut into chunks	1/2	(1-envelope) beef stew seasoning mix

Arrange roast, celery, carrots, onion and potatoes in 9x13-inch baking pan. Combine tomato juice, tapioca, sugar, salt, pepper, garlic and seasoning mix in bowl and mix well. Pour over roast mixture. Bake, covered with foil, at 250 degrees for 5 hours.

Approx Per Serving: Cal 365; Prot 35 g; Carbo 27 g; T Fat 14 g; 33% Calories from Fat; Chol 109 mg; Fiber 3 g; Sod 664 mg

Mary Campbell, Siouxland HFH, Sioux City, IA

GONE-ALL-DAY STEW

YIELD: 8 SERVINGS

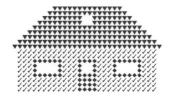

1	(2-pound) beef chuck roast, trimmed, cut into bite-size pieces	2	beef bouillon cubes
3	medium carrots, cut into 1-inch diagonal slices	1	tablespoon Italian seasoning mix
6	small onions	1	bay leaf
4	medium potatoes, cut into 1- to 1½-inch chunks		Freshly ground pepper to taste
½	cup (1-inch) slices celery	1	(10-ounce) can tomato soup
12	whole fresh mushrooms	1	cup water
		¼	cup flour

Combine beef, carrots, onions, potatoes, celery, mushrooms, bouillon cubes, seasoning mix, bay leaf and pepper in roasting pan. Combine soup, water and flour in bowl and mix well. Pour over beef mixture, stirring to mix. Bake, covered, at 275 degrees for 4 to 5 hours. Discard bay leaf. Adjust seasonings if needed. Serve over noodles or with crusty French bread to soak up the gravy and coleslaw. May substitute a mixture of 1 tablespoon leaf oregano, 1 tablespoon thyme and 1 tablespoon rosemary for Italian seasoning mix and red wine for the water.

Approx Per Serving: Cal 345; Prot 28 g; Carbo 33 g; T Fat 11 g; 29% Calories from Fat; Chol 82 mg; Fiber 4 g; Sod 558 mg

Jacqueline Bell, St. Joseph County HFH, South Bend, IN

ONE-TWO-THREE STEW

YIELD: 6 SERVINGS

1	pound beef stew meat	1	(10-ounce) can onion soup
1	(10-ounce) can cream of mushroom soup		

Combine stew meat and soups in bowl and mix well. Spoon into 2-quart baking dish. Bake, covered, at 300 degrees for 3 hours. May add peeled and sliced potatoes and carrots 1 hour before end of cooking process.

Approx Per Serving: Cal 183; Prot 17 g; Carbo 7 g; T Fat 10 g; 48% Calories from Fat; Chol 47 mg; Fiber 1 g; Sod 976 mg

Carolyn Nemec, Schuylkill County HFH, Auburn, PA

I exhort therefore, that, first of all, supplications, prayers, intercessions, and giving of thanks, be made for all men.

1 Timothy 2:1

PARAGUAYAN RICE STEW

YIELD: 6 SERVINGS

1	medium onion, chopped	2	quarts water
¼	cup vegetable oil	1	tablespoon oregano
1½	pounds beef, cubed	1	tablespoon salt
1	pimento pepper or red bell pepper, chopped	3	bay leaves
		½	teaspoon pepper
4	tomatoes, peeled, chopped	16	ounces rice
1	(6-ounce) can tomato paste		

Sauté onion in oil in saucepan. Add beef and mix well. Sauté until beef is brown and juices are absorbed. Stir in pimento pepper, tomatoes and tomato paste. Sauté for several minutes. Add water, oregano, salt, bay leaves and pepper and mix well. Simmer, covered, until beef is tender, stirring occasionally. Stir in rice. Simmer, covered, for 25 minutes or until rice is tender. The stew should be moist, not dry. Discard bay leaves. Spoon into individual bowls. Serve with grated Parmesan cheese or finely chopped onion marinated in vinegar and olive oil.

Approx Per Serving: Cal 555; Prot 31 g; Carbo 72 g; T Fat 15 g; 25% Calories from Fat; Chol 72 mg; Fiber 4 g; Sod 1341 mg

Alicia and Victor Martinez, HFHI Board of Directors
Guatemala, Guatemala

Photo by Chris McGranahan

Photograph at right by Robert Baker

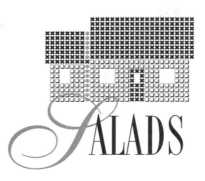

SALADS

"In everything give thanks: for this is the will of
God in Christ Jesus concerning you."

1 Thessalonians 5:18

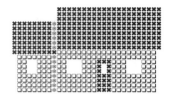

APPLE DOT SLAW

YIELD: 8 SERVINGS

3	cups shredded cabbage	1	tablespoon salad oil
1	cup chopped unpeeled red apple	1	tablespoon cider vinegar
		1	tablespoon sugar
¹/₂	teaspoon celery seeds	¹/₄	teaspoon salt

Mix cabbage, apple and celery seeds in bowl. Whisk salad oil, vinegar, sugar and salt in bowl until blended. Pour over cabbage mixture, tossing to coat. Chill, covered, until serving time.

Approx Per Serving: Cal 39; Prot <1 g; Carbo 6 g; T Fat 2 g; 40% Calories from Fat; Chol 0 mg; Fiber 1 g; Sod 72 mg

Donna Godfrey, York HFH, York, PA

APPLE NUT SALAD

YIELD: 10 SERVINGS

1	(8-ounce) can juice-pack crushed pineapple	1	egg, lightly beaten
		4	cups chopped peeled Granny Smith apples
¹/₂	cup sugar		
2	tablespoons vinegar	8	ounces whipped topping
1	tablespoon flour	1	cup Spanish peanuts

Drain pineapple, reserving juice. Cook reserved juice, sugar, vinegar, flour and egg in saucepan over low heat until thickened, stirring constantly. Cool. Mix pineapple, apples, whipped topping and half the peanuts in bowl. Fold in dressing. Sprinkle with remaining peanuts.

Approx Per Serving: Cal 249; Prot 5 g; Carbo 30 g; T Fat 14 g; 47% Calories from Fat; Chol 21 mg; Fiber 2 g; Sod 13 mg

Helen J. Lien, La Crosse Area HFH, La Crosse, WI

APRICOT SALAD

YIELD: 15 SERVINGS

1	(15-ounce) can crushed pineapple	3	tablespoons sugar
		2	cups buttermilk
1	(6-ounce) package apricot gelatin	8	ounces whipped topping
		1	cup chopped pecans

Mix undrained pineapple, gelatin and sugar in saucepan. Heat until gelatin dissolves. Let stand until cool. Stir in buttermilk, whipped topping and pecans. Spoon into shallow dish. Chill until set.

Approx Per Serving: Cal 187; Prot 3 g; Carbo 25 g; T Fat 10 g; 44% Calories from Fat; Chol 1 mg; Fiber 1 g; Sod 64 mg

Henrietta Pliner, Webster County HFH, Fort Dodge, IA

CRAN-PINEAPPLE SALAD

YIELD: 10 SERVINGS

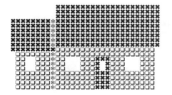

1	(8-ounce) can juice-pack crushed pineapple	1	(6-ounce) package cherry gelatin
1	(16-ounce) package fresh cranberries, rinsed	2	cups chopped pecans

Drain pineapple, reserving juice. Combine reserved juice with enough water to measure 1 cup. Combine juice mixture and cranberries in saucepan. Cook for 10 minutes or until tender, stirring occasionally. Add gelatin and mix well. Cook until gelatin dissolves, stirring constantly. Stir in pineapple and chopped pecans. Spoon into 9x13-inch dish. Chill until set. Cut into 10 portions. Serve on lettuce-lined salad plates.

Approx Per Serving: Cal 256; Prot 4 g; Carbo 28 g; T Fat 16 g; 53% Calories from Fat; Chol 0 mg; Fiber 3 g; Sod 55 mg

Virginia Brewer, Denton HFH, Denton, TX

FRUIT SALAD

YIELD: 12 SERVINGS

1	(20-ounce) can juice-pack chunk pineapple	1	(11-ounce) can mandarin oranges, drained
1	(6-ounce) package vanilla instant pudding mix	2	bananas, sliced
1	(16-ounce) can fruit cocktail, drained		

Drain pineapple, reserving 1 cup of the juice. Combine reserved juice and pudding mix in bowl, stirring until blended. Fold in pineapple, fruit cocktail, mandarin oranges and bananas. Spoon into shallow dish. Chill for 1 to 2 hours or until set. May substitute juices of fruit cocktail or mandarin oranges for pineapple juice or use a combination of the juices.

Approx Per Serving: Cal 135; Prot 1 g; Carbo 35 g; T Fat <1 g; 2% Calories from Fat; Chol 0 mg; Fiber 1 g; Sod 209 mg

Susan Kruspe, Ontario County NY HFH, Shortsville, NY

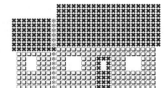

CONGEALED LIME SALAD

YIELD: 10 SERVINGS

2	(3-ounce) packages lime gelatin	1	(20-ounce) can crushed pineapple
2	cups boiling water	1	(14-ounce) can sweetened condensed milk
1	envelope unflavored gelatin	1	cup chopped pecans
1/4	cup cold water	1/2	cup mayonnaise
8	ounces cream cheese, finely chopped, softened		

Dissolve lime gelatin in boiling water in bowl and mix well. Soften unflavored gelatin in cold water in bowl and mix well. Add to lime gelatin mixture, stirring until dissolved. Add cream cheese, stirring until blended. Let stand until cool. Stir in undrained pineapple, condensed milk, pecans and mayonnaise. Spoon into mold or shallow dish. Chill until set. May substitute raspberry gelatin for lime gelatin for a holiday look.

Approx Per Serving: Cal 474; Prot 8 g; Carbo 51 g; T Fat 28 g; 52% Calories from Fat; Chol 45 mg; Fiber 1 g; Sod 229 mg

Emma Stout, Thomasville HFH, Thomasville, NC

MANDARIN ORANGE SALAD

YIELD: 6 SERVINGS

1	(15-ounce) can pineapple tidbits, drained	1 1/2	cups miniature marshmallows
1	(11-ounce) can mandarin oranges, drained	1	cup light sour cream
1	(3-ounce) jar maraschino cherries, drained		

Photo by Raul Ribiera

Combine pineapple, mandarin oranges and cherries in glass bowl and mix gently. Stir in marshmallows. Fold in sour cream. Chill, covered, for 2 to 10 hours.

Approx Per Serving: Cal 175; Prot 3 g; Carbo 34 g; T Fat 4 g; 17% Calories from Fat; Chol 13 mg; Fiber 1 g; Sod 36 mg

Rita C. Anderson, Horry County HFH Myrtle Beach, SC

Orange and Lettuce Salad
Yield: 8 servings

3   (11-ounce) cans mandarin oranges, drained
1½ heads iceberg lettuce, torn into bite-size pieces
2   cups chopped celery
¾   cup slivered almonds, toasted
6   green onions, chopped
3   tablespoons minced fresh parsley
6   tablespoons sugar
6   tablespoons tarragon vinegar
1½ teaspoons salt
¾   teaspoon Tabasco sauce
¾   cup salad oil

Combine mandarin oranges, lettuce, celery, almonds, green onions and parsley in salad bowl and mix well. Chill, covered, in refrigerator for 1 hour. Combine sugar, tarragon vinegar, salt and Tabasco sauce in bowl and mix well. Whisk in oil until blended. Add to chilled lettuce mixture and toss just before serving.

Approx Per Serving: Cal 385; Prot 5 g; Carbo 35 g; T Fat 27 g; 61% Calories from Fat; Chol 0 mg; Fiber 3 g; Sod 450 mg

Cincy Camp, Canton HFH, Canton, OH

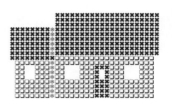

Raspberry Pecan Salad
Yield: 15 servings

1   (6-ounce) package raspberry gelatin
2   cups boiling water
2   (16-ounce) cans whole cranberry sauce
1   (20-ounce) can crushed pineapple, drained
3   large bananas, cut into ⅛- to ¼-inch slices
½   to 1 cup pecan halves

Dissolve gelatin in boiling water in bowl and mix well. Add cranberry sauce, stirring until mixed. Stir in pineapple and bananas. Pour into 9x13-inch dish. Top with pecan halves, pressing to cover slightly. Chill until set. May use sugar-free raspberry gelatin.

Approx Per Serving: Cal 226; Prot 2 g; Carbo 46 g; T Fat 5 g; 19% Calories from Fat; Chol 0 mg; Fiber 2 g; Sod 44 mg

Jane Stewart, Merced County HFH, Merced, CA

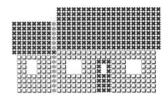

MOTHER'S SUNDAY SALAD

YIELD: 15 SERVINGS

1	(6-ounce) package lemon gelatin	2	large bananas, sliced
2	cups boiling water	1	cup shredded Cheddar cheese
2	cups lemon-lime soda	1	teaspoon butter buds
1	(20-ounce) can crushed pineapple	1/2	cup sugar
1	cup miniature marshmallows	1	cup whipped cream

Dissolve gelatin in boiling water in bowl and mix well. Stir in soda. Chill until partially set. Fold in undrained pineapple, marshmallows and bananas. Spoon into 9x13-inch dish. Chill until set. Combine cheese and butter buds in bowl and mix well. Fold sugar into whipped cream in bowl. Fold into cheese mixture. Spread over prepared layer. Chill until serving time.

Approx Per Serving: Cal 195; Prot 3 g; Carbo 35 g; T Fat 6 g; 25% Calories from Fat; Chol 19 mg; Fiber 1 g; Sod 95 mg

Linda Reeder, Rogue Valley HFH, Medford, OR

CHICKEN RICE SALAD

YIELD: 6 SERVINGS

1	(6-ounce) package long grain and wild rice, cooked	1	cup seedless grapes
		1/2	to 1 cup finely chopped onion
2	cups chopped cooked chicken	1/2	cup chopped pecans
1	cup chopped celery	1/4	to 3/4 cup low-fat mayonnaise

Combine rice, chicken, celery, grapes, onion and pecans in bowl and mix gently. Add just enough mayonnaise to moisten, stirring until mixed. Serve immediately or chill until serving time. May substitute chopped apple for the grapes and nonfat mayonnaise for the low-fat mayonnaise. May omit pecans to reduce fat grams.

Approx Per Serving: Cal 409; Prot 18 g; Carbo 40 g; T Fat 20 g; 44% Calories from Fat; Chol 49 mg; Fiber 1 g; Sod 784 mg

Candy Morris, Walton Co. HFH, Monroe, GA

FRUITY TURKEY SALAD

YIELD: 2 SERVINGS

4	ounces leftover turkey, chopped	1/8	teaspoon thyme
1/2	medium peach, chopped	1	teaspoon mayonnaise
1/2	cup finely chopped celery		Leaf lettuce

Combine turkey, peach, celery and thyme in bowl and mix well. Stir in mayonnaise. Spoon onto lettuce-lined salad plates.

Approx Per Serving: Cal 127; Prot 17 g; Carbo 4 g; T Fat 5 g; 34% Calories from Fat; Chol 44 mg; Fiber 1 g; Sod 79 mg

Ruth Bauman, Richland County HFH, Mansfield, OH

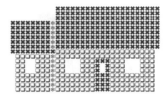

SURPRISING TUNA FISH

YIELD: 2 SERVINGS

1	(6-ounce) can water-pack albacore tuna, drained	1/4	cup finely chopped celery
1/2	apple, peeled, chopped	2	tablespoons mayonnaise
1/4	cup chopped pecans	1	teaspoon Dijon mustard
1/4	cup chopped scallions	1/4	teaspoon dillweed
		1/4	teaspoon cinnamon

Combine tuna, apple, pecans, scallions and celery in bowl and mix well. Sir in mixture of mayonnaise, Dijon mustard, dillweed and cinnamon. Chill, covered, until serving time. Use as sandwich spread with bleu cheese or Cheddar cheese for tuna melt. May use low-fat mayonnaise.

Approx Per Serving: Cal 316; Prot 22 g; Carbo 10 g; T Fat 22 g; 61% Calories from Fat; Chol 31 mg; Fiber 2 g; Sod 420 mg

Joe Casale, HFHI, Midland Park, NJ

After a couple of years of hard work developing our chapter, raising money, locating a homeowner, and organizing volunteers, we dedicated our first home. All those long hours were well worth the effort. Our prayers were answered—our first home was completed! The feeling of that moment when the Bible and house keys were passed over to the new homeowner was wonderful. Every time I drive by that home, those same feelings come back, and I will treasure them forever.

Candy Morris
Walton Co. HFH

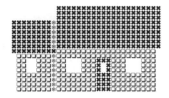

Jeanie's Tuna Potato Salad
Yield: 12 servings

1	(6-ounce) can water-pack tuna, drained	2	tablespoons prepared mustard
4	carrots, grated	1	tablespoon sugar
4	ribs celery, chopped		Salt and pepper to taste
1	small onion, finely chopped	2	(2-ounce) cans shoestring potatoes
2	cups mayonnaise-type salad dressing		

Combine tuna, carrots, celery and onion in bowl and mix well. Combine salad dressing, mustard, sugar, salt and pepper in bowl and mix well. Add to tuna mixture, stirring until mixed. Chill, covered, for 3 to 4 hours. Stir in shoestring potatoes just before serving.

Approx Per Serving: Cal 238; Prot 5 g; Carbo 19 g; T Fat 16 g; 60% Calories from Fat; Chol 14 mg; Fiber 1 g; Sod 436 mg

Sheilla W. Snell, HFHI, Americus, GA

Four-Bean Salad
Yield: 12 servings

Great for potluck dinners. The flavor is enhanced if the salad is made 1 day in advance.

1	(16-ounce) can green beans, drained	1	green bell pepper, chopped
1	(16-ounce) can yellow wax beans, drained	1	(6-ounce) can mushrooms, drained
1	(16-ounce) can kidney beans, drained	1/2	cup sugar
1	(16-ounce) can garbanzo beans, drained	1/2	cup red wine vinegar
1	ripe tomato, chopped	1/2	cup salad oil
1	red onion, chopped	2	tablespoons tarragon vinegar
1	(7-ounce) jar sliced green olives, drained	1	teaspoon salt
		1/2	teaspoon dry mustard
		1/2	teaspoon oregano
		1/4	teaspoon pepper

Layer the green beans, wax beans, kidney beans, garbanzo beans, tomato, onion, olives, green pepper and mushrooms in a gallon glass jar. Combine remaining ingredients in bowl and mix well. Pour over vegetables; seal tightly. Shake to coat. Marinate in refrigerator for 24 hours or longer, shaking every few hours. Marinating in glass jar instead of stirring assures that the vegetables will be marinated evenly without the possibility of breaking up the beans.

Approx Per Serving: Cal 251; Prot 6 g; Carbo 31 g; T Fat 12 g; 42% Calories from Fat; Chol 0 mg; Fiber 5 g; Sod 940 mg

Rose Waite, Payson Area HFH, Payson, AZ

Broccoli Bacon Salad

Yield: 12 servings

Florets of 1 bunch broccoli
1 pound bacon, crisp-fried, drained, crumbled
1 cup chopped celery
1/2 cup chopped red onion
1/2 cup sunflower kernels
1/2 cup raisins
3/4 cup mayonnaise
1/4 cup sugar
2 tablespoons vinegar

Combine broccoli, bacon, celery, onion, sunflower kernels and raisins in bowl and mix well. Combine mayonnaise, sugar and vinegar in bowl and mix well. Stir dressing into broccoli mixture. Chill, covered, until serving time.

Approx Per Serving: Cal 242; Prot 6 g; Carbo 13 g; T Fat 20 g; 71% Calories from Fat; Chol 18 mg; Fiber 1 g; Sod 271 mg

Jill Olen, St. Lucie HFH, Fort Pierce, FL

Mixed Broccoli Salad

Yield: 12 servings

Florets of 1 bunch broccoli
Florets of 1 head cauliflower
1 red onion, finely chopped
1/2 cup golden raisins
1/2 cup light mayonnaise
1/4 cup sugar
3 tablespoons white wine vinegar

Combine broccoli, cauliflower, onion and raisins in salad bowl and mix gently. Combine mayonnaise, sugar and wine vinegar in bowl and mix well. Add to broccoli mixture, stirring to coat. Chill, covered, until serving time.

Approx Per Serving: Cal 72; Prot 1 g; Carbo 13 g; T Fat 2 g; 25% Calories from Fat; Chol 3 mg; Fiber 1 g; Sod 60 mg

Deb Schulte, Southeast New Hampshire HFH, New Castle, NH

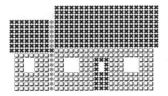

A few weeks after moving into their new home, HFH homeowners Trish and Marc Allain of Somersworth, NH, offered to help my family restore our old family home. Habitat for Humanity builds homes, but equally as important, it builds lasting friendships between home-owners and volunteers.

Deb Schulte
Southeast
New Hampshire HFH

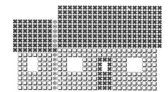

BROCCOLI GRAPE SALAD

YIELD: 10 SERVINGS

4	cups broccoli florets, cut into bite-size pieces	1/2	cup thinly sliced red onion, chopped
12	slices crisp-fried bacon, crumbled	1	cup mayonnaise
1	cup seedless red grapes	2	tablespoons sugar
1/2	cup sunflower kernels	2	tablespoons raspberry vinegar

Combine broccoli, bacon, grapes, sunflower kernels and onion in bowl and mix gently. Stir in mixture of mayonnaise, sugar and raspberry vinegar. Serve immediately or chill. Store, covered, in refrigerator for up to 1 week. May substitute nonfat raspberry yogurt for mayonnaise mixture and bacon bits for crisp-fried bacon.

Approx Per Serving: Cal 273; Prot 5 g; Carbo 9 g; T Fat 25 g; 80% Calories from Fat; Chol 19 mg; Fiber 1 g; Sod 252 mg

Lucy S. Woodhouse, Georgetown County SC HFH, Georgetown, SC

PEANUTTY CABBAGE SALAD

YIELD: 10 SERVINGS

Leslie Linton, Bob Hope's chef, shared one of Bob Hope's favorite salads with us.

2	tablespoons rice vinegar	1	tablespoon brown sugar
2	tablespoons sesame oil		Boiling water
1	tablespoon fresh organic peanut butter with oil	1	head cabbage, shredded
1	tablespoon soy sauce	1/2	cup chopped peanuts

Combine rice vinegar, sesame oil, peanut butter, soy sauce and brown sugar in bowl and mix well. Add enough boiling water to make of sauce consistency and mix well. Pour over cabbage in bowl, tossing to coat. Sprinkle with peanuts. May sprinkle with chopped fresh gingerroot.

Approx Per Serving: Cal 130; Prot 5 g; Carbo 9 g; T Fat 10 g; 62% Calories from Fat; Chol 0 mg; Fiber 3 g; Sod 121 mg

Bob Hope, No. Hollywood, CA

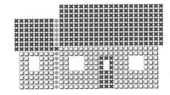

PENNSYLVANIA DUTCH SLAW

YIELD: 9 SERVINGS

3	cups finely shredded cabbage	1/3	cup vinegar
1	small green bell pepper, finely chopped	2	tablespoons sugar
1	small red bell pepper, finely chopped	1	teaspoon salt

Toss cabbage, green pepper and red pepper in bowl. Combine vinegar, sugar and salt in bowl, stirring until sugar and salt dissolve. Pour over cabbage mixture, tossing to coat. May omit salt and substitute artificial sweetener for sugar. Add celery seeds and/or grated carrots for variety.

Approx Per Serving: Cal 21; Prot <1 g; Carbo 5 g; T Fat <1 g; 3% Calories from Fat; Chol 0 mg; Fiber 1 g; Sod 241 mg

Jane S. Oleksak, Cambria County HFH, Johnstown, PA

MARINATED CARROT SALAD

YIELD: 8 SERVINGS

Makes a wonderful tasty addition to buffet tables during any season of the year. This salad travels well and is, therefore, perfect for picnics and potluck suppers. Or take it to your building site.

1	pound carrots, julienned	1/2	cup vegetable oil
1	medium red onion, thinly sliced	1/3	cup cider vinegar
1	cup gherkins, julienned	1/4	cup sugar
1/2	(10-ounce) can tomato soup	1/2	teaspoon salt
		1/4	teaspoon freshly ground pepper

Steam carrots in steamer for 8 minutes or until tender-crisp; drain. Combine carrots, onion and pickles in glass bowl and mix gently. Whisk soup, oil, vinegar, sugar, salt and pepper in bowl until blended. Pour over carrot mixture, tossing to coat. Marinate, covered, in refrigerator for 8 to 10 hours or longer, stirring occasionally. Serve using a slotted spoon. May store, covered, in refrigerator for several weeks. May substitute dill pickles for gherkins, olive oil for vegetable oil and wine vinegar for cider vinegar.

Approx Per Serving: Cal 215; Prot 1 g; Carbo 23 g; T Fat 14 g; 57% Calories from Fat; Chol 0 mg; Fiber 2 g; Sod 422 mg
Nutritional information includes entire amount of marinade.

Betty Jane Rose, Waterloo Region HFH, Waterloo, Ontario, Canada

Our sponsored Habitat partner is Jamaica. Since our affiliate began in 1987, I always joked that I wanted to deliver our tithe. I did that in February of 1996. I had the wonderful experience of working in Majesty Garden, Kingston, Jamaica, for two weeks with the Habitat Canadian team. It was a real mountaintop experience for me!

Betty Jane Rose
Waterloo Region HFH

SALADS

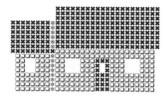

Last summer our affiliate was challenged to raise $5,000 in less than one month in order to receive a matching $5,000 from a local resident. This was quite a stretch for our fund-raising skills. Not only did we reach our $5,000 goal, we raised $12,500. What a wonderful affirmation of the belief in, and support of, Habitat for Humanity.

Sally A. Conard
Emporia Area HFH

COUSCOUS SALAD

YIELD: 6 SERVINGS

1½	cups cooked couscous	¾	cup lemon juice
1½	cups canned garbanzo beans, heated	¼	to ½ cup olive oil
1	cup chopped fresh parsley	1	teaspoon Dijon mustard
2	medium tomatoes, chopped	1	teaspoon mint
1	cup chopped cucumber	½	teaspoon salt
6	green onions, chopped	½	teaspoon garlic powder
		¼	teaspoon ground pepper

Combine couscous, beans, parsley, tomatoes, cucumber and green onions in bowl and mix gently. Whisk lemon juice, olive oil, Dijon mustard, mint, salt, garlic powder and pepper in bowl until blended. Stir into couscous mixture. Chill, covered, until serving time.

Approx Per Serving: Cal 296; Prot 5 g; Carbo 27 g; T Fat 20 g; 58% Calories from Fat; Chol 0 mg; Fiber 6 g; Sod 353 mg

Patricia A. Frazar, Broward HFH, Ft. Lauderdale, FL

EMPORIA SALAD

YIELD: 12 SERVINGS

Giving this recipe to new female residents of Emporia has been a tradition for the past fifty years.

2	(10-ounce) cans tomato soup	1	green bell pepper, chopped
2	(3-ounce) packages lemon gelatin	3	or 4 green onions, minced
1	cup mayonnaise-type salad dressing	1	cup cottage cheese
8	ounces cream cheese, cubed	3	ounces cream cheese, softened
1½	cups chopped celery	1	envelope ranch salad dressing mix
1	cup chopped pecans	1	(8-ounce) can clams, drained
			Lettuce leaves

Heat soup in saucepan just to the boiling point. Remove from heat. Add gelatin, salad dressing and 8 ounces cream cheese, stirring until blended. Let stand until cool. Stir in celery, pecans, green pepper and green onions. Spoon into ring mold. Chill until set. Beat cottage cheese, 3 ounces cream cheese and salad dressing mix in mixer bowl until blended. Stir in clams. Invert mold onto lettuce-lined platter. Fill center with cottage cheese mixture.

Approx Per Serving: Cal 377; Prot 12 g; Carbo 30 g; T Fat 24 g; 56% Calories from Fat; Chol 49 mg; Fiber 1 g; Sod 910 mg

Sally A. Conard, Emporia Area HFH, Emporia, KS

GTO SALAD

Yield: 2 servings

4	ounces sliced fresh green beans
1	fresh tomato, chopped
1/3	cup chopped onion or sweet cipollini
1	tablespoon vegetable oil

1 1/2	teaspoons lemon juice
1/8	teaspoon salt
1/8	teaspoon white pepper
2	slices crisp-fried bacon, crumbled

Combine greeen beans with enough water to cover in saucepan. Cook for 4 to 5 minutes or until tender-crisp; drain. Plunge into ice water in bowl to cool; drain. Combine green beans, tomato and onion in bowl and mix gently. Stir in mixture of oil, lemon juice, salt and white pepper just before serving. Sprinkle with bacon. Add 5 ounces cooked peeled shrimp for a hearty salad.

Approx Per Serving: Cal 138; Prot 4 g; Carbo 10 g; T Fat 10 g; 63% Calories from Fat; Chol 5 mg; Fiber 3 g; Sod 244 mg

Joyce Lind, Windsor HFH, Eaton, CO

"LA PITAYAHA" POTATO SALAD

Yield: 25 servings

10	pounds small unpeeled white or red potatoes
2	cups chopped scallions with tops
1/2	cup white vinegar
2	cups thinly sliced radishes
2	large jicama, peeled, chopped

2	cups mayonnaise
2	cups plain low-fat yogurt
1	large bunch cilantro, chopped
1	tablespoon salt
1	pint cherry tomatoes, cut into halves

Combine potatoes with enough water to cover in stockpot. Cook over open fire or on stove for 20 minutes or until tender; drain. Cool slightly and slice; do not peel. Combine potatoes and scallions in bowl and mix gently. Pour vinegar over potato mixture. Let stand until cool. Stir in radishes and jicama. Combine mayonnaise, yogurt, cilantro and salt in bowl and mix well. Add to potato mixture, stirring gently to mix. Top with tomatoes. May substitute 2 cups chopped celery for jicama.

Approx Per Serving: Cal 356; Prot 6 g; Carbo 52 g; T Fat 15 g; 36% Calories from Fat; Chol 12 mg; Fiber 7 g; Sod 394 mg

Brenda Mleziva and Cinda McKinney, Habitat Northeast, Acton, MA

The challenge was to provide lunch the last day of our Global Village Short Term Mission Project in Mexico. The menu was to be easy enough to be prepared without a kitchen. The potatoes were cooked over an open fire. Vegetables were chopped with Swiss army knives from our backpacks and a borrowed machete. Members of our group and residents of the village of La Pitayaha pitched in for the feast preparation. The potato salad was a rather humble addition. Cooking in partnership is a wonderful way to build relationships, as is the building of homes.

Brenda Mleziva and Cinda McKinney Habitat Northeast

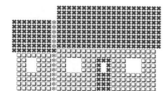

New Potato Salad

YIELD: 10 SERVINGS

6	unpeeled medium new potatoes, coarsely chopped	1	tablespoon Dijon mustard
1	small onion, chopped	1/2	teaspoon chopped garlic
1/3	cup olive oil	1/2	teaspoon hot pepper sauce
1/4	cup cider vinegar	1/2	teaspoon salt
		1/2	teaspoon dillweed
		1/2	teaspoon tarragon

Combine potatoes with enough water to cover in saucepan. Cook until tender but firm; drain. Let stand until cool. Pour mixture of onion, olive oil, vinegar, Dijon mustard, garlic, hot pepper sauce, salt, dillweed and tarragon over potatoes in bowl, tossing gently to mix.

Approx Per Serving: Cal 149; Prot 2 g; Carbo 20 g; T Fat 7 g; 44% Calories from Fat; Chol 0 mg; Fiber 2 g; Sod 151 mg

Bonnie Watson, HFHI and Former International Partner, Americus, GA

Spinach Salad

YIELD: 10 SERVINGS

2	pounds spinach, trimmed, torn into bite-size pieces	1/2	cup sliced green onions
16	ounces fresh strawberries, sliced	1/2	cup snipped fresh mint
1	cucumber, sliced	1/2	cup Poppy Seed Dressing

Toss spinach, strawberries, cucumber, green onions and mint in salad bowl. Drizzle with 1/2 cup of the Poppy Seed Dressing just before serving.

Approx Per Serving: Cal 107; Prot 3 g; Carbo 9 g; T Fat 8 g; 60% Calories from Fat; Chol 0 mg; Fiber 3 g; Sod 63 mg

Poppy Seed Dressing

YIELD: 24 TABLESPOONS

1	cup olive oil	1	teaspoon poppy seeds
1/3	cup sugar	1/2	teaspoon dry mustard
1/4	cup vinegar	1/8	teaspoon salt
1	teaspoon paprika		

Combine olive oil, sugar, vinegar, paprika, poppy seeds, dry mustard and salt in jar with tightfitting lid and shake to mix.

Approx Per Tablespoon: Cal 91; Prot <1 g; Carbo 3 g; T Fat 10 g; 87% Calories from Fat; Chol 0 mg; Fiber <1 g; Sod 11 mg

Paulette House, Rogue Valley HFH, Medford, OR

TOMATO AVOCADO SALAD

YIELD: 8 SERVINGS

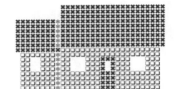
2	ripe avocados, sliced	1	cup Italian salad dressing
2	large tomatoes, cut into wedges		Lettuce leaves
1	medium onion, cut into wedges		

Combine avocados, tomatoes and onion in salad bowl and mix gently. Add salad dressing, tossing to coat. Chill, covered, for 20 to 30 minutes. Spoon onto a lettuce-lined serving platter.

Approx Per Serving: Cal 235; Prot 2 g; Carbo 11 g; T Fat 24 g; 81% Calories from Fat; Chol 0 mg; Fiber 3 g; Sod 242 mg

Rusleen Maurice, Bryan/College Station HFH, Bryan, TX

MARINATED VEGETABLES

YIELD: 10 SERVINGS

1	(1-pound) bunch broccoli	1	medium red onion, sliced, separated into rings
	Florets of 1 small head cauliflower	1/4	cup minced fresh parsley
1/2	(14-ounce) package frozen crinkle-cut carrots		Lemon Salad Dressing (page 58)
1	(9-ounce) can marinated artichoke hearts, drained	1	(16-ounce) can pitted black olives, drained
1	large green bell pepper, julienned	4	ounces bleu cheese, crumbled

Separate broccoli into florets. Peel stems; cut into 1-inch pieces. Cook broccoli and cauliflower in boiling water in separate saucepans for 5 to 7 minutes or until tender-crisp; drain. Cook carrots using package directions; drain. Combine broccoli, cauliflower, carrots, artichokes, green pepper, onion and parsley in bowl and mix gently. Add Lemon Salad Dressing, tossing to coat. Marinate, covered, for 4 to 10 hours, stirring occasionally. Stir in olives and bleu cheese just before serving. May substitute 10 ounces frozen cooked broccoli and cauliflower for fresh broccoli and fresh cauliflower.

Approx Per Serving: Cal 274; Prot 5 g; Carbo 11 g; T Fat 25 g; 77% Calories from Fat; Chol 9 mg; Fiber 4 g; Sod 934 mg

Celine Wicks, Lake Villa, IL

Photo by Robert Baker

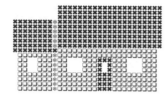

FRENCH DRESSING

YIELD: 12 (¹/₄-CUP) SERVINGS

1	(10-ounce) can tomato soup	2	tablespoons Worcestershire sauce
³/₄	cup sugar	1	teaspoon salt
³/₄	cup vegetable oil	1	teaspoon dry mustard
¹/₂	cup vinegar		Minced onion to taste

Mix soup, sugar, oil, vinegar, Worcestershire sauce, salt, dry mustard and onion in jar with tightfitting lid. Shake well. Store in refrigerator.

Approx Per Serving: Cal 191; Prot <1 g; Carbo 17 g; T Fat 14 g; 64% Calories from Fat; Chol 0 mg; Fiber <1 g; Sod 382 mg

Linda K. Gehl, Orleans County HFH, Albion, NY

LEMON SALAD DRESSING

YIELD: 1 CUP

¹/₃	cup fresh lemon juice	¹/₂	teaspoon prepared mustard
1	teaspoon salt		
1	teaspoon sugar	¹/₄	teaspoon freshly ground pepper
1	teaspoon oregano		
1	teaspoon basil	²/₃	cup salad oil

Combine lemon juice, salt, sugar, oregano, basil, prepared mustard and pepper in bowl and mix well. Whisk in salad oil until blended.

Approx Per Serving: Cal 83; Prot <1 g; Carbo 1 g; T Fat 9 g; 97% Calories from Fat; Chol 0 mg; Fiber <1 g; Sod 135 mg

Celine Wicks, Lake Villa, IL

Photograph at right by Robert Baker

Entrees

"A generous man will himself be blessed,
for he shares his food with the poor."

Proverbs 84:3

ENTREES

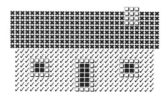

ESTHER'S POT ROAST

YIELD: 10 SERVINGS

1	(4- to 5-pound) chuck or rump beef roast	1/2	to 1 envelope onion soup mix
1/4	cup flour	1	cup (or more) water
1	tablespoon vegetable shortening	1	(10-ounce) can cream of mushroom soup
	Salt and pepper to taste	1	to 2 tablespoons soy sauce

Coat roast with flour. Brown in shortening in Dutch oven on all sides. Season with salt and pepper. Sprinkle with onion soup mix. Pour mixture of water, cream of mushroom soup and soy sauce over roast. Bake, covered, at 325 degrees for 2 1/2 to 3 hours or until done to taste. May add onions and carrot pieces during the last hour of baking.

Approx Per Serving: Cal 394; Prot 43 g; Carbo 5 g; T Fat 21 g; 50% Calories from Fat; Chol 142 mg; Fiber <1 g; Sod 611 mg

University of Maryland College Park (CC), College Park, MD

ITALIAN BEEF

YIELD: 8 SERVINGS

1	(12-ounce) bottle beer	1	envelope Italian salad dressing mix
1	(3-pound) chuck roast, trimmed, cut into large pieces		

Pour beer over roast in slow cooker. Cook on Medium for 2 to 3 hours or until tender; roast should fall apart. Remove roast to platter with slotted spoon, reserving drippings; shred beef. Skim reserved drippings. Combine beef, reserved drippings and dressing mix in slow cooker and mix well. Cook on Low until heated through; mixture should be moist but not runny. May add additional liquid if desired. Serve on rolls or French bread with green salad and hot peppers. May substitute one 14-ounce can beef broth or 2 cups water for beer. May cook in covered cast-iron skillet over low heat.

Approx Per Serving: Cal 329; Prot 31 g; Carbo 2 g; T Fat 20 g; 55% Calories from Fat; Chol 113 mg; Fiber <1 g; Sod 194 mg

Arthur Woodward, Flower City HFH, Rochester, NY

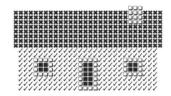

ROUND STEAK BAKE

YIELD: 6 SERVINGS

1	(2-pound) round steak, cut into 1-inch cubes	5	carrots, sliced
4	medium potatoes, cut into quarters	2	(10-ounce) cans cream of mushroom soup
		1	envelope onion soup mix

Combine steak, potatoes and carrots in 3-quart baking dish. Pour mixture of soup and soup mix over steak mixture. Bake, covered, at 325 degrees for 2½ hours.

Approx Per Serving: Cal 370; Prot 32 g; Carbo 32 g; T Fat 12 g; 30% Calories from Fat; Chol 76 mg; Fiber 3 g; Sod 1009 mg

Donna Holter, Mercer County HFH, West Middlesex, PA

SESAME FLANK STEAK

YIELD: 4 SERVINGS

¼	cup sesame seeds	1	tablespoon minced fresh gingerroot
¼	cup thinly sliced green onions	1	tablespoon minced garlic
3	tablespoons soy sauce	1	teaspoon dry mustard
2	tablespoons sesame or vegetable oil	1	teaspoon Worcestershire sauce
1	tablespoon vinegar	1	(1½-pound) flank steak
1	tablespoon brown sugar		

Toast sesame seeds in skillet until golden brown. Combine sesame seeds, green onions, soy sauce, sesame oil, vinegar, brown sugar, gingerroot, garlic, dry mustard and Worcestershire sauce in bowl and mix well. Pour over steak in sealable plastic bag. Marinate in refrigerator for 8 to 10 hours, turning occasionally. Grill steak over hot coals for 6 to 7 minutes per side or until done to taste. Cut cross grain into thin slices. Serve immediately.

Approx Per Serving: Cal 347; Prot 30 g; Carbo 8 g; T Fat 22 g; 57% Calories from Fat; Chol 67 mg; Fiber 1 g; Sod 872 mg

Joyce Lind, Windsor HFH, Eaton, CO

Photo by Robert Baker

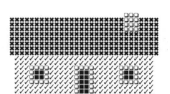

DINNER IN FOIL

YIELD: 4 SERVINGS

I attended a little country day school during my younger years. Each fall brought bushel baskets of golden yellow, rust, and orange-colored leaves that, for some reason, our teacher considered in the way. To coax us children into raking them up, when the last of the leaves were in the bin, we all got to participate in cooking a meal outdoors. An oven rack was placed on the top of the smoldering leaves, followed by foil-wrapped lunches, steamed until done. This delicious meal had a wonderful way of soothing aching back muscles and seemingly made it worth it! While I no longer rake up leaves, I still make this tasty and nutritious meal every couple of weeks—mostly because I get so many requests for it. I hope you like it, too!

1	pound beef, cut into bite-size pieces	1/2	teaspoon salt
4	potatoes, peeled, chopped	1/2	teaspoon pepper
1	large onion, chopped		Basil to taste
2	large carrots, cut into 1/8-inch slices		Garlic salt to taste
2	cups (1-inch) string bean pieces	4	teaspoons butter
		1	cup water

Cut four 12x12-inch sheets of foil. Combine beef, potatoes, onion, carrots and beans in bowl and mix gently. Spoon 1/4 of mixture in center of each foil square. Turn foil up around ingredients to form a pouch. Season with salt, pepper, basil and garlic salt; dot with butter. Add 1/4 cup water to each pouch; pinch foil to seal. Grill over hot coals for 20 minutes. Open pouch and serve.

Approx Per Serving: Cal 374; Prot 25 g; Carbo 38 g; T Fat 14 g; 33% Calories from Fat; Chol 81 mg; Fiber 6 g; Sod 912 mg

Bettie B. Youngs, PhD, Author, *Gifts of the Heart*, Del Mar, CA

NO-PEEK BEEF STROGANOFF

YIELD: 6 SERVINGS

2	pounds beef stew meat, cut into 1-inch pieces	1	(4-ounce) can mushrooms
1	(10-ounce) can cream of mushroom soup	1	envelope onion soup mix
		1	cup sour cream

Mix stew meat, soup, mushrooms and soup mix in slow cooker. Cook on Low for 8 to 12 hours or on High for 5 to 6 hours; do not peek. Stir in sour cream just before serving. Serve over noodles.

Approx Per Serving: Cal 351; Prot 30 g; Carbo 7 g; T Fat 22 g; 57% Calories from Fat; Chol 108 mg; Fiber 1 g; Sod 884 mg

JoAnn Wolfe, St. Joseph County HFH, Granger, IN

No-Peek Casserole

Yield: 4 servings

2	pounds beef stew meat, cut into bite-size pieces	1	onion, chopped
1	(10-ounce) can cream of celery soup	1	(6-ounce) can mushroom pieces
		2	carrots, chopped

Mix all ingredients in bowl. Spoon into baking pan. Bake, tightly covered, for 3 hours; do not peek. Serve over hot cooked rice.

Approx Per Serving: Cal 405; Prot 44 g; Carbo 13 g; T Fat 19 g; 42% Calories from Fat; Chol 144 mg; Fiber 3 g; Sod 1170 mg

Clara Short, Southeast New Hampshire HFH, Portsmouth, NH

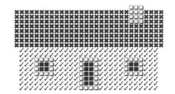

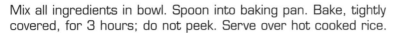

Mom Lupke's Barbecue

Yield: 6 servings

1	pound ground beef	1	cup water
	Onion salt to taste	1	tablespoon Worcestershire sauce
1	cup catsup		
1	cup packed brown sugar		

Brown ground beef in skillet, stirring until crumbly; drain. Sprinkle with onion salt. Stir in catsup, brown sugar, water and Worcestershire sauce. Bring to a boil; reduce heat. Simmer until of the desired consistency, stirring occasionally. Serve on hamburger buns.

Approx Per Serving: Cal 324; Prot 17 g; Carbo 41 g; T Fat 11 g; 29% Calories from Fat; Chol 56 mg; Fiber 1 g; Sod 564 mg

Sherri Ritter, Okeechobee HFH, Okeechobee, FL

Beef and Rice Bake

Yield: 6 servings

6	slices bacon, chopped	1	teaspoon salt
1½	pounds ground beef	1	cup rice, rinsed, drained
1	onion, chopped	4	cups tomato juice, heated

Sauté bacon in skillet until crisp. Drain most of pan drippings. Add ground beef and onion. Cook until ground beef is brown and onion is tender, stirring constantly; drain. Stir in salt, rice and 1½ cups of the tomato juice. Spoon into greased 2-quart baking dish. Bake at 350 degrees for 1 hour or until rice is tender, adding remaining tomato juice as liquid is absorbed.

Approx Per Serving: Cal 432; Prot 31 g; Carbo 33 g; T Fat 19 g; 40% Calories from Fat; Chol 90 mg; Fiber 1 g; Sod 1106 mg

Helen Steinberg, Will County HFH, Joliet, IL

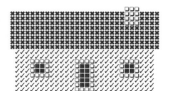

BEAN BURGERS

YIELD: 8 SERVINGS

1	pound ground beef	¹/₄	cup catsup
1	(10-ounce) can bean and bacon soup	1	to 2 teaspoons prepared mustard

Brown ground beef in skillet, stirring until crumbly; drain. Stir in soup, catsup and mustard. Cook until heated through. Serve on buns.

Approx Per Serving: Cal 186; Prot 15 g; Carbo 9 g; T Fat 10 g; 47% Calories from Fat; Chol 43 mg; Fiber 3 g; Sod 426 mg

Elaine M. Wuethrich, Richland County HFH, Mansfield, OH

HOBO BURGERS

YIELD: 4 SERVINGS

1	pound lean ground chuck	2	onions, sliced
2	carrots, thinly sliced		Salt and pepper to taste
2	potatoes, thinly sliced		

Cut four 12x12-inch sheets of heavy-duty foil. Shape ground chuck into 4 thick patties. Place 1 patty on each foil square. Arrange carrots, potatoes and onions on and around beef patties. Season with salt and pepper. Seal foil to enclose. Place foil pouches on baking sheet. Bake at 400 degrees for 40 minutes. Open foil and serve.

Approx Per Serving: Cal 341; Prot 27 g; Carbo 22 g; T Fat 16 g; 42% Calories from Fat; Chol 84 mg; Fiber 3 g; Sod 78 mg

Edwin Stephens, Burke County HFH, Sardis, GA

SPICY BURGERS

YIELD: 8 SERVINGS

¹/₃	cup crumbled bleu cheese	1	tablespoon brown sugar
4	scallions with tops, minced	1	tablespoon Worcestershire sauce
1	red bell pepper, chopped	1	tablespoon prepared horseradish
1	small yellow onion, minced		
2	large cloves of garlic, crushed	1	teaspoon pepper
2	tablespoons soy sauce	2	pounds lean ground beef

Combine first 10 ingredients in bowl and mix well. Add ground beef, stirring until mixed. Chill, covered, for 1 hour or longer. Shape into 8 patties. Grill over hot coals until cooked through.

Approx Per Serving: Cal 284; Prot 27 g; Carbo 5 g; T Fat 17 g; 55% Calories from Fat; Chol 88 mg; Fiber 1 g; Sod 407 mg

Jennifer A. Oliver, HFHI, Americus, GA

EL DORADO CASSEROLE

Yield: 6 servings

1	pound ground beef
1	(15-ounce) can tomato sauce
1	small onion, chopped
10	black olives, chopped
10	green olives, chopped
1	cup sour cream
1	cup cottage cheese
8	ounces Cheddar cheese, shredded
1	(9-ounce) package taco-flavor tortilla chips

Brown ground beef in skillet, stirring until crumbly; drain. Stir in tomato sauce, onion and olives. Combine sour cream and cottage cheese in bowl and mix well. Layer ground beef mixture, sour cream mixture, Cheddar cheese and chips alternately in 2-quart baking dish until all ingredients are used. Bake at 350 degrees for 30 minutes.

Approx Per Serving: Cal 682; Prot 36 g; Carbo 37 g; T Fat 45 g; 58% Calories from Fat; Chol 120 mg; Fiber 4 g; Sod 1422 mg

Ruth Hazelton, Las Vegas HFH, Las Vegas, NM

ENCHILADA CASSEROLE

Yield: 12 servings

2	pounds ground beef
1	(16-ounce) can ranch-style beans
1	onion, chopped
1	teaspoon garlic powder
1	teaspoon cumin
1	teaspoon chili powder
½	teaspoon salt
12	corn tortillas, torn
16	ounces Velveeta cheese, shredded
1	(10-ounce) can cream of chicken soup
1	(10-ounce) can tomatoes with green chiles

Brown ground beef in skillet, stirring until crumbly; drain. Add beans, onion, garlic powder, cumin, chili powder and salt and mix well. Layer ½ of the corn tortillas, ground beef mixture, cheese and remaining corn tortillas in order listed in 9x13-inch baking pan. Spread with soup; top with tomatoes. Bake, covered with foil, at 350 degrees for 1 hour.

Approx Per Serving: Cal 439; Prot 30 g; Carbo 27 g; T Fat 23 g; 48% Calories from Fat; Chol 90 mg; Fiber 2 g; Sod 1119 mg

Mary Ruth Rhodenbaugh, Brazoria County HFH, Brazoria, TX

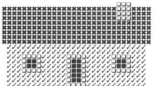

Watching relationships develop and grow is an exciting part of Habitat for me. I recall two young men working on an HFH house. They did not speak the same language. One owned a $200,000 home and one was earning sweat equity. They were both thirty-three years old and each had three children. One was an electrical engineer; one was a day laborer. Both were ambitious and energetic and wanted the best for their families. They had come to respect and admire each other. I wondered that evening...how would these two young men have become acquainted without Habitat?

Mary Ruth
Rhodenbaugh
Brazoria County HFH

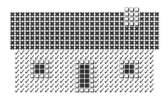

TAMALE CORN BREAD PIE

YIELD: 6 SERVINGS

8	ounces extra-lean ground chuck	1/4	teaspoon ground red pepper
3	cups whole kernel corn	2	cups tomato juice
2	cups canned tomatoes	1/4	cup unbleached flour
1	cup finely chopped green bell pepper	1 1/2	cups cornmeal
1	onion, finely chopped	1	tablespoon baking powder
1	tablespoon chili powder	3/4	cup skim milk
1	teaspoon cumin	2	eggs
		2	tablespoons olive oil

Brown ground chuck in skillet, stirring until crumbly; drain. Stir in
corn, tomatoes, green pepper, onion, chili powder, cumin and ground
red pepper. Add mixture of tomato juice and flour and mix well.
Simmer, covered, over low heat for 5 minutes, stirring occasionally.
Spoon into 9x13-inch baking dish. Combine cornmeal and baking
powder in bowl and mix well. Whisk skim milk, eggs and olive oil in
bowl until blended. Stir into cornmeal mixture until mixed. Spread
evenly over prepared layer. Bake at 425 degrees for 20 to 25
minutes or until corn bread topping is cooked through.

Approx Per Serving: Cal 404; Prot 18 g; Carbo 58 g; T Fat 13 g;
28% Calories from Fat; Chol 95 mg; Fiber 7 g; Sod 745 mg

Suzanne Wood, Macon Area HFH, Macon, GA

HAM-TO-CO-RI

YIELD: 4 SERVINGS

*May double this recipe to serve a larger crew. Prepare one day in
advance to enhance the flavor.*

1	medium onion, chopped	1	(8-ounce) can tomato sauce
1	tablespoon vegetable oil	3/4	cup medium salsa
1	pound lean ground beef	1	cup rice, cooked
1	teaspoon salt		
1/2	teaspoon pepper		
1	(15-ounce) can whole kernel corn, drained		

Sauté onion in oil in skillet until brown; push to one side of skillet. Add
ground beef. Cook until brown and crumbly. Stir in salt and pepper;
drain. Add corn, tomato sauce and salsa. Simmer for 10 to 15
minutes or until of the desired consistency, stirring occasionally.
Serve over hot cooked rice.

Approx Per Serving: Cal 576; Prot 32 g; Carbo 66 g; T Fat 21 g;
32% Calories from Fat; Chol 84 mg; Fiber 5 g; Sod 1763 mg

Judi Dilworth, Montgomery County HFH, Roslyn, PA

ENTREES

KURT'S ITALIAN SANDWICH

YIELD: 12 SERVINGS

2	pounds ground beef	1/2	teaspoon oregano
1	large onion, chopped	1 1/3	cups milk
1/4	teaspoon salt	2	eggs
1/4	teaspoon pepper	3	cups flour
2	(10-ounce) cans tomato soup	2	teaspoons baking powder
		1/2	teaspoon onion salt
1	cup catsup	1/2	teaspoon salt
2	teaspoons Worcestershire sauce	12	slices American cheese

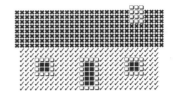

Brown ground beef with onion in skillet, stirring until ground beef is crumbly; drain. Stir in next 6 ingredients. Simmer for 20 minutes, stirring occasionally. Whisk milk and eggs in bowl until blended. Add flour, baking powder, onion salt and salt and mix well. Spread 1/2 of the flour mixture in 9x13-inch baking pan. Layer 1/2 of the ground beef mixture, cheese slices and remaining ground beef mixture over prepared layer. Spread with remaining flour mixture. Bake at 350 degrees for 30 minutes or until brown.

Approx Per Serving: Cal 449; Prot 28 g; Carbo 39 g; T Fat 20 g; 40% Calories from Fat; Chol 115 mg; Fiber 2 g; Sod 1251 mg

Avis Norton, North Saint Louis Co. HFH, Gilbert MN

MEATBALLS AND FRANKS

YIELD: 8 SERVINGS

1	cup fresh bread crumbs	1	cup chili sauce
1/2	cup milk	3/4	cup grape jelly
2	eggs	1/4	cup water
2	pounds ground chuck	1	tablespoon lemon juice
2	teaspoons salt	1	teaspoon Worcestershire sauce
1	teaspoon onion flakes		
1/4	teaspoon pepper	1/2	teaspoon dry mustard
2	tablespoons vegetable shortening	8	ounces frankfurters, sliced diagonally

Soak bread crumbs in milk in bowl for 2 to 3 minutes. Stir in eggs. Add ground chuck, salt, onion flakes and pepper and mix well. Shape into meatballs. Brown meatballs in shortening in skillet over high heat; drain. Mix next 6 ingredients in skillet. Add meatballs and mix gently. Simmer, covered, for 30 minutes. Stir in frankfurters. Spoon into 2-quart baking dish. Bake at 350 degrees for 30 minutes.

Approx Per Serving: Cal 500; Prot 30 g; Carbo 34 g; T Fat 27 g; 49% Calories from Fat; Chol 146 mg; Fiber 1 g; Sod 1435 mg

R'Gean Lillibridge, Silver Valley HFH, Pinehurst, ID

ENTREES

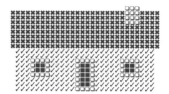

PIQUANT SAUCED MEAT LOAF   YIELD: 8 SERVINGS

1¹/₂	pounds ground beef	¹/₈	teaspoon pepper
1	cup milk	¹/₄	cup catsup
²/₃	cup bread crumbs	3	tablespoons brown sugar
¹/₄	cup grated onion	1	teaspoon dry mustard
2	eggs, beaten	¹/₄	teaspoon nutmeg
¹/₄	teaspoon salt		

Combine ground beef, milk, bread crumbs, onion, eggs, salt and pepper in bowl and mix well. Shape into round flat loaf in 9x9-inch baking pan. Spoon mixture of catsup, brown sugar, dry mustard and nutmeg over top. Bake at 350 degrees for 1¹/₄ hours or until cooked through.

Approx Per Serving: Cal 281; Prot 23 g; Carbo 14 g; T Fat 15 g; 47% Calories from Fat; Chol 120 mg; Fiber 1 g; Sod 307 mg

Linda Caley, Winchester-Frederick Co. HFH, Winchester, VA

COMPANY MEAT LOAF   YIELD: 4 SERVINGS

1¹/₂	pounds ground beef	¹/₂	green bell pepper, chopped
1	(10-ounce) can vegetable beef soup	1	cup sliced fresh mushrooms
1¹/₂	cups cracker crumbs		
1	tomato, chopped		
¹/₂	onion, chopped		

Combine ground beef, soup, cracker crumbs, tomato, onion and green pepper in bowl and mix well. Shape into loaf in 6x9-inch baking dish, allowing 1 inch space between meat loaf and edges of dish. Sprinkle with mushrooms. Bake at 350 degrees for 1 hour. May omit mushrooms. May substitute ground turkey for ground beef, vegetable soup for vegetable beef soup, bread crumbs for cracker crumbs and canned mushrooms for fresh mushrooms.

Approx Per Serving: Cal 577; Prot 45 g; Carbo 33 g; T Fat 29 g; 45% Calories from Fat; Chol 129 mg; Fiber 3 g; Sod 1087 mg

Elaine Lombardo, East Polk County HFH, Winter Haven, FL

QUICK TACO BAKE

YIELD: 8 SERVINGS

1	pound ground beef	1	(15-ounce) can green beans, drained
1/2	cup chopped onion	2	cups shredded Cheddar cheese
1	envelope taco seasoning mix	2	cups baking mix
1	(15-ounce) can tomato sauce	1	cup milk
1	(15-ounce) can whole kernel corn, drained	2	eggs

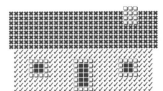

Brown ground beef with onion in skillet, stirring until ground beef is crumbly; drain. Remove from heat. Stir in taco seasoning mix. Add tomato sauce, corn and beans and mix well. Spoon into ungreased 9x13-inch baking pan. Sprinkle with cheese. Combine baking mix, milk and eggs in bowl, stirring until blended. Spread over prepared layers. Bake at 350 degrees for 35 minutes.

Approx Per Serving: Cal 491; Prot 28 g; Carbo 40 g; T Fat 25 g; 45% Calories from Fat; Chol 129 mg; Fiber 4 g; Sod 1439 mg

Eileen Nuss, Muscatine County HFH, Muscatine, IA

EASY SHEPHERD'S PIE

YIELD: 12 SERVINGS

12	potatoes, peeled Salt and pepper to taste	1	envelope beef onion soup mix
2	to 2 1/2 pounds lean ground beef	1	(10-ounce) can beef gravy

Combine potatoes with enough water to cover in saucepan. Cook until tender; drain. Mash potatoes in bowl. Season with salt and pepper. Brown ground beef in skillet, stirring until crumbly; drain. Stir in soup mix and beef gravy. Spoon into 9x13-inch baking pan. Spread with mashed potatoes. Bake at 400 degrees for 30 minutes or until light brown and bubbly.

Approx Per Serving: Cal 322; Prot 22 g; Carbo 29 g; T Fat 13 g; 36% Calories from Fat; Chol 64 mg; Fiber 2 g; Sod 387 mg

Betty Powell, Salem County HFH, Woodstown, NJ

Several years ago Salem County Habitat blitz-built a new home in one week. My husband and I were responsible for a noon meal for the workers and were told how many to plan for. So many extra volunteers showed up that we had to bring in extra food. We were happy they had so many volunteers and that the house was completed on schedule.

Betty Powell
Salem County HFH

BISON OSSO BUCO

YIELD: *4 SERVINGS*

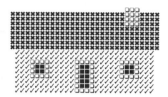

This is actually our favorite special-occasion meal. Slow cooking on low heat makes this relatively inexpensive cut of meat quite tender. You'll be amazed at the wonderful taste of such a low-fat meat. For information on obtaining bison, write North American Bison Cooperative, RR1, Box 162B, New Rockford, North Dakota 58356. Call (701) 947-2505 or fax (701) 947-2105.

1/2 cup unbleached flour	1/4 cup chopped fresh rosemary
1 teaspoon dried oregano	
1 teaspoon dried basil	1/4 cup chopped fresh sage
1 teaspoon dried rosemary	2 tablespoons finely grated lemon zest
1 teaspoon dried sage	
1 teaspoon salt	8 cloves of garlic, minced
1 teaspoon ground pepper	1/2 cup balsamic vinegar
4 pounds bison shanks, trimmed, cut into 2-inch pieces	3 cups chicken stock
	1/4 cup chopped fresh Italian parsley
1 tablespoon olive oil	

Photo by Joe Matthews

Combine flour, oregano, basil, dried rosemary, dried sage, salt and pepper in shallow dish and mix well. Add bison, tossing to coat. Sauté bison in olive oil in Dutch oven over medium heat for 5 minutes or until brown. Add fresh rosemary, fresh sage, lemon zest and garlic and mix well. Sauté for 2 minutes. Stir in balsamic vinegar and 1 cup of the stock. Simmer for 20 minutes or until liquid is almost absorbed. Add remaining stock and mix well. Cook, covered, over low heat for 40 minutes, stirring occasionally. Bake, covered, at 350 degrees for 2 hours, spooning pan drippings over bison every 15 minutes. Spoon onto dinner plates; sprinkle with parsley. May substitute veal shanks, beef chuck roast or beef rump roast for bison and low-sodium chicken broth for chicken stock.

Approx Per Serving: Cal 544; Prot 82 g; Carbo 23 g; T Fat 11 g; 20% Calories from Fat; Chol 219 mg; Fiber 1 g; Sod 1279 mg

Jane Fonda, Fonda, Inc., Atlanta, GA

Alaskan Swedish Meatballs *Yield: 4 servings*

2   slices sourdough or white bread, crusts trimmed, crumbled
1   egg, beaten
1   large onion, chopped
1/4 cup butter
1   pound ground moose
1/4 teaspoon nutmeg
1/2 cup nonfat sour cream
     Salt and pepper to taste
1   (14-ounce) can beef consommé
1   (10-ounce) can cream of mushroom soup
1 1/2 tablespoons flour

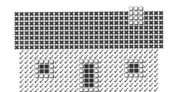

Soften bread crumbs in egg in bowl. Sauté onion in butter in skillet until tender. Mix bread crumbs, onion, moose, sour cream, nutmeg, salt and pepper in bowl. Shape into meatballs. Brown in skillet; drain. Add beef consommé. Simmer for 5 minutes, stirring occasionally. Remove meatballs with slotted spoon to bowl, reserving pan drippings. Add mixture of soup and flour to pan drippings and mix well. Return meatballs to skillet and mix gently. Spoon into baking pan. Bake at 350 degrees for 1 hour or until meatballs are cooked through.

Approx Per Serving: Cal 374; Prot 37 g; Carbo 19 g; T Fat 16 g; 38% Calories from Fat; Chol 154 mg; Fiber 1 g; Sod 1351 mg

Debbie Adamson, Central Peninsula HFH, Kenai, AK

Dry-Rub Barbecue Pork *Yield: 10 servings*

1   (8- to 10-pound) Boston butt roast
5   tablespoons lemon pepper seasoned salt
1   teaspoon Hungarian paprika
1   teaspoon ground black pepper
1   teaspoon ground red pepper
1   teaspoon cumin
1   teaspoon chili powder

Soak hickory chips in water for 30 minutes. Pat pork with paper towel. Rub entire surface with mixture of remaining ingredients, wearing a plastic or rubber glove, or placing a sandwich bag over your hand, to make the process easier. Toss hickory chips onto gray-ashed coals. Place pork on rack in smoker. Slow-smoke for 5 to 6 hours or until cooked through, turning every hour and never allowing fire to flame; smoker should be cool enough to touch quickly with palm of hand. Pork will develop dark, crusty exterior and a 1/2- to 1-inch reddish smoke ring will penetrate into the pork; pork will remain moist. Chop into bite-size pieces, discarding bone. Serve with your favorite barbecue sauce.

Approx Per Serving: Cal 597; Prot 36 g; Carbo 1 g; T Fat 50 g; 75% Calories from Fat; Chol 161 mg; Fiber <1 g; Sod 3955 mg

Dick Byrd, HFHI, Americus, GA

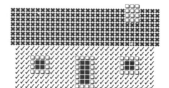

PORK STEAK BUNDLES

YIELD: *4 SERVINGS*

12	slices bacon	1	large green bell pepper, cut into quarters
4	(1/2- to 3/4-inch) boneless pork steaks	4	(1-ounce) slices American cheese
4	(1/2-inch) slices white onion		

Arrange 2 slices of bacon in shape of cross on hard surface. Place 1 slice diagonally through the center of cross. Layer 1 pork steak, 1 slice onion and 1 green pepper quarter over bacon. Crisscross bacon over center; secure with wooden pick. Repeat process with remaining bacon, pork steaks, onion and green pepper. Grill over medium-hot coals for 20 to 30 minutes or until cooked through. Top each bundle with 1 slice of cheese 3 minutes before end of cooking time.

Approx Per Serving: Cal 531; Prot 49 g; Carbo 5 g; T Fat 34 g; 59% Calories from Fat; Chol 166 mg; Fiber 1 g; Sod 745 mg

Sara R. Franing, Knox HFH (CC), Moline, IL

PORK CHOP BAKE

YIELD: *4 SERVINGS*

4	carrots, cut into 1-inch slices	1	(10-ounce) package frozen peas
1	large onion, sliced	1	teaspoon sugar
3	small potatoes, cut into quarters	1/2	teaspoon salt
1	(16-ounce) can stewed tomatoes	1/2	teaspoon pepper
		8	(1/2-inch) pork chops

Combine carrots, onion, potatoes, undrained tomatoes, peas, sugar, salt and pepper in bowl and mix well. Spoon into roasting pan. Arrange pork chops over vegetable mixture. Bake, covered, at 350 degrees for 1 hour; turn pork chops. Bake, covered, for 30 minutes; remove cover. Bake for 15 minutes longer. May increase or decrease recipe to serve 2 to 10 people.

Approx Per Serving: Cal 429; Prot 43 g; Carbo 40 g; T Fat 11 g; 23% Calories from Fat; Chol 104 mg; Fiber 8 g; Sod 738 mg

Mary Louise Heimbach, Lehigh Valley HFH, Emmaus, PA

PORK CHOPS SUPREME

YIELD: 8 SERVINGS

8	pork chops	2	tablespoons catsup
1	(10-ounce) can cream of chicken soup	2	tablespoons Worcestershire sauce

Arrange pork chops in single layer in 9x13-inch baking pan. Combine soup, catsup and Worcestershire sauce in bowl and mix well. Spread over pork chops. Bake, covered with foil, at 325 degrees for 1½ to 2 hours or until pork chops are cooked through.

Approx Per Serving: Cal 166; Prot 19 g; Carbo 5 g; T Fat 7 g; 41% Calories from Fat; Chol 55 mg; Fiber <1 g; Sod 425 mg

Elnora Woline, Henry County HFH, Mt. Pleasant, IA

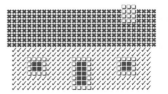

SEASONED PORK CHOPS

YIELD: 4 SERVINGS

2	tablespoons flour	4	(¾-inch) pork chops, trimmed
1	teaspoon basil		
1	teaspoon oregano	1	tablespoon vegetable oil
¼	teaspoon garlic powder	6	to 10 olive-oil-pack
⅛	teaspoon pepper		sun-dried tomatoes

Combine flour, basil, oregano, garlic powder and pepper in shallow dish and mix well. Add pork chops, turning to coat. Cook pork chops in oil in skillet over medium heat for 5 minutes; turn. Spoon sun-dried tomatoes over pork chops. Cook for 5 minutes longer or until pork chops are cooked through.

Approx Per Serving: Cal 184; Prot 19 g; Carbo 5 g; T Fat 10 g; 48% Calories from Fat; Chol 52 mg; Fiber 1 g; Sod 58 mg

Barbara Reina, Monroe County HFH, Stroudsburg, PA

He who regards one day as special, does so to the Lord. He who eats meat, eats to the Lord, for he gives thanks to God; and he who abstains, does so to the Lord and gives thanks to God.

Romans 14:6

SLOW-COOKER PORK CHOPS

YIELD: 6 SERVINGS

6	pork chops	1	(10-ounce) can chicken and rice soup
1	tablespoon vegetable oil		

Brown pork chops in oil in skillet; drain. Place in slow cooker sprayed with nonstick cooking spray. Pour soup over pork chops. Cook on Low for 6 to 8 hours or until pork chops are cooked through.

Approx Per Serving: Cal 168; Prot 20 g; Carbo 3 g; T Fat 8 g; 45% Calories from Fat; Chol 54 mg; Fiber <1 g; Sod 368 mg

Ruth G. Harris, Rapides HFH, Pineville, LA

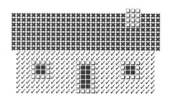

SAUSAGE AND POTATOES

YIELD: 8 SERVINGS

1	teaspoon salt	1	head cabbage, chopped
3	sausage links		Salt and pepper to taste
6	potatoes, peeled or unpeeled, coarsely chopped		

Fill Dutch oven 2/3 full of water. Bring to a boil. Add 1 teaspoon salt. Cut sausage into small pieces; shape into balls. Add sausage, potatoes and cabbage to boiling water. Cook for 45 to 60 minutes or until potatoes are tender and sausage is cooked through. Season with salt and pepper to taste. Spoon into bowls. Serve with crackers and milk.

Approx Per Serving: Cal 131; Prot 4 g; Carbo 26 g; T Fat 2 g; 12% Calories from Fat; Chol 4 mg; Fiber 4 g; Sod 355 mg

Karen Morra-Mesh, Westchester HFH, White Plains, NY

BREAKFAST CASSEROLE

YIELD: 6 SERVINGS

4	slices bread, torn	2	cups milk
16	ounces pork sausage	6	eggs
1	cup shredded sharp Cheddar cheese	1	teaspoon salt
		1/8	teaspoon pepper

Arrange bread in single layer in greased 9x13-inch baking dish. Brown sausage in skillet, stirring until crumbly; drain. Spoon over bread. Sprinkle with cheese. Whisk milk, eggs, salt and pepper in bowl until blended. Pour over prepared layers; do not stir. Bake at 350 degrees for 35 to 40 minutes or until set. May substitute bacon and/or mushrooms for sausage or omit meat altogether. May add 1/2 chopped sautéed onion and 1 chopped sautéed rib celery to egg mixture.

Approx Per Serving: Cal 354; Prot 21 g; Carbo 14 g; T Fat 24 g; 60% Calories from Fat; Chol 267 mg; Fiber <1 g; Sod 1032 mg

Keith Branson, Habitat Southwest, Waco, TX

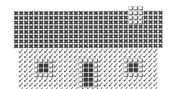

SAUSAGE GRITS CASSEROLE
YIELD: 6 SERVINGS

16	ounces pork sausage	1/4	cup butter or margarine
4	cups water	4	eggs, lightly beaten
1/2	teaspoon salt	1/2	cup milk
1	cup quick-cooking grits		
1 1/2	cups shredded sharp Cheddar cheese		

Brown sausage in skillet, stirring until crumbly; drain. Bring water and salt to a boil in saucepan. Stir in grits gradually; reduce heat. Cook, covered, for 5 minutes, stirring occasionally. Remove from heat. Add 1 cup of the cheese and butter, stirring until blended. Stir in eggs, milk and sausage. Spoon into greased 3-quart baking dish. Sprinkle with remaining 1/2 cup cheese. Bake at 350 degrees for 1 hour or until golden brown. Let stand for 10 minutes before serving.

Approx Per Serving: Cal 443; Prot 20 g; Carbo 23 g; T Fat 30 g; 61% Calories from Fat; Chol 218 mg; Fiber 3 g; Sod 845 mg

Pat Evans, Nashville Area HFH, Nashville, TN

SAUSAGE AND BEAN MEAL
YIELD: 6 SERVINGS

16	ounces pork sausage	1	(29-ounce) can pork and beans
1	small onion, chopped		
1/4	cup catsup		

Brown sausage with onion in skillet, stirring until sausage is crumbly; drain. Stir in catsup and beans. Simmer for 5 minutes, stirring frequently. Serve with potatoes.

Approx Per Serving: Cal 270; Prot 13 g; Carbo 33 g; T Fat 11 g; 35% Calories from Fat; Chol 33 mg; Fiber 6 g; Sod 944 mg

Annabelle Woods, Hamilton County HFH, Noblesville, IN

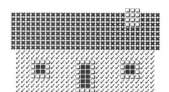

SAUSAGE SKILLET MEAL

YIELD: 6 SERVINGS

16 ounces mild or hot pork sausage, cut into 1/2-inch slices
1 large onion, finely chopped
6 medium potatoes, coarsely chopped
1 (46-ounce) can tomato juice

Place sausage in cold cast-iron skillet. Cook until light brown on both sides. Drain, discarding pan drippings. Add onion to skillet. Cook until brown, stirring frequently. Add potatoes and mix well. Add enough tomato juice to cover over potato mixture. Arrange sausage slices over top. Simmer, covered, until potatoes are tender; do not stir. Remove sausage to platter. Spoon potato mixture into serving bowl; arrange sausage over top.

Approx Per Serving: Cal 263; Prot 10 g; Carbo 38 g; T Fat 9 g; 30% Calories from Fat; Chol 23 mg; Fiber 3 g; Sod 1153 mg
Nutritional information includes entire amount of tomato juice.

Judith Kirby Shearer, Garrard County HFH, Lancaster, KY

IMPOSSIBLE QUICHE

YIELD: 6 SERVINGS

1 1/2 cups milk
1/2 cup baking mix
1/4 cup melted butter
3 eggs
1 cup cubed ham
1 cup shredded Swiss cheese
1 (4-ounce) can mushrooms, drained

Process milk, baking mix, butter and eggs in blender until smooth. Combine with ham, cheese and mushrooms in bowl and mix well. Spoon into 9- or 10-inch round baking dish. Bake at 350 degrees for 1 hour. May add chopped onion, chopped bell peppers, chopped spinach and/or any of your favorite vegetables as desired. May substitute bacon or sausage for ham.

Approx Per Serving: Cal 294; Prot 17 g; Carbo 11 g; T Fat 20 g; 61% Calories from Fat; Chol 165 mg; Fiber 1 g; Sod 704 mg

Anne L. Bishop, Greater Bucks County HFH, Chalfont, PA

HAM LOAVES

YIELD: 12 SERVINGS

2	pounds ground ham	1	cup packed brown sugar
2	pounds ground pork	1/2	cup vinegar
2	cups graham cracker crumbs	1/2	cup water
1/2	cup milk	1/2	teaspoon prepared mustard
3	eggs, lightly beaten		
1	(10-ounce) can tomato soup		

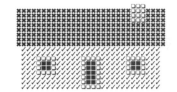

Combine ground ham, ground pork, graham cracker crumbs, milk and eggs in bowl and mix well. Divide into 2 equal portions. Shape each portion into a loaf in 5x9-inch loaf pan. Combine soup, brown sugar, vinegar, water and mustard in saucepan and mix well. Cook over low heat until heated through. Spoon some of the glaze over each loaf. Bake at 325 degrees for 2 hours, basting with remaining glaze every 30 minutes.

Approx Per Serving: Cal 443; Prot 35 g; Carbo 35 g; T Fat 18 g; 37% Calories from Fat; Chol 140 mg; Fiber 1 g; Sod 1365 mg

Julia H. Lifer, Fairfield County HFH, Lancaster, OH

CHICKEN FRICASSEE

YIELD: 6 SERVINGS

1	(4- to 5-pound) hen, skinned	4	or 5 carrots, peeled, sliced
1	onion, cut into quarters	2	(10-ounce) cans reduced-fat cream of celery soup
2	ribs celery with leaves	1 1/2	cups rice
1/2	teaspoon thyme		Baking mix

Rinse chicken. Combine chicken, onion, celery and thyme in stockpot. Add water to cover chicken by 1/2; cover with lid. Bring to a boil; reduce heat. Simmer for 1 1/2 hours or until chicken is cooked through. Remove chicken to a bowl. Strain broth, discarding onion and celery. Return broth to stockpot. Stir in carrots and soup. Simmer until carrots are tender-crisp. Stir in rice. Cook until rice is tender; mixture will be soupy. Add additional water if needed for desired consistency. Chop chicken into bite-size pieces, discarding bone. Add to stockpot and mix gently. Prepare dumplings using package directions on baking mix package. Add to chicken mixture 20 minutes before end of cooking time, adding additional water if needed. May substitute mixture of equal portions of canned low-fat low-sodium chicken broth and water for additional water.

Nutritional information for this recipe is not available.

Cathy Belatti, Dunwoody, GA

ENTREES

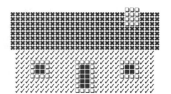

PERFECTLY BAKED CHICKEN

YIELD: 4 SERVINGS

Crisp and moist, this chicken will almost fall off the bone.

1	(3-pound) chicken	Salt and pepper to taste

Rinse chicken and pat dry. Sprinkle with salt and pepper. Place in 2-quart baking dish. Bake at 400 degrees for 1 hour. Decrease oven temperature to 300 degrees. Bake for 1 hour longer. Do not open oven door during cooking time.

Approx Per Serving: Cal 323; Prot 49 g; Carbo 0 g; T Fat 13 g; 37% Calories from Fat; Chol 151 mg; Fiber 0 g; Sod 146 mg

Eugenie S. Crandall, Monroe County HFH, Monroeville, AL

CHICKEN RIGANATO

YIELD: 4 SERVINGS

1	(2½-pound) chicken, cut into quarters	¼	teaspoon pepper
		1	clove of garlic, crushed
½	cup vegetable oil	4	large potatoes, cut into quarters
	Juice of 1 lemon		
2	teaspoons oregano	1½	cups water
1½	teaspoons salt	¼	cup butter or margarine

Rinse chicken and pat dry. Whisk oil, lemon juice, oregano, salt, pepper and garlic in bowl until mixed. Coat chicken with oil mixture. Place skin side down in baking pan. Arrange potatoes around chicken. Add water; dot potatoes with butter. Bake at 375 degrees for 1 hour, basting chicken with remaining oil mixture and turning chicken and potatoes frequently to promote even browning. If baking chicken without potatoes, decrease water to 1 cup and omit butter.

Approx Per Serving: Cal 787; Prot 45 g; Carbo 41 g; T Fat 49 g; 56% Calories from Fat; Chol 157 mg; Fiber 3 g; Sod 1048 mg

University of Maryland College Park (CC), College Park, MD

SPICED ROAST CHICKEN

Yield: 4 servings

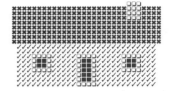

1	(3½-pound) chicken Mushroom Stuffing	⅔ cup marsala Salt and pepper to taste
¼	cup water	Sprigs of fresh thyme and
1	tablespoon margarine	fresh watercress

Rinse chicken and pat dry. Stuff with Mushroom Stuffing; truss. Place breast side down in roasting pan. Add water. Roast at 375 degrees for 45 minutes; turn chicken breast side up. Dot with margarine. Roast 45 minutes longer or until meat thermometer inserted in thickest part of thigh (not touching bone) registers 185 degrees. Transfer chicken to serving platter, reserving pan drippings. Cover to keep warm. Skim pan drippings. Deglaze remaining pan drippings with marsala. Bring to a boil over high heat. Boil for 1 minute to reduce slightly, stirring constantly. Season with salt and pepper. Remove skin from chicken and carve. Garnish with thyme and watercress sprigs. Serve with flavored pan drippings and seasonal vegetables.

MUSHROOM STUFFING

1	onion, finely chopped	1	cup fresh white bread
2	tablespoons olive oil		crumbs
1	teaspoon garam masala	¼	cup minced walnuts
4	ounces button or brown mushrooms, chopped	2	teaspoons chopped fresh thyme
1	cup coarsely grated parsnip	1	egg, beaten Salt and pepper to taste
1	cup coarsely grated carrot		

Sauté onion in olive oil in saucepan for 2 minutes or until tender. Stir in garam masala. Cook for 1 minute, stirring frequently. Add mushrooms, parsnip and carrot and mix well. Cook for 5 minutes, stirring constantly. Remove from heat. Stir in bread crumbs, walnuts, thyme, egg, salt and pepper.

Approx Per Serving: Cal 699; Prot 63 g; Carbo 30 g; T Fat 31 g; 40% Calories from Fat; Chol 230 mg; Fiber 5 g; Sod 299 mg

Tipper Gore, Office of the Vice President, Washington, DC

ENTREES

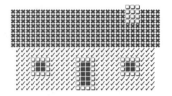

CHICKEN AND DUMPLINGS

YIELD: 6 SERVINGS

Like Grandma made!

1	(2½- to 3-pound) chicken, cut up	2	tablespoons butter
1	cup flour	¼	cup flour
1	teaspoon baking soda	⅔	cup milk
¼	cup milk		Salt and pepper to taste

Rinse chicken. Combine chicken with enough water to cover in stockpot. Cook until tender. Drain, reserving broth. Chill broth until fat becomes firm. Skim off fat, reserving ¼ cup of fat and broth. Chop chicken, discarding skin and bone. Combine 1 cup flour and baking soda in bowl and mix well. Stir in ¼ cup reserved chicken fat and ¼ cup milk. Drop by teaspoonfuls into boiling reserved broth in stockpot. Simmer for 5 to 10 minutes or until tender. Heat butter in saucepan until melted. Stir in ¼ cup flour until blended. Add 1 cup hot broth from dumplings and ⅔ cup milk. Cook until thickened, stirring constantly. Stir into dumpling mixture. Add chicken, salt and pepper and mix gently. Cook just until heated through.

Approx Per Serving: Cal 444; Prot 37 g; Carbo 22 g; T Fat 22 g; 46% Calories from Fat; Chol 124 mg; Fiber 1 g; Sod 365 mg

Rona Branson, Habitat Southwest, Waco, TX

ORIENTAL CHICKEN

YIELD: 4 SERVINGS

1	(3-pound) chicken, cut up	⅛	teaspoon pepper
¼	cup soy sauce	⅛	teaspoon garlic powder
¾	teaspoon dry mustard	2	cups hot cooked rice
¼	teaspoon ground ginger		

Rinse chicken and pat dry. Combine soy sauce, dry mustard, ginger, pepper and garlic powder in bowl and mix well. Brush chicken with soy sauce mixture. Arrange chicken in greased 10x15-inch baking pan. Let stand for 30 minutes. Brush with soy sauce mixture. Bake at 350 degrees for 1 hour, turning and basting with remaining soy sauce mixture every 20 minutes. Serve with hot cooked rice.

Approx Per Serving: Cal 469; Prot 53 g; Carbo 31 g; T Fat 13 g; 26% Calories from Fat; Chol 151 mg; Fiber 1 g; Sod 1176 mg

Vienna C. Snodgrass, Pearl River County HFH, Picayune, MS

EASY OVEN CHICKEN

YIELD: 4 SERVINGS

1	cup margarine		Salt and pepper to taste
1	(3-pound) chicken, cut up	3	cups flour

Heat margarine in 9x13-inch baking pan until melted, tilting pan to coat bottom. Rinse chicken and pat dry. Sprinkle with salt and pepper. Coat chicken generously with flour. Arrange skin side down in prepared pan. Sprinkle with salt and pepper. Bake at 425 degrees for 45 minutes; turn chicken. Bake for 15 minutes longer or until chicken is cooked through. Drain on paper towel before serving. Serve with pan drippings if desired.

Approx Per Serving: Cal 1073; Prot 59 g; Carbo 72 g; T Fat 59 g; 50% Calories from Fat; Chol 151 mg; Fiber 3 g; Sod 684 mg

Sunny Johnson, Menominee River HFH, Iron Mountain, MI

ARROZ CON POLLO

YIELD: 8 SERVINGS

4	to 6 boneless skinless chicken breast halves	3/4	cup salsa
1 1/4	cups uncooked rice	1/2	cup chopped onion
1	(14-ounce) can chicken broth	2	cups sliced fresh mushrooms
1	(8-ounce) can tomato sauce	2	cups shredded Monterey Jack cheese

Rinse chicken and pat dry. Chop into bite-size pieces. Spread rice evenly over bottom of 9x13-inch baking pan sprayed with nonstick cooking spray. Arrange chicken over rice. Combine broth, tomato sauce, salsa and onion in bowl and mix well. Pour over prepared layers. Top with mushrooms. Bake, covered with foil, at 350 degrees for 1 hour. Remove foil; sprinkle with cheese. Bake for 10 minutes longer. May serve with warm flour tortillas. May substitute canned mushrooms for fresh mushrooms and Cheddar cheese for Monterey Jack cheese.

Approx Per Serving: Cal 357; Prot 32 g; Carbo 29 g; T Fat 12 g; 30% Calories from Fat; Chol 80 mg; Fiber 1 g; Sod 789 mg

Cindy Schultz, South Puget Sound HFH, Olympia, WA

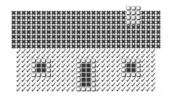

During a Habitat potluck held in our honor as we walked across America in 1996, Daniel, aged nine and son of a new homeowner, told us his story. "Well, our landlord said 'you're out of here' and we didn't know what to do, but then we heard about Habitat and BOOMO, we had a house."

Cindy Schultz
South Puget
Sound HFH

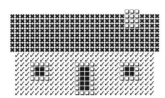

AWESOME CHICKEN

YIELD: 8 SERVINGS

2½	to 3 pounds boneless skinless chicken breast halves	1	(6-ounce) package seasoned croutons
	Salt and pepper to taste	½	cup melted margarine
½	cup shredded Cheddar cheese	1	(10-ounce) can cream of chicken soup
		1	soup can milk

Rinse chicken and pat dry. Sprinkle with salt and pepper. Arrange chicken in buttered 9x13-inch baking dish. Top with cheese. Toss croutons with margarine in bowl. Sprinkle over prepared layers. Pour mixture of soup and milk over top. Bake, covered with foil, at 350 degrees for 45 minutes. May be prepared in advance, stored in refrigerator and baked just before serving.

Approx Per Serving: Cal 497; Prot 46 g; Carbo 18 g; T Fat 26 g; 47% Calories from Fat; Chol 124 mg; Fiber 1 g; Sod 852 mg

Julie Vallorano, New Castle County HFH, Wilmington, DE

BAKED CHICKEN

YIELD: 6 SERVINGS

6	boneless skinless chicken breast halves	1	(10-ounce) can cream of mushroom soup
1	ounce chipped dried beef	1	cup sour cream
3	slices bacon, cut into halves		

Rinse chicken and pat dry. Layer beef, chicken and bacon in shallow baking pan. Combine soup and sour cream in bowl and mix well. Spread over prepared layers. Bake at 275 degrees for 3 hours. May cover with foil to prevent overbrowning.

Photo by Robert Baker

Approx Per Serving: Cal 302; Prot 31 g; Carbo 6 g; T Fat 17 g; 51% Calories from Fat; Chol 95 mg; Fiber <1 g; Sod 710 mg

Shirley Skirvin, Pueblo HFH, Pueblo, CO

Broccoli Cheese Chicken

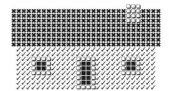

4   boneless skinless chicken
    breast halves
1   tablespoon margarine
1   (10-ounce) can broccoli
    cheese soup
1/3 cup milk
2   cups broccoli florets

Rinse chicken and pat dry. Cook chicken in margarine in skillet over medium heat for 10 minutes or until brown on both sides; drain. Add soup and milk and mix well. Simmer, covered, for 10 minutes, stirring occasionally. Add broccoli. Simmer for 5 to 10 minutes longer or until broccoli is tender, stirring occasionally.

Approx Per Serving: Cal 260; Prot 29 g; Carbo 8 g; T Fat 11 g; 41% Calories from Fat; Chol 76 mg; Fiber 1 g; Sod 651 mg

Dee Dee Ritchie, Pensacola HFH, Pensacola, FL

Chicken Casino

Yield: 4 servings

4   boneless skinless chicken
    breast halves
1   medium onion, sliced
2   teaspoons olive oil
1   (15-ounce) can sliced
    tomatoes
1/4 cup lemon juice
1   teaspoon oregano
1   teaspoon basil
1/2 teaspoon cumin
1/2 teaspoon crushed red
    pepper
1   (4-ounce) can mushrooms
2   cups hot cooked rice

Rinse chicken and pat dry. Sauté chicken and onion in olive oil; drain. Process tomatoes in blender until puréed. Add to chicken mixture and mix well. Add mixture of lemon juice, oregano, basil, cumin and red pepper. Add undrained mushrooms and mix well. Simmer over low heat for 1 1/2 hours, stirring occasionally. Serve over hot cooked rice.

Approx Per Serving: Cal 337; Prot 31 g; Carbo 39 g; T Fat 6 g; 16% Calories from Fat; Chol 73 mg; Fiber 3 g; Sod 359 mg

Frances L. Daily, Alliance Area HFH, Alliance, OH

TIM ALLEN'S CHICKEN DIVAN

YIELD: 8 SERVINGS

Mom gave me this recipe.

2	or 3 (10-ounce) packages frozen broccoli spears	½	cup shredded Cheddar cheese
8	boneless skinless chicken breast halves, poached	1	teaspoon lemon juice
2	(10-ounce) cans cream of chicken soup	⅛	teaspoon curry powder
1	cup mayonnaise	½	cup fresh bread crumbs
		1	tablespoon melted butter
			Pimento strips to taste

Cook broccoli using package directions; drain. Spread in 9x13-inch baking dish. Top with chicken. Mix next 5 ingredients in bowl. Spread over chicken. Toss bread crumbs with butter in bowl. Sprinkle over prepared layers. Bake at 350 degrees for 1½ hours. Garnish with pimento.

Approx Per Serving: Cal 485; Prot 34 g; Carbo 13 g; T Fat 34 g; 62% Calories from Fat; Chol 107 mg; Fiber 3 g; Sod 914 mg

Tim Allen, Tool Time, Detroit, MI

CHICKEN DIVAN

YIELD: 4 SERVINGS

4	chicken breasts	2	tablespoons lemon juice
8	ounces broccoli spears	1	cup stuffing mix
1	(10-ounce) can cream of chicken soup	¾	cup shredded sharp Cheddar cheese
½	cup mayonnaise		

Rinse chicken. Combine chicken with enough water to cover in saucepan. Parboil for 15 minutes. Drain, reserving broth. Debone chicken and discard skin. Cook broccoli in reserved broth in saucepan for 5 minutes; drain. Wrap each chicken breast around several spears of broccoli. Arrange in single layer in baking dish. Combine soup, mayonnaise and lemon juice in bowl and mix well. Spread over prepared layer. Sprinkle with stuffing mix; top with cheese. Bake at 350 degrees until brown and bubbly.

Approx Per Serving: Cal 579; Prot 38 g; Carbo 24 g; T Fat 37 g; 58% Calories from Fat; Chol 118 mg; Fiber 2 g; Sod 1245 mg

Gail Creed, Northeast Connecticut HFH, Putnam, CT

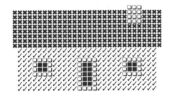

CHICKEN TORTILLA CASSEROLE *YIELD: 4 SERVINGS*

2	whole chicken breasts, split, skinned	1/2	(9-ounce) package tortilla chips
1	(10-ounce) can cream of chicken soup	1	(4-ounce) can chopped green chiles, drained
1/4	cup chicken stock	1	small onion, chopped
1/4	teaspoon oregano	8	ounces Monterey Jack cheese, shredded
1/8	teaspoon cumin	8	ounces longhorn cheese, shredded
1/8	teaspoon sage		
1/8	teaspoon chili powder		
1/8	teaspoon garlic		

Rinse chicken and pat dry. Broil, microwave or cook in pressure cooker until almost done. Chop, discarding bone. Combine chicken, soup and stock in saucepan and mix well. Stir in oregano, cumin, sage, chili powder and garlic. Cook over low heat until heated through, stirring frequently. Line 1 1/2- to 2-quart baking dish with tortilla chips. Layer chicken mixture, green chiles, onion, Monterey Jack cheese and longhorn cheese over tortilla chips. Bake, covered, at 350 degrees for 35 minutes. May substitute corn tortillas softened in oil for tortilla chips. Grease baking dish before lining with tortillas. May substitute one 2-pound chicken for chicken breasts and 1 chicken bouillon cube dissolved in 1/4 cup hot water for chicken stock.

Approx Per Serving: Cal 829; Prot 60 g; Carbo 30 g; T Fat 52 g; 57% Calories from Fat; Chol 189 mg; Fiber 3 g; Sod 1870 mg

Celine Wicks, Lake Villa, IL

CRANBERRY CHICKEN *YIELD: 4 SERVINGS*

4	chicken breast halves	1	(8-ounce) bottle creamy French salad dressing
1	(16-ounce) can whole cranberry sauce	1	envelope onion soup mix

Rinse chicken and pat dry. Arrange in shallow baking pan. Combine cranberry sauce, salad dressing and soup mix in bowl and mix well. Spoon over chicken. Bake, covered, at 350 degrees for 1 hour.

Approx Per Serving: Cal 562; Prot 27 g; Carbo 55 g; T Fat 25 g; 41% Calories from Fat; Chol 106 mg; Fiber 1 g; Sod 1032 mg

University of Maryland College Park (CC), College Park, MD

ENTREES

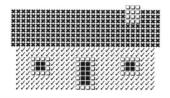

MEXICAN CHICKEN CASSEROLE YIELD: 4 SERVINGS

1/2	(9-ounce) package tortilla chips, crushed	1	(10-ounce) can cream of mushroom soup
2	or 3 boneless skinless chicken breast halves, cooked, chopped	1	cup shredded Cheddar cheese
1	(10-ounce) can tomatoes with green chiles		

Cover bottom of baking pan with some of the crushed tortilla chips. Combine chicken, undrained tomatoes and soup in bowl and mix well. Spoon over prepared layer. Sprinkle with remaining tortilla chips; top with cheese. Bake at 350 degrees for 15 to 20 minutes or until hot and bubbly.

Approx Per Serving: Cal 469; Prot 31 g; Carbo 29 g; T Fat 26 g; 49% Calories from Fat; Chol 85 mg; Fiber 3 g; Sod 1293 mg

Melissa Knapp, Heartland Regional Center, Springfield, MO

TIPSY CHICKEN YIELD: 8 SERVINGS

8	boneless skinless chicken breast halves	1	cup shredded reduced-fat Swiss cheese
1	to 1 1/2 cups white wine		Paprika to taste
2	(10-ounce) cans reduced-fat cream of mushroom soup		

Rinse chicken and pat dry. Pour white wine into baking dish to depth of 1/4 inch. Arrange chicken in prepared baking dish. Spread with soup; sprinkle with cheese and paprika. Bake at 375 degrees for 40 minutes. May substitute grated Parmesan cheese for Swiss cheese.

Approx Per Serving: Cal 232; Prot 31 g; Carbo 7 g; T Fat 5 g; 20% Calories from Fat; Chol 81 mg; Fiber 0 g; Sod 559 mg

Maria McCarthy, Halifax HFH, Daytona Beach, FL

CHICKEN CASSEROLE

YIELD: 6 SERVINGS

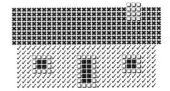

1	(8-ounce) package stuffing mix		1	(10-ounce) can chicken broth
1/2	cup melted margarine		1	(10-ounce) can cream of mushroom soup
4	boneless skinless chicken breast halves, cooked, chopped		1	(10-ounce) can cream of chicken soup

Combine stuffing mix and margarine in bowl and mix well. Spread 1/2 of the stuffing mixture in 9x13-inch baking pan. Combine chicken, broth and soups in bowl and mix well. Spoon over prepared layer. Top with remaining stuffing mixture. Bake at 350 degrees for 45 minutes or until bubbly.

Approx Per Serving: Cal 485; Prot 26 g; Carbo 37 g; T Fat 26 g; 48% Calories from Fat; Chol 54 mg; Fiber <1 g; Sod 1929 mg

Catherine S. Bream, Richmond County HFH, Hamlet, NC

CHICKEN RICE CASSEROLE

YIELD: 4 SERVINGS

1	(10-ounce) can cream of chicken soup		3/4	cup chopped celery
1 1/2	cups chopped cooked chicken		1/2	cup almonds, toasted
1	cup sour cream		1/2	(8-ounce) can water chestnuts, drained
1	cup cooked instant rice			Salt and pepper to taste
			1	cup crushed cornflakes

Combine soup, chicken, sour cream, rice, celery, almonds, water chestnuts, salt and pepper in bowl and mix well. Spoon into buttered 9x13-inch baking dish. Sprinkle with cornflakes. Bake at 350 degrees for 30 minutes or until bubbly.

Approx Per Serving: Cal 537; Prot 25 g; Carbo 41 g; T Fat 31 g; 52% Calories from Fat; Chol 73 mg; Fiber 4 g; Sod 911 mg

Emma Stout, Thomasville HFH, Thomasville, NC

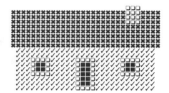

ENTREES

EASY CHICKEN CASSEROLE

YIELD: 8 SERVINGS

2	(16-ounce) cans whole green beans, drained	1	(8-ounce) can sliced water chestnuts, drained
2	cups chopped cooked chicken	1	tablespoon lemon juice
1	(10-ounce) can cream of chicken soup	1½	teaspoons curry powder
¾	cup mayonnaise	1	cup shredded sharp Cheddar cheese

Cover bottom of greased 9x13-inch baking dish with beans. Top with chicken. Combine soup, mayonnaise, water chestnuts, lemon juice and curry powder in bowl and mix well. Spoon over prepared layers. Sprinkle with cheese. Bake at 350 degrees for 30 minutes or until bubbly. May add additional cheese if desired.

Approx Per Serving: Cal 345; Prot 16 g; Carbo 12 g; T Fat 26 g; 67% Calories from Fat; Chol 61 mg; Fiber 4 g; Sod 823 mg

Evelyn A. Young, Highlands County HFH, Sebring, FL

CHICKEN PIE

YIELD: 6 SERVINGS

Serve with a fruit salad or tomato pudding.

2½	cups chopped cooked chicken	1	teaspoon salt
1	(10-ounce) can cream of mushroom soup	1	teaspoon pepper
1	(10-ounce) can cream of chicken soup	1	cup self-rising flour
1	(9-ounce) can Veg-All	1	cup milk
		6	tablespoons melted margarine

Combine chicken, soups, Veg-All, salt and pepper in bowl and mix well. Spoon into greased 2-quart baking dish. Combine flour, milk and margarine in bowl and mix well. Spread over prepared layer. Bake at 350 degrees for 30 minutes or until golden brown.

Approx Per Serving: Cal 427; Prot 23 g; Carbo 28 g; T Fat 24 g; 52% Calories from Fat; Chol 62 mg; Fiber 3 g; Sod 1730 mg

Mary R. Barrera, Newnan-Coweta HFH, Newnan, GA

HOT CHICKEN SALAD

YIELD: 6 SERVINGS

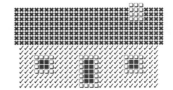

2	cups chopped cooked chicken	1	(10-ounce) can cream of chicken soup
1	(6-ounce) can mushrooms, drained	3/4	cup mayonnaise-type salad dressing
1	cup cooked rice	1	cup bread cubes
1	cup chopped celery	2	tablespoons melted butter
1/2	cup sliced almonds		
1/4	cup chopped onion		

Combine chicken, mushrooms, rice, celery, almonds and onion in bowl and mix well. Stir in soup and salad dressing. Spoon into buttered 9x13-inch baking dish. Sprinkle with mixture of bread cubes and butter. Bake at 350 degrees for 30 minutes. May substitute cream of mushroom soup for cream of chicken soup and crushed cornflakes for bread cubes.

Approx Per Serving: Cal 408; Prot 19 g; Carbo 28 g; T Fat 25 g; 54% Calories from Fat; Chol 53 mg; Fiber 2 g; Sod 867 mg

Lois J. Clark, Wabash Valley HFH, Vincennes, IN

HOT CHICKEN SANDWICHES

YIELD: 4 SERVINGS

8	slices white bread, crusts trimmed	3	hard-cooked eggs, chopped
4	teaspoons butter, softened	1/2	onion, grated
3	cups chopped cooked chicken	1/2	cup mayonnaise
		1	(10-ounce) can cream of chicken soup
1/2	cup chopped black olives	3/4	to 1 cup sour cream
1	(4-ounce) can mushrooms, drained, chopped		

Spread 1 side of 4 slices of bread with butter. Combine chicken, black olives, mushrooms, eggs and onion in bowl and mix gently. Stir in mayonnaise. Spoon chicken mixture over unbuttered side of buttered bread slices. Top with remaining bread slices. Arrange butter side down in 9x9-inch baking dish. Spread with mixture of soup and sour cream. Bake at 350 degrees for 25 minutes.

Approx Per Serving: Cal 825; Prot 43 g; Carbo 33 g; T Fat 58 g; 63% Calories from Fat; Chol 311 mg; Fiber 3 g; Sod 1471 mg

Rosemary Sellers, Three Rivers HFH, Alexander City, AL

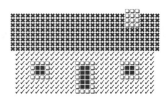

TEX-MEX CHICKEN

YIELD: 6 SERVINGS

3	slices bacon, chopped	2/3	cup picante sauce
1/2	cup chopped onion	1/4	cup sliced green olives
1/2	cup chopped celery	1/4	teaspoon garlic powder
2	(28-ounce) cans tomatoes	1/4	teaspoon white pepper
2	cups chopped cooked chicken	3	cups hot cooked rice

Fry bacon in skillet until crisp. Drain, reserving 1 tablespoon bacon drippings. Sauté onion and celery in reserved bacon drippings. Add bacon, undrained tomatoes, chicken, picante sauce, green olives, garlic powder and white pepper and mix well. Simmer, covered, for 30 minutes. Serve over hot cooked rice.

Approx Per Serving: Cal 320; Prot 20 g; Carbo 44 g; T Fat 7 g; 20% Calories from Fat; Chol 45 mg; Fiber 4 g; Sod 845 mg

Walton Garrett, Haywood HFH, Lake Junaluska, NC

We were ready to start the foundation for a HFH house, but our regular mason could not do the work. When the new homeowner, a single parent, stated that her father wanted to help and he was a mason, we were overjoyed. Our prayers were answered.

Walton Garrett, Haywood HFH

TURKEY ENCHILADAS

YIELD: 10 SERVINGS

1	cup chopped cooked turkey	1	(8-ounce) can mild green chile salsa
1	cup sour cream		
1	cup shredded Monterey Jack cheese	1/2	cup shredded Monterey Jack cheese
10	flour tortillas		

Combine turkey, sour cream and 1 cup cheese in bowl and mix well. Spoon 2 tablespoons of the turkey mixture onto each tortilla; roll to enclose filling. Arrange seam side down in 9x13-inch baking dish. Spoon green chile salsa over enchiladas; sprinkle with 1/2 cup cheese. Bake at 350 degrees for 30 to 35 minutes or until bubbly. May substitute Cheddar cheese for Monterey Jack cheese.

Approx Per Serving: Cal 258; Prot 12 g; Carbo 22 g; T Fat 13 g; 46% Calories from Fat; Chol 36 mg; Fiber 1 g; Sod 431 mg

Doris B. Smith, National Association of Homebuilders, Danville, CA

THANKSGIVING DELIGHT

YIELD: 12 SERVINGS

This recipe is not simple, but the results will be well worth the effort.

1	(20-pound) turkey	6	tablespoons margarine
	Salt to taste	1½	cups hot water
	Turkey Stuffing		Turkey Gravy

Rinse turkey and pat dry. Sprinkle generously with salt. Fill turkey cavity with Turkey Stuffing. Place turkey on rack in roasting pan. Dot with margarine. Cover wing tips with foil. Bake at 575 degrees for 45 minutes or until turkey is very brown; reduce oven temperature to 350 degrees. Add hot water to roasting pan. Bake, covered tightly with foil, for 2½ to 3 hours or until juices run clear. Remove turkey to serving platter. Let stand for several minutes before carving. Drain pan drippings into bowl for gravy. Serve turkey and dressing with Turkey Gravy.

TURKEY STUFFING

	Turkey gizzards	1	medium onion, chopped
1	large package seasoned stuffing mix	1	(6-ounce) can mushrooms, drained
	Chopped celery		Chopped nuts

Rinse turkey gizzards. Combine with enough water to cover in saucepan. Simmer until tender. Drain, reserving broth. Chop gizzards. Combine gizzards, broth, stuffing mix, celery, onion, mushrooms and nuts in bowl and mix using package directions on stuffing mix.

TURKEY GRAVY

	Flour	½	teaspoon curry powder
2	teaspoons salt	1	(6-ounce) can mushrooms, drained
1	teaspoon paprika		
½	teaspoon pepper	1	tablespoon sour cream

Combine ½ of cooled turkey pan drippings with enough flour to thicken in bowl. Combine with remaining pan drippings in saucepan and mix well. Bring to a boil; reduce heat. Simmer until thickened, stirring constantly. Stir in salt, paprika, pepper and curry powder. Add mushrooms and sour cream and mix well. Heat until the sour cream is blended, stirring constantly. Adjust measurements according to taste and amount of gravy available.

Nutritional information for this recipe is not available.

Cordella Faye Rice, Sumter County Florida HFH, Wildwood, FL

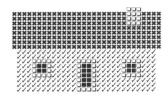

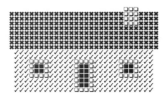

TURKEY LOAF

YIELD: 6 SERVINGS

2	pounds ground turkey	1	carrot, shredded
1	cup Cheerios	1	small onion, chopped
1	green bell pepper, chopped	1	egg, lightly beaten
1	potato, shredded		

Combine ground turkey, Cheerios, green pepper, potato, carrot, onion and egg in bowl and mix well. Shape into loaf. Place in 9x12-inch baking pan. Bake at 375 degrees for 1 hour. May substitute ground beef for ground turkey.

Approx Per Serving: Cal 326; Prot 33 g; Carbo 10 g; T Fat 16 g; 45% Calories from Fat; Chol 151 mg; Fiber 1 g; Sod 179 mg

Donna Holter, Mercer County HFH, West Middlesex, PA

JAKE'S TURKEY AND RICE

YIELD: 4 SERVINGS

1	pound ground turkey	1	envelope taco seasoning
2	(8-ounce) cans tomato sauce		mix
2	tomato sauce cans water	1½	cups rice
1	(11-ounce) can vegetable juice cocktail		

Brown ground turkey in skillet, stirring until crumbly; drain. Stir in tomato sauce, water, vegetable juice cocktail and seasoning mix. Bring to a boil. Add rice and mix well. Boil for 1 minute; reduce heat. Simmer for 10 minutes or until rice is tender, stirring occasionally. May substitute lean ground beef for ground turkey.

Approx Per Serving: Cal 542; Prot 31 g; Carbo 75 g; T Fat 12 g; 21% Calories from Fat; Chol 87 mg; Fiber 3 g; Sod 1936 mg

Craig Jacob, Lawrence HFH, Lawrence, KS

STIR-FRIED FISH

YIELD: 8 SERVINGS

Don't let the amount of ingredients scare you. It just requires a little more time.

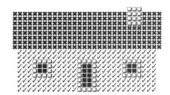

2	pounds frozen white fish, thawed			Sugar to taste
1	egg white	3	cups vegetable oil
1½	teaspoons wine	2	tablespoons vegetable oil
½	teaspoon salt	1	bunch spring onions, chopped
1	(8-ounce) can bamboo shoots	2	pieces gingerroot, chopped
1	(½-ounce) package dried black mushrooms	2	tablespoons soup stock
8	ounces broccoli, chopped	1½	teaspoons wine
2	tablespoons vegetable oil	1	teaspoon soy sauce
1	teaspoon wine	1	teaspoon cornstarch
	Salt to taste	1	teaspoon sesame oil
		½	teaspoon salt
		½	teaspoon sugar

Cut fish into ¼-inch-thick 1x1½-inch portions. Combine egg white, 1½ teaspoons wine and ½ teaspoon salt in bowl and mix well. Add fish. Let stand at room temperature for 30 minutes. Heat bamboo shoots in saucepan. Drain and slice. Soak mushrooms in enough warm water to cover in bowl until softened; drain. Remove stems. Cut each mushroom into 2 or 3 pieces. Cook broccoli in boiling water in saucepan for 2 minutes; drain. Plunge immediately into cold water in bowl. Drain and pat dry. Heat mixture of 2 tablespoons oil, 1 teaspoon wine, salt to taste and sugar to taste in skillet. Add broccoli. Stir-fry until of desired crispness. Remove to platter with slotted spoon. Heat 3 cups oil in skillet over high heat until hot. Fry fish in hot oil for 10 seconds. Drain, discarding oil. Reheat skillet. Add 2 tablespoons oil. Stir-fry spring onions and gingerroot in hot oil. Add mushrooms, bamboo shoots and broccoli and mix well. Stir-fry for a few seconds. Add fish and mix well. Stir in mixture of soup stock, 1½ teaspoons wine, soy sauce, cornstarch, sesame oil, ½ teaspoon salt and ½ teaspoon sugar. Stir-fry just until heated through. Serve immediately. May be prepared 1 day in advance and reheated just before serving but the vegetables will not be as crisp.

Approx Per Serving: Cal 974; Prot 24 g; Carbo 5 g; T Fat 96 g; 88% Calories from Fat; Chol 70 mg; Fiber 2 g; Sod 403 mg
Nutritional information includes entire amount of oil.

Diana Villiers Negroponte, HFHI Board of Directors, Washington, DC

ENTREES

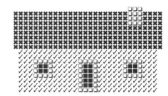

When we were building our first house the backhoe's large tire went flat. We had to stop work. When we were wondering what to do, a neighbor drove up for lunch with his emergency truck. He saw our trouble and used the on-board compressed air to inflate the tire, so we could complete our work. God provided help.

Douglas Carrol Thomas
Washington County
HFH

BAKED HADDOCK IN FOIL

YIELD: 4 SERVINGS

1	pound haddock, cut into 4 equal portions	1/2	teaspoon thyme
1/4	cup white wine	1/2	teaspoon pepper
1/4	cup vegetable oil	1/2	teaspoon paprika
		4	lemon slices

Cut 4 large squares of heavy-duty foil. Place 1 portion of haddock on each square. Drizzle each portion with 1 tablespoon white wine and 1 tablespoon oil. Sprinkle each portion with 1/8 teaspoon thyme, 1/8 teaspoon pepper and 1/8 teaspoon paprika. Top with lemon slices; seal tightly. Place on baking sheet. Bake at 425 degrees for 15 minutes or until fish flakes easily. May substitute any type of fish for haddock and lemon juice for lemon slices.

Approx Per Serving: Cal 234; Prot 22 g; Carbo 1 g; T Fat 14 g; 56% Calories from Fat; Chol 67 mg; Fiber 0 g; Sod 80 mg

Virginia Brennan, Cumberland Valley HFH, Carlisle, PA

KENAI, ALASKA HALIBUT

YIELD: 4 SERVINGS

1 1/2	pounds Alaska halibut steaks	1/4	cup minced green onions
1 1/2	cups dry white wine	1	tablespoon finely chopped onion
2	teaspoons salt	1	(4-ounce) can sliced mushrooms, drained
1/4	cup fine dry bread crumbs		Paprika to taste
3/4	cup sour cream		
3/4	cup mayonnaise		

Arrange halibut steaks in shallow dish. Pour mixture of white wine and salt over fish, turning to coat. Marinate, covered, in refrigerator for 2 hours or longer, turning occasionally; drain. Pat dry with paper towel. Coat with bread crumbs. Arrange in 7x12-inch baking dish sprayed with nonstick cooking spray. Combine sour cream, mayonnaise, green onions, onion and mushrooms in bowl and mix well. Spread over fish; sprinkle with paprika. Bake at 450 degrees for 10 minutes per inch of thickness of fillets measured at thickest part or until fish flakes easily. May decrease recipe by 1/2. May substitute other types of fish fillets for halibut steaks.

Approx Per Serving: Cal 674; Prot 40 g; Carbo 10 g; T Fat 47 g; 62% Calories from Fat; Chol 99 mg; Fiber 1 g; Sod 1598 mg

Douglas Carroll Thomas, Washington County HFH, Hagerstown, MD

RED SNAPPER

Yield: 2 servings

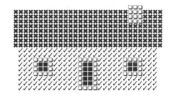

1/2	cup chopped onion	1	small clove of garlic, minced
1	green bell pepper, chopped		
2	tablespoons vegetable oil	1	(1-pound) red snapper fillet
2	tomatoes, chopped	3	tablespoons butter or margarine
1	teaspoon tomato paste		

Sauté onion and green pepper in oil in skillet until tender. Add tomatoes, tomato paste and garlic. Simmer, covered, for 30 minutes, stirring occasionally. Sauté red snapper in butter in skillet for 5 minutes or until fish begins to flake. Add tomato mixture. Simmer for 5 minutes; do not overcook. May substitute other types of fish for red snapper but adjust cooking times accordingly.

Approx Per Serving: Cal 560; Prot 50 g; Carbo 12 g; T Fat 35 g; 56% Calories from Fat; Chol 132 mg; Fiber 3 g; Sod 314 mg

Jacqueline Nice, Greater Portland HFH, Portland, ME

SALMON IN PUFF PASTRY

Yield: 4 servings

1	cup frozen chopped spinach, thawed, drained	1	large shallot, finely chopped
		1	large leek, chopped
1	clove of garlic, crushed	1	tablespoon lemon juice
2	tablespoons anisette liqueur		Salt and pepper to taste
		2	sheets puff pastry, thawed
2	tablespoons unsalted butter	2	egg yolks, beaten
		1	(1 1/2-pound) salmon fillet

Squeeze moisture from spinach. Sauté garlic in mixture of liqueur and butter for 1 minute. Add shallot and mix well. Sauté for 1 minute. Stir in spinach and leek. Sauté until leek is almost tender. Stir in lemon juice, salt and pepper. Spread 1 sheet of puff pastry on hard surface and roll to size necessary to accommodate salmon fillet. Place on parchment paper on baking sheet. Brush with egg yolks. Spread spinach mixture evenly over pastry to within 1 inch of edges. Place salmon over spinach mixture. Brush remaining pastry with remaining egg yolks. Cut into strips. Arrange pastry strips egg yolk side down in crisscross pattern over salmon. Roll edges to seal. Chill, covered, until just before baking. Bake, uncovered, at 375 degrees for 30 minutes or until golden brown and salmon flakes easily.

Approx Per Serving: Cal 1114; Prot 50 g; Carbo 68 g; T Fat 71 g; 57% Calories from Fat; Chol 240 mg; Fiber 4 g; Sod 443 mg

Deanna Cranston, Bend Area HFH, Bend, OR

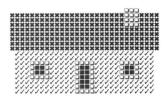

In 1995, Home Depot graciously sponsored the Florida Open in Broward County, benefiting Broward HFH. When they heard that funds were extremely tight and the staff was going unpaid, the regional manager, Terry Kinskey, personally called twelve of their vendors to help raise additional funds. He was responsible for raising $17,000. It is one great company to Habitat!

Kit Rains
Broward HFH

BAKED SALMON IN FOIL

YIELD: 4 SERVINGS

2	tablespoons mayonnaise		Juice of 1 lemon
2	pounds salmon fillets	1	onion, thinly sliced

Cut sheet of heavy-duty foil large enough for salmon fillets. Spread foil with 1/2 of the mayonnaise. Lay fillets on mayonnaise. Spread with remaining mayonnaise; drizzle with lemon juice. Top with onion slices. Cover with another sheet of foil; roll edges to seal. Place on 11x17-inch baking sheet. Bake at 400 degrees for 30 minutes or until salmon flakes easily. May substitute haddock for salmon.

Approx Per Serving: Cal 455; Prot 50 g; Carbo 4 g; T Fat 26 g; 52% Calories from Fat; Chol 162 mg; Fiber 1 g; Sod 160 mg

Miriam Morrell, Mount Washington Valley HFH, North Conway, NH

SPICY AND SWEET SALMON

YIELD: 4 SERVINGS

1/2	cup water	1/2	to 1 teaspoon red pepper flakes
6	tablespoons maple syrup		
2	tablespoons minced gingerroot	4	(6-ounce) salmon fillets, 1 inch thick
2	cloves of garlic, minced	1/4	teaspoon kosher salt

Combine water, maple syrup, gingerroot, garlic and red pepper flakes in saucepan and mix well. Simmer until reduced by 1/2, stirring frequently. Let stand until cool. Arrange salmon skin side down on oiled broiler rack in broiler pan. Sprinkle with kosher salt. Broil 4 inches from heat source for 5 minutes. Brush with maple syrup mixture. Broil for 6 to 10 minutes longer or until salmon flakes easily, basting with remaining maple syrup mixture occasionally.

Approx Per Serving: Cal 377; Prot 37 g; Carbo 21 g; T Fat 15 g; 37% Calories from Fat; Chol 118 mg; Fiber <1 g; Sod 213 mg

Kit Rains, Broward HFH, Lighthouse Point, FL

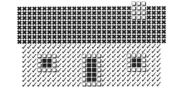

TUNA CASSEROLE

YIELD: 8 SERVINGS

1	(12-ounce) package medium egg noodles
¹⁄₄	to ¹⁄₂ cup chopped onion
1	(28-ounce) can chopped tomatoes
1	(10-ounce) can cream of mushroom soup

Salt and pepper to taste
2 (6-ounce) cans water-pack tuna, drained
1 cup shredded Cheddar cheese

Cook noodles using package directions; drain. Sauté onion in nonstick skillet until tender. Combine noodles, onion, undrained tomatoes, soup, salt and pepper in bowl and mix gently. Stir in tuna. Spoon into 9x13-inch baking pan. Sprinkle with cheese. Bake at 350 degrees for 35 to 50 minutes or until brown and bubbly.

Approx Per Serving: Cal 171; Prot 22 g; Carbo 38 g; T Fat 10 g; 28% Calories from Fat; Chol 103 mg; Fiber 1 g; Sod 709 mg

Elizabeth Poirier, Edmonton HFH, Edmonton, AB, Canada

CURRIED TUNA

YIELD: 4 SERVINGS

1	(10-ounce) can cream of mushroom soup
1	(6-ounce) can water-pack tuna, drained

¹⁄₃ cup milk
1 teaspoon curry powder
2 cups hot cooked rice

Spoon soup into saucepan. Stir in tuna, milk and curry powder. Bring to a boil, stirring frequently. Spoon over hot cooked rice. Serve with assorted curry accompaniments such as raisins, peanuts, pineapple chunks, chopped tomatoes and/or mango chutney. May use reduced-fat cream of mushroom soup and skim milk to reduce fat grams.

Approx Per Serving: Cal 274; Prot 16 g; Carbo 36 g; T Fat 7 g; 24% Calories from Fat; Chol 16 mg; Fiber 1 g; Sod 772 mg

Carl W. Umland, HFHI Board of Directors, Houston, TX

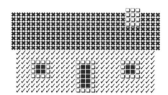

CRAWFISH ETOUFFE

YIELD: 6 SERVINGS

1/2	cup chopped onion	1	(10-ounce) can cream of celery soup
1/2	cup chopped green bell pepper	1/4	teaspoon Cajun or Creole seasoning
1/2	teaspoon minced garlic	1	pound frozen crawfish tails, thawed, peeled, deveined
1/2	cup margarine		
1	(10-ounce) can cream of mushroom soup	3	cups hot cooked rice

Sauté onion, green pepper and garlic in margarine in saucepan for 5 minutes. Stir in soups and Cajun seasoning. Cook until heated through, stirring frequently. Add crawfish and mix gently. Simmer for 10 minutes or until crawfish are cooked through, stirring frequently. Spoon over hot cooked rice. May substitute shrimp for crawfish.

Approx Per Serving: Cal 419; Prot 15 g; Carbo 38 g; T Fat 22 g; 49% Calories from Fat; Chol 87 mg; Fiber 1 g; Sod 1053 mg

Michelle Hays, Pearl River County HFH, Picayune, MS

CRAB QUICHE

YIELD: 6 SERVINGS

4	slices bacon	3	eggs
1	(6- to 8-ounce) can crab meat	1/8	teaspoon salt
1 1/2	cups milk	1/8	teaspoon pepper
1/2	cup baking mix	2	cups shredded Swiss cheese
1/3	cup melted butter		

Fry bacon in skillet until crisp; drain. Crumble bacon. Drain crab meat, reserving 1/4 cup liquid. Beat reserved liquid, milk, baking mix, butter, eggs, salt and pepper in mixer bowl until smooth. Pour into greased 9-inch pie plate. Sprinkle crab meat, bacon and cheese over top and press gently. Bake at 350 degrees for 35 to 40 minutes or until set.

Approx Per Serving: Cal 405; Prot 25 g; Carbo 11 g; T Fat 29 g; 64% Calories from Fat; Chol 212 mg; Fiber <1 g; Sod 624 mg

Wilma Wood, Middletown HFH, Middletown, OH

CRAB CAKES

YIELD: 6 SERVINGS

ENTREES

Lorraine M. Ornelas, chef for former President and Mrs. Gerald R. Ford, shares one of the favorite recipes of the Ford family.

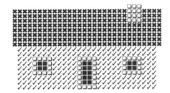

1	pound fresh or frozen crab meat	1	tablespoon bread crumbs
1	rib celery, chopped	2	egg whites, lightly beaten
2	green onions, chopped	1	teaspoon chopped fresh basil
1	tablespoon chopped fresh cilantro	1	cup bread crumbs
1	tablespoon reduced-fat mayonnaise		Mixed baby greens
		12	lemon wedges

Combine crab meat, celery, green onions, cilantro, mayonnaise, bread crumbs, egg whites and basil in bowl and mix gently. If using fresh crab meat, do not overmix—chunks should be kept intact. Shape by 1/4 cupfuls into 6 patties. Coat with 1 cup bread crumbs. Heat 12-inch sauté pan coated heavily with nonstick olive oil cooking spray over medium heat until hot. Add 3 of the crab cakes. Cook for 2 minutes or until golden brown; turn. Cook for 2 minutes longer or until golden brown. Remove to a baking sheet. Repeat process with remaining crab cakes. Bake at 400 degrees for 15 minutes or until cooked through. Serve immediately on platter lined with mixed baby greens. Top with lemon wedges.

Approx Per Serving: Cal 191; Prot 18 g; Carbo 15 g; T Fat 6 g; 30% Calories from Fat; Chol 71 mg; Fiber 1 g; Sod 599 mg

Betty Ford, Rancho Mirage, CA

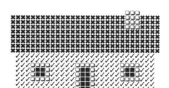

MEAT MARINADE

YIELD: 3/4 CUP

1/2 cup soy sauce	1 tablespoon vinegar
2 tablespoons water	1 teaspoon ginger
2 tablespoons brown sugar	1/2 teaspoon pepper
1 tablespoon vegetable oil	1 clove of garlic, minced

Combine soy sauce, water, brown sugar, oil, vinegar, ginger, pepper and garlic in jar with tightfitting lid and shake to mix. Pour over 1 1/2 pounds beef chuck steak, moose or caribou in shallow dish, turning to coat. Marinate, covered, in refrigerator for 1 hour, turning occasionally. Grill over hot coals until done to taste.

Approx Per Serving: Cal 23; Prot 1 g; Carbo 3 g; T Fat 1 g; 44% Calories from Fat; Chol 0 mg; Fiber <1 g; Sod 686 mg

Debbie Adamson, Central Peninsula HFH, Kenai, AK

MAGIC MARINADE

YIELD: 1 CUP

1 clove of garlic, crushed	1 tablespoon finely chopped
1/2 cup canola oil	gingerroot
1/4 cup Worcestershire sauce	1 tablespoon salt
2 tablespoons lemon juice	1 tablespoon honey
2 tablespoons Dijon mustard	1/4 teaspoon pepper

Cook garlic in canola oil in saucepan over low heat until light brown, stirring constantly. Remove from heat. Stir in Worcestershire sauce, lemon juice, Dijon mustard, gingerroot, salt, honey and pepper. Coat skinless chicken breasts with marinade. Grill over medium-hot coals until cooked through, turning and basting occasionally with marinade.

Approx Per Serving: Cal 70; Prot <1 g; Carbo 2 g; T Fat 7 g; 87% Calories from Fat; Chol 0 mg; Fiber <1 g; Sod 489 mg

Georgia Fuller, HFHI, Americus, GA

HABITAT WIDOWER'S DELIGHT

YIELD: VARIABLE

Step 1: Find your car keys. **Step 2:** Mix dollar bills in with your wallet. **Step 3:** Stir yourself to the car. **Step 4:** Start engine. **Step 5:** Drive to favorite local restaurant. **Step 6:** Order any affordable item. How's that for simple, decent and affordable?

Kristina Pekock, HFHI, Americus, GA

Photograph at right by Robert Baker

VEGETARIAN

"Is it not to share your food with the hungry
and to provide the poor wanderer with shelter—
when you see the naked, to clothe him,
and not to turn away from your own flesh and blood?"

Isaiah 58:7

ARROZ FRIJOLES ENCHILADAS   *YIELD: 6 SERVINGS*

2	cloves of garlic, minced		1	teaspoon cumin
1	tablespoon vegetable oil		1/2	teaspoon oregano
1	(16-ounce) can black beans, rinsed, drained		3/4	cup chopped green bell pepper
1	(8-ounce) can whole tomatoes, chopped		3	green onions with tops, sliced
1	cup instant rice		2	cups shredded Cheddar cheese
1/2	cup picante sauce		12	(6- to 7-inch) flour tortillas
1/3	cup water		1	cup picante sauce
1	teaspoon chicken bouillon granules			

Sauté garlic in oil in 10-inch skillet for 2 minutes. Stir in beans, undrained tomatoes, rice, 1/2 cup picante sauce, water, bouillon granules, cumin and oregano. Bring to a boil; reduce heat. Simmer, covered, for 1 minute. Remove from heat. Let stand for 5 minutes. Stir in green pepper, green onions and 1 cup of the cheese. Spoon about 1/3 cup of bean mixture down center of each tortilla; roll to enclose filling. Arrange seam side down in 9x13-inch baking dish. Spoon 1 cup picante sauce over enchiladas. Bake, covered with foil, at 350 degrees for 20 minutes or until heated through. Sprinkle with remaining 1 cup cheese. Serve with additional picante sauce.

Approx Per Serving: Cal 534; Prot 21 g; Carbo 67 g; T Fat 20 g; 34% Calories from Fat; Chol 40 mg; Fiber 7 g; Sod 1339 mg

Linda C. Fauth, Adams County HFH, Gettysburg, PA

HEAVENLY BEANS AND RICE   *YIELD: 4 SERVINGS*

1	(16-ounce) can black beans		1/4	cup chopped onion
2	tablespoons salsa		1/2	cup sour cream
5	large cloves of garlic, crushed		1	cup shredded sharp Cheddar cheese
1/8	teaspoon red pepper			
2	cups hot cooked saffron rice			

Combine beans, salsa, garlic and red pepper in saucepan and mix well. Cook just until heated through, stirring frequently. Spoon over rice in individual bowls. Top each serving with onion and sour cream; sprinkle with cheese.

Approx Per Serving: Cal 391; Prot 16 g; Carbo 41 g; T Fat 19 g; 42% Calories from Fat; Chol 42 mg; Fiber 7 g; Sod 1090 mg

Michelle Gordon Dalva, HFHI, Americus, GA

CHEESE SOUFFLE

4   slices bread
4   teaspoons butter, softened
1   cup cubed sharp Cheddar cheese
2   cups milk
3   eggs, lightly beaten
1/4   teaspoon prepared mustard
    Salt and pepper to taste

Spread 1 side of each slice of bread with 1 teaspoon butter; cut into cubes. Layer bread cubes and cheese 1/2 at a time in 1 1/2-quart baking dish. Whisk milk, eggs, prepared mustard, salt and pepper in bowl until blended. Pour over prepared layers. Bake at 350 degrees for 45 minutes. May be prepared 1 day in advance, stored in refrigerator and baked just before serving. Let stand at room temperature for 1 hour before baking. May add 1 cup chopped cooked ham, chopped cooked chicken, chopped cooked turkey, cooked sausage or crumbled crisp-fried bacon to egg mixture.

Approx Per Serving: Cal 374; Prot 19 g; Carbo 21 g; T Fat 24 g; 57% Calories from Fat; Chol 222 mg; Fiber 1 g; Sod 498 mg

Herman Shiplett, Kingston, PA

COTTAGE CHEESE LOAF

YIELD: 8 SERVINGS

2   cups low-fat cottage cheese
6   cups Special-K
1   envelope onion soup mix
1/2   cup melted butter or margarine
3   eggs, lightly beaten
1/2   cup crushed walnuts

Combine cottage cheese, cereal and soup mix in bowl and mix well. Stir in butter and eggs. Add walnuts and mix well. Shape into loaf in 5x9-inch loaf pan. Bake at 350 degrees for 1 hour. Let stand for 10 minutes before serving.

Approx Per Serving: Cal 314; Prot 16 g; Carbo 20 g; T Fat 19 g; 55% Calories from Fat; Chol 116 mg; Fiber 1 g; Sod 649 mg

Patsy Kneller, San Angelo HFH, San Angelo, TX

A young boy was talking in his nursery school class about professions. His teacher had previously told the class about construction workers. He shared that they were not called construction workers...they were called Habitat volunteers.

Patsy Kneller
San Angelo HFH

VEGETARIAN

BLACK BEAN CHILI

YIELD: 6 SERVINGS

4	large onions, chopped
1	large green bell pepper, chopped
3	tablespoons vegetable oil
1	tablespoon minced garlic
1	(16-ounce) can Mexican stewed tomatoes
3	(16-ounce) cans black beans
1	cup water
1	(6-ounce) can tomato paste
1	tablespoon chili powder
1	teaspoon cumin seeds
1/2	cup chopped fresh tomato
1/2	cup chopped green chiles
1/2	cup chopped onion
1/2	cup chopped jalapeños
1	cup sour cream
1	cup shredded Cheddar cheese
1	(9-ounce) package tortilla chips

Sauté 4 onions and green pepper in oil in 6-quart saucepan over medium-high heat for 3 minutes or until tender. Add garlic and mix well. Sauté for 1 minute. Stir in undrained canned tomatoes, undrained beans, water, tomato paste, chili powder and cumin seeds. Simmer for 45 minutes, stirring occasionally. Ladle into chili bowls. Top with 1/2 cup fresh tomato, chiles, 1/2 cup chopped onion, jalapeños, sour cream and cheese. Serve with tortilla chips.

Approx Per Serving: Cal 719; Prot 25 g; Carbo 84 g; T Fat 35 g; 42% Calories from Fat; Chol 37 mg; Fiber 20 g; Sod 1604 mg

Rebecca Holt, Bulloch County HFH, Statesboro, GA

SSU VEGETARIAN CHILI

YIELD: 100 SERVINGS

4	pounds onions, chopped
1	pound celery, chopped
1	pound green bell peppers, chopped
5	ounces salt
3	ounces pepper
2 1/2	ounces chili powder
2	ounces garlic powder
1 1/2	ounces cumin
1 1/2	ounces oregano
1/2	cup olive oil
16	pounds whole tomatoes
1	pound carrots, chopped
20	pounds canned kidney beans

Sauté first 9 ingredients in olive oil in stockpot until vegetables are tender. Add tomatoes and carrots and mix well. Simmer until carrots are tender, stirring occasionally. Add beans and mix well. Bring to a boil; reduce heat. Simmer for 20 minutes, stirring occasionally. Ladle into chili bowls.

Approx Per Serving: Cal 121; Prot 6 g; Carbo 22 g; T Fat 2 g; 15% Calories from Fat; Chol 0 mg; Fiber 8 g; Sod 880 mg

Lynne Prettyman, Maryland's Lower Shore HFH, Salisbury, MD

VEGETARIAN CHILI

YIELD: 6 SERVINGS

1	onion, chopped	1	green bell pepper, chopped
2	cloves of garlic, chopped	1	cup chopped celery
1	tablespoon olive oil	2	tablespoons vinegar
1	(28-ounce) can chopped tomatoes	1	tablespoon chili powder
1	(16-ounce) can kidney beans, rinsed, drained	1/2	teaspoon each pepper, basil, oregano and cumin
1	(16-ounce) can garbanzo beans, rinsed, drained	1/4	teaspoon allspice
		1	bay leaf

Sauté onion and garlic in olive oil in saucepan for 2 minutes. Stir in undrained tomatoes, beans, green pepper and celery. Add remaining ingredients and mix well. Simmer, covered, over medium-low heat for 1 hour or until of the desired consistency, adding water as needed and stirring occasionally. Discard bay leaf.

Approx Per Serving: Cal 225; Prot 10 g; Carbo 38 g; T Fat 5 g; 18% Calories from Fat; Chol 0 mg; Fiber 13 g; Sod 410 mg

Maureen Phelan, Mahoning County HFH, Boardman, OH

VEGGIE CHILI

YIELD: 16 SERVINGS

2	cups chopped onions	1	tablespoon cumin
2	cups chopped peeled carrots	2	(28-ounce) cans chopped tomatoes
1/4	cup olive oil	4	cups each drained cooked black beans and pinto beans
2	cups chopped zucchini		
2	cups chopped yellow squash		
2	tablespoons minced garlic	4	cups water
2	poblanos, seeded, chopped	1	cup chopped fresh cilantro
4	jalapeños, seeded, chopped		Salt and pepper to taste
4	cups fresh or frozen whole kernel corn	1/4	cup cornstarch
		1	tablespoon cold water

Sauté onions and carrots in olive oil in stockpot for 5 minutes or until tender. Stir in next 5 ingredients. Cook for 3 minutes or until zucchini and squash are tender. Add corn and cumin and stir in undrained tomatoes, beans, 4 cups water and cilantro. Simmer over medium-low heat for 30 minutes. Season with salt and pepper. Stir in mixture of cornstarch and 1 tablespoon water. Cook for 5 minutes. Ladle into chili bowls. Serve with corn bread and soft drinks.

Approx Per Serving: Cal 230; Prot 11 g; Carbo 40 g; T Fat 5 g; 18% Calories from Fat; Chol 0 mg; Fiber 11 g; Sod 175 mg

Dorothy A. Murdock, DuPage HFH, Warrenville, IL

WINE-POACHED EGGS

YIELD: 2 SERVINGS

1	tablespoon butter	4	mushrooms, chopped
1	tablespoon vegetable oil	1/2	cup dry white wine
2	tomatoes, chopped	4	eggs
1	onion, chopped		

Heat butter and oil in skillet until hot. Sauté tomatoes, onion and mushrooms in butter mixture until tender. Stir in white wine. Simmer for several minutes, stirring constantly. Break eggs into tomato mixture. Simmer until set. Serve with hot crusty bread.

Approx Per Serving: Cal 356; Prot 15 g; Carbo 14 g; T Fat 23 g; 58% Calories from Fat; Chol 441 mg; Fiber 3 g; Sod 202 mg

Elizabeth H. Stewart, Flower City HFH, Rochester, NY

VEGETARIAN LASAGNA

YIELD: 12 SERVINGS

1	(26-ounce) jar wine and herb spaghetti sauce	2	cups cottage cheese
1	(8-inch) zucchini, chopped	1	cup white wine
1	(8-inch) yellow squash, chopped	1	cup grated Parmesan cheese
8	ounces fresh mushrooms, sliced	12	uncooked lasagna noodles
4	cups shredded mozzarella cheese	1	pound fresh spinach, trimmed

Photo by Robert Baker

Combine spaghetti sauce, zucchini, yellow squash, mushrooms, 3 cups of the mozzarella cheese, cottage cheese, white wine and Parmesan cheese in bowl and mix well. Spread thin layer of spaghetti sauce mixture in 9x13-inch baking pan. Layer noodles, spinach and remaining spaghetti sauce mixture 1/4 at a time over prepared layer. Bake, covered with foil, at 350 degrees for 45 minutes. Sprinkle with remaining 1 cup mozzarella cheese. Bake for 15 minutes longer. Let stand for 15 minutes before serving.

Approx Per Serving: Cal 356; Prot 21 g; Carbo 31 g; T Fat 16 g; 39% Calories from Fat; Chol 41 mg; Fiber 4 g; Sod 767 mg

Deborah Rupprecht, Emporia Area HFH, Emporia, KS

MIDDLE EASTERN LENTILS

YIELD: 6 SERVINGS

1	large onion, cut into 1/4-inch slices, separated into rings	2	cups lentils	
		7	cups water	
3	tablespoons vegetable oil	1	tablespoon salt	
		1	cup rice	

Sauté onion in oil in skillet until golden brown. Drain, reserving pan drippings. Sort and rinse lentils. Bring water and salt to a boil in saucepan. Add lentils. Boil for 10 minutes. Stir rice into lentils; reduce heat. Simmer over medium-low heat for 20 minutes; do not stir. Fold rice and lentils if necessary. Fold in reserved pan drippings. Spoon into serving bowl. Top with sautéed onion. Serve with warm pita bread, kalamata olives and hummus if desired. May also top lentils with a chopped salad prepared with the vegetables of choice and a dressing of balsamic vinegar or lemon juice, salt and salad oil.

Approx Per Serving: Cal 376; Prot 18 g; Carbo 60 g; T Fat 8 g; 18% Calories from Fat; Chol 0 mg; Fiber 8 g; Sod 1071 mg

Cynthia D. Rahal, Central South Carolina HFH, Vienna, VA

LENTILS AND BROWN RICE

YIELD: 4 SERVINGS

3/4	cup lentils	1/4	teaspoon oregano, crushed
2 1/2	cups chicken or vegetable broth	1/4	teaspoon thyme, crushed
		1/4	teaspoon garlic powder
3/4	cup chopped onion	1/8	teaspoon pepper
1/2	cup brown rice	1/2	cup shredded mozzarella cheese
1/4	cup dry white wine		
1/2	teaspoon basil, crushed	8	thin strips mozzarella cheese
1/4	teaspoon salt		

Sort and rinse the lentils. Combine broth, lentils, onion, brown rice, white wine, basil, salt, oregano, thyme, garlic powder, pepper and shredded cheese in bowl and mix well. Spoon into ungreased 1 1/2-quart baking pan. Bake, covered, at 350 degrees for 1 1/2 to 2 hours or until lentils and rice are tender, stirring twice. Top with mozzarella cheese strips. Bake for 2 to 3 minutes longer or until cheese melts. Decrease oven temperature to 325 degrees if using a glass baking dish.

Approx Per Serving: Cal 360; Prot 22 g; Carbo 41 g; T Fat 11 g; 28% Calories from Fat; Chol 33 mg; Fiber 6 g; Sod 782 mg

Marlene J. Tobias, Black Hills Area HFH, Rapid City, SD

QUINOA DISH

YIELD: 5 SERVINGS

One cup of uncooked quinoa equals five cups cooked quinoa. Quinoa is a good source of minerals, vitamins and protein. Add your favorite herbs for variety.

1	cup quinoa	1/4	teaspoon curry
1	onion, chopped	1/8	teaspoon capsicum
1	tablespoon chives	1	bay leaf
1/2	teaspoon parsley	1	clove of garlic, minced
1/4	teaspoon rosemary		Sea salt to taste
1/4	teaspoon ginger		

Rinse quinoa several times; drain. Bring about 2 cups of water to a boil in saucepan. Add onion, chives, parsley, rosemary, ginger, curry, capsicum, bay leaf and garlic. Simmer for several minutes. Stir in quinoa and sea salt. Simmer for 20 minutes or until tender. Discard bay leaf.

Approx Per Serving: Cal 137; Prot 5 g; Carbo 26 g; T Fat 2 g; 13% Calories from Fat; Chol 0 mg; Fiber 2 g; Sod 8 mg

Mae Boudreau Pedersen, Moncton HFH, Moncton, NB, Canada

SPINACH PIE

YIELD: 12 SERVINGS

2	(10-ounce) packages frozen spinach, cooked, drained	1/2	cup raisins
		1/2	teaspoon red pepper flakes
1/4	cup minced onion	2	unbaked (10-inch) deep-dish pie shells
3	cloves of garlic, minced		
1/2	cup chopped green bell pepper	12	ounces mozzarella cheese, shredded
3	tablespoons olive oil	1	tablespoon olive oil
8	to 10 black olives, sliced		Salt and pepper to taste

Cook onion, garlic and green pepper in 3 tablespoons olive oil in skillet over low heat for 10 minutes, stirring frequently. Add olives and raisins and mix well. Cook for 2 minutes, stirring constantly. Stir in spinach and red pepper flakes. Cook for 5 minutes, stirring constantly. May be prepared to this point 1 day in advance and stored, covered, in refrigerator. Spoon spinach mixture into 1 pie shell. Top with mixture of cheese, 1 tablespoon olive oil, salt and pepper. Top with remaining pie pastry. Brush with a small amount of water, sealing edge and cutting 3 vents. Bake at 400 degrees for 35 minutes. Serve warm or at room temperature.

Approx Per Serving: Cal 338; Prot 9 g; Carbo 25 g; T Fat 23 g; 61% Calories from Fat; Chol 22 mg; Fiber 2 g; Sod 388 mg

Patricia (Ed) Lindell, HFHI Board of Directors, Edina, MN

Harvest Stew

4	potatoes, peeled, chopped	1	teaspoon salt
2	sweet potatoes, chopped	1	(16-ounce) can hominy, drained
1	medium acorn squash, chopped	1	(16-ounce) can kidney beans, drained
1	medium onion, chopped	1	(15-ounce) can stewed tomatoes
1	green bell pepper, chopped		
3	cloves of garlic, minced	1	(15-ounce) can tomato sauce
2	jalapeños, seeded, minced		
1	teaspoon canola oil	1	cup water
3	tablespoons chili powder	50	pumpkin seeds, toasted
1½	teaspoons cumin		

Combine first 3 ingredients with enough water to cover in stockpot. Cook until tender-crisp; drain. Sauté onion, green pepper, garlic and jalapeños in oil in skillet, adding chili powder, cumin and salt before onion is tender. Combine onion mixture, hominy, beans, undrained tomatoes, tomato sauce and water in stockpot. Stir in potatoes, sweet potatoes and acorn squash. Cook over medium heat for 10 to 15 minutes. Ladle into soup bowls. Sprinkle with pumpkin seeds.

Approx Per Serving: Cal 278; Prot 9 g; Carbo 59 g; T Fat 2 g; 7% Calories from Fat; Chol 0 mg; Fiber 13 g; Sod 879 mg

John D. Borders, Metro Louisville HFH, Louisville, KY

Tofu Onion Torte

35	saltines, crushed	1¼	teaspoons salt
⅓	cup melted margarine	¼	teaspoon black pepper or cayenne
5	medium onions, sliced		
3	tablespoons margarine	¼	teaspoon bitters
1	pound tofu	2	to 3 cups shredded Cheddar cheese
4	eggs		
1	tablespoon parsley		Paprika to taste

Mix cracker crumbs and ⅓ cup margarine in bowl. Press over bottom of 8- or 9-inch springform pan. Chill in refrigerator. Sauté onions in 3 tablespoons margarine in skillet until golden brown. Spread onions evenly over prepared layer. Process tofu, eggs, parsley, salt, black pepper and bitters in food processor until blended. Mix tofu mixture with cheese in bowl. Spread over onions. Sprinkle with paprika. Bake at 350 degrees for 50 to 60 minutes or until set.

Approx Per Serving: Cal 588; Prot 27 g; Carbo 23 g; T Fat 44 g; 66% Calories from Fat; Chol 201 mg; Fiber 3 g; Sod 1259 mg

Linda Fuller, HFHI, Americus, GA

One winter day, a woman was taping newspaper over a broken window of a dilapidated trailer she shared with her sickly husband and several children. Printed on the newspaper was an article about Habitat for Humanity. The article gave the phone number of the local affiliate. Within months her family had moved into a brand new Habitat home.

Linda Fuller
HFHI

SCRAMBLED TOFU

YIELD: 2 SERVINGS

1	cup sliced mushrooms	1/4	teaspoon turmeric
1	large green onion, sliced	1/8	teaspoon white pepper
1	teaspoon peanut oil	1	small tomato, chopped
10	to 11 ounces tofu, drained, crumbled	1/2	green bell pepper, chopped
1/2	cup shredded Cheddar cheese		

Sauté mushrooms and green onion in peanut oil in skillet until tender. Add tofu, cheese, turmeric and white pepper. Cook over low heat for 2 1/2 to 5 minutes, stirring frequently. Stir in tomato and green pepper. Cook for 2 1/2 to 5 minutes longer or until tofu is heated through, stirring frequently. Serve with whole wheat toast or muffins.

Approx Per Serving: Cal 278; Prot 21 g; Carbo 9 g; T Fat 19 g; 59% Calories from Fat; Chol 30 mg; Fiber 3 g; Sod 193 mg

Marian Seagren Hall, Wausau HFH, Wausau, WI

TORTILLA CAKE

YIELD: 6 SERVINGS

1	cup shredded Cheddar cheese	2	cups cooked red kidney beans
1/2	cup ricotta cheese	1	clove of garlic, chopped
1/2	cup crumbled tofu	1	teaspoon chili powder
1	cup shredded celery	1/4	cup salsa
1/2	cup shredded carrot	2	green onions, sliced
1/4	cup chopped black olives	6	to 12 tortillas
1/4	cup salsa	1/4	cup to 1/3 cup shredded Cheddar cheese
1/4	cup chopped fresh cilantro		

Combine 1 cup Cheddar cheese, ricotta cheese and tofu in bowl and mix well. Stir in celery, carrot, olives and 1/4 cup salsa. Mash cilantro, beans, garlic and chili powder in bowl. Stir in 1/4 cup salsa and green onions. Place 1 tortilla on greased baking sheet. Spread tortilla with some of bean mixture. Layer with tortilla. Spread with some of cheese mixture. Layer with tortilla. Continue the stacking process with remaining bean mixture, remaining cheese mixture and remaining tortillas. Bake at 350 degrees for 15 to 30 minutes or until heated through. Sprinkle with 1/4 to 1/3 cup Cheddar cheese. Bake for 2 minutes longer. Let stand for 5 minutes. Cut into wedges. Serve with tossed green salad.

Approx Per Serving: Cal 483; Prot 22 g; Carbo 58 g; T Fat 18 g; 33% Calories from Fat; Chol 37 mg; Fiber 8 g; Sod 695 mg

Thea deGroot, Sarnia, ONT, Canada

SEVEN-LAYER TORTILLA

YIELD: 8 SERVINGS

This dish may take a little more time, but you will be pleased with the results.

1	cup shredded low-fat Monterey Jack cheese	1	teaspoon oregano	

1　cup shredded low-fat Monterey Jack cheese
1　cup shredded sharp Cheddar cheese
1　cup chopped red bell pepper
3/4　cup chopped green bell pepper
1/2　cup chopped red onion
1　(4-ounce) can chopped green chiles, drained
2　tablespoons minced fresh cilantro

1　teaspoon oregano
1　teaspoon chili powder
1/2　teaspoon cumin
1　tablespoon olive oil
2　cups tomato juice
2　(15-ounce) cans black beans, drained
2　(15-ounce) cans cannellini or other white beans, drained
7　(8-inch) flour tortillas
　Sprigs of cilantro

Crisscross 2 sheets of foil in 9-inch pie plate to extend 6 inches over edge of pie plate. Spray with nonstick cooking spray. Combine Monterey Jack cheese and Cheddar cheese in bowl and mix well. Sauté red pepper, green pepper, onion, chiles, 2 tablespoons cilantro, oregano, chili powder and cumin in olive oil in nonstick skillet over medium heat for 5 minutes or until vegetables are tender. Stir in tomato juice. Cook for 8 minutes or until reduced to 2 1/2 cups, stirring frequently. Combine black beans and 1/2 of tomato juice mixture in bowl and mix well. Stir cannellini into remaining tomato juice mixture. Arrange 1 tortilla in prepared pie plate. Spread with 1 cup of the cannellini mixture; sprinkle with 1/4 cup of the cheese mixture. Cover with tortilla, pressing lightly. Spread with 1 cup of the black bean mixture; sprinkle with 1/4 cup of the cheese mixture. Repeat layers with remaining tortillas, remaining cannellini mixture, remaining black bean mixture and remaining cheese mixture, ending with cannellini mixture and cheese mixture. Bring edges of foil to center and seal. Bake at 350 degrees for 40 minutes or until heated through. Remove tortilla stack to serving platter with spatula. Cut into wedges. Top each serving with fresh cilantro.

Approx Per Serving: Cal 444; Prot 25 g; Carbo 60 g; T Fat 12 g; 24% Calories from Fat; Chol 25 mg; Fiber 13 g; Sod 1070 mg

Dorothy Davis, Metro Denver HFH, Denver, CO

Women's Build is a Habitat home planned, funded, and built by women. In addition to providing a home for a single-mother family, Women's Build also empowers the hundreds of women who build each year.

Dorothy Davis
Metro Denver HFH

VEGETARIAN TACO SALAD

YIELD: 4 SERVINGS

1	small onion, chopped	1	head lettuce, separated into leaves
1	teaspoon olive oil		
2	carrots, chopped	4	medium tomatoes, chopped
3	cloves of garlic, minced		
1	(16-ounce) can kidney beans, rinsed, drained	1/2	red onion, chopped
		1/4	cup chopped fresh cilantro
1	(16-ounce) can black beans, rinsed, drained	2	teaspoons lemon juice
		1	teaspoon olive oil
1	(16-ounce) can navy beans, rinsed, drained	6	corn tortillas, cut into strips
1	(16-ounce) can crushed tomatoes	1/4	teaspoon cumin
		1/4	teaspoon salt
1	(8-ounce) can corn, drained	1/4	teaspoon paprika
1	green bell pepper, chopped	1	(16-ounce) can jumbo black olives, drained
1	envelope taco seasoning mix		
		1	cup chopped green onions
3	tablespoons salsa		

Photo by Erin Hooper

Sauté onion in 1 teaspoon olive oil in skillet until tender. Add carrots and garlic and mix well. Sauté until carrots are tender-crisp. Combine carrot mixture, beans, undrained tomatoes, corn, green pepper, seasoning mix and salsa in 5-quart saucepan and mix well. Cook for 30 minutes or until of the consistency of chili, stirring occasionally. Arrange lettuce on large plates or in chili bowls, leaving room in center for chili. Sprinkle tomatoes, onion and cilantro over lettuce; drizzle with lemon juice. Add 1 teaspoon olive oil to skillet 10 minutes before serving. Add tortilla strips to skillet, tossing to coat. Sprinkle with cumin, salt and paprika. Fry tortilla strips until crisp; drain. Ladle 1 cup of chili in center of each plate or bowl. Top each serving with 4 olives; sprinkle with green onions. Serve with warm tortilla strips. May top with sour cream, guacamole and/or salsa.

Approx Per Serving: Cal 792; Prot 34 g; Carbo 132 g; T Fat 19 g; 21% Calories from Fat; Chol 0 mg; Fiber 35 g; Sod 2397 mg

Jennifer Moorhead, Alfred University Chapter, Syracuse, NY

Photograph at right by Don Hall

PASTA

"And who gives food to every creature.
His love endures forever."

Psalms 136:25

MACARONI SALAD

YIELD: 4 SERVINGS

8	ounces elbow macaroni	1	tablespoon (scant)
1	cup chopped celery		prepared mustard
1	cup chopped green bell	1	teaspoon sugar
	pepper	3/4	teaspoon salt
1/4	cup chopped onion	1/8	teaspoon pepper
3/4	cup mayonnaise	4	lettuce leaves
1 3/4	tablespoons cider vinegar	2	tomatoes, cut into quarters

Cook macaroni using package directions; drain. Rinse with cold water; drain. Combine macaroni, celery, green pepper and onion in bowl and mix gently. Combine mayonnaise, vinegar, mustard, sugar, salt and pepper in bowl and mix well. Stir into macaroni mixture. Spoon onto lettuce-lined salad plates. Arrange 2 tomato wedges on each plate.

Approx Per Serving: Cal 546; Prot 9 g; Carbo 52 g; T Fat 35 g; 56% Calories from Fat; Chol 24 mg; Fiber 3 g; Sod 722 mg

Leora Schermerhorn, Haywood HFH, Canton, NC

LAYERED SPINACH SALAD

YIELD: 10 SERVINGS

9	ounces fresh cheese	1/2	cup sliced green onions
	tortellini	1	(8-ounce) bottle ranch
2	cups shredded red		salad dressing
	cabbage	8	slices bacon, crisp-fried,
6	cups torn fresh spinach		crumbled
2	cups cherry tomato halves		

Cook tortellini using package directions; drain. Rinse with cold water; drain. Layer cabbage, spinach, tortellini, cherry tomatoes and green onions in glass salad bowl. Pour salad dressing over top. Sprinkle with bacon. Chill, covered, for 1 hour or longer. May use reduced-fat ranch salad dressing and omit bacon to reduce fat grams.

Approx Per Serving: Cal 211; Prot 7 g; Carbo 16 g; T Fat 13 g; 56% Calories from Fat; Chol 23 mg; Fiber 2 g; Sod 284 mg

Betty J. Petron, HFHI, Williston, ND

Pasta Tuna Salad

YIELD: 4 SERVINGS

8	ounces small pasta shells, cooked, drained	1/4	cup chopped green onions
1	(7-ounce) can water-pack tuna, drained, flaked	1	cup mayonnaise
		2	tablespoons lemon juice
1/2	cup chopped celery	1	tablespoon horseradish
1/2	cup chopped cucumber	1/2	teaspoon salt
		1/8	teaspoon pepper

Combine pasta, tuna, celery, cucumber and green onions in bowl and mix gently. Combine mayonnaise, lemon juice, horseradish, salt and pepper in bowl and mix well. Add to pasta mixture, stirring until mixed. Chill, covered, until serving time.

Approx Per Serving: Cal 675; Prot 21 g; Carbo 47 g; T Fat 46 g; 60% Calories from Fat; Chol 47 mg; Fiber 2 g; Sod 770 mg

Margo Rosen, Omaha HFH, Omaha, NE

Raisin Pasta Salad

YIELD: 8 SERVINGS

16	ounces rotelle or rotini	1	teaspoon dillweed
1	large tomato, chopped	1	teaspoon chives
3	tablespoons raisins	1/4	teaspoon garlic powder
2	tablespoons sunflower kernels	1	(8- to 12-ounce) bottle Italian salad dressing
2	teaspoons oregano		

Cook pasta using package directions; drain. Combine pasta, tomato, raisins, sunflower kernels, oregano, dillweed, chives and garlic powder in bowl and mix gently. Add salad dressing, tossing to coat. Chill, covered, for 8 to 10 hours, stirring occasionally.

Approx Per Serving: Cal 438; Prot 8 g; Carbo 51 g; T Fat 25 g; 49% Calories from Fat; Chol 0 mg; Fiber 2 g; Sod 341 mg

Brenda K. White, Somerset-Pulaski County HFH, Somerset, KY

Photo by Robert Baker

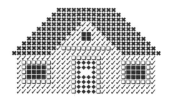

CHICKEN CAPELLINI

YIELD: 4 SERVINGS

5	ounces capellini	1/4	teaspoon pepper
1	(10-ounce) can cream of celery soup	1/4	teaspoon thyme
1/4	cup margarine	2	cups chopped cooked chicken breast
1/2	teaspoon onion powder		

Cook capellini using package directions; drain. Cover to keep warm. Combine soup, margarine, onion powder, pepper and thyme in skillet and mix well. Cook over medium heat until blended, stirring frequently. Stir in chicken. Cook until heated through, stirring frequently. Add pasta and mix well. Cook just until heated through, stirring constantly.

Approx Per Serving: Cal 404; Prot 27 g; Carbo 32 g; T Fat 18 g; 40% Calories from Fat; Chol 68 mg; Fiber 1 g; Sod 765 mg

Julie Vallorano, New Castle County HFH, Wilmington, DE

CHICKEN LINGUINI

YIELD: 6 SERVINGS

16	ounces linguini	1/2	cup olive oil
2	or 3 boneless skinless chicken breast halves	2	cups chopped roasted red peppers
1 1/2	to 2 cloves of garlic, chopped	1	(6-ounce) can black olives, drained, cut into halves

Cook linguini using package directions; drain. Cover to keep warm. Rinse chicken and pat dry. Cut into thin slices. Sauté garlic in olive oil in skillet. Add chicken and mix well. Sauté until cooked through. Stir in red peppers. Cook, covered, over low heat for 15 minutes, stirring occasionally. Remove from heat. Stir in olives. Spoon over linguini on serving platter. Serve immediately with grated Parmesan cheese.

Approx Per Serving: Cal 558; Prot 23 g; Carbo 61 g; T Fat 24 g; 39% Calories from Fat; Chol 37 mg; Fiber 3 g; Sod 458 mg

Donna Holter, Mercer County HFH, West Middlesex, PA

CHICKEN SPEZZATTA

2   cups orzo
      Salt to taste
      Grated Parmesan cheese
         to taste
      Butter to taste
      Chopped fresh parsley to
         taste
      Lemon juice to taste
      Pepper to taste
10   ounces boneless skinless
         chicken breasts
      Olive oil

1/2   cup dry white wine
      Crushed garlic to taste
1   cup Velouté Sauce
1/2   tomato, cut into 1/2-inch
         pieces
1/2   medium green bell pepper,
         cut into 1/2-inch pieces
1/2   medium Spanish onion, cut
         into 1/2-inch pieces
3   large mushrooms, cut into
         1/2-inch pieces

Cook orzo in boiling salted water in saucepan using package directions; drain. Stir in Parmesan cheese, butter, parsley, lemon juice and pepper. Cover to keep warm. Rinse chicken and pat dry. Cut into bite-size pieces. Heat olive oil, white wine, garlic, lemon juice, parsley and Velouté Sauce in skillet until hot. Sauté chicken, tomato, green pepper, onion and mushrooms in olive oil mixture for 6 to 8 minutes or until chicken is cooked through; reduce heat. Simmer for 1 to 2 minutes or until thickened. Spoon orzo into shape of ring on serving platter. Spoon chicken mixture into center. Sprinkle with Parmesan cheese, parsley and pepper.

VELOUTE SAUCE

2   cups chicken broth
      Flour
1   teaspoon finely chopped
         fresh parsley

1   teaspoon lemon juice
1/8   teaspoon salt
1/8   teaspoon pepper

Bring broth just to boiling point in saucepan. Add mixture of flour and a small amount of water, stirring until of consistency of pancake batter. Add parsley, lemon juice, salt and pepper and mix well.

Nutritional information for this recipe is not available.

Frank and Vincent Console, West Philadelphia HFH, Philadelphia, PA

PASTA

BLACK BEAN LASAGNA

YIELD: 12 SERVINGS

8	ounces low-fat cream cheese, softened
1	cup low-fat cottage cheese
2	tablespoons low-fat sour cream
1	(26-ounce) jar spaghetti sauce
16	ounces lasagna noodles, cooked, drained
1	(16-ounce) can black beans, drained, mashed
1	(16-ounce) can black beans, drained
2	(16-ounce) cans spinach, drained
1/2	cup grated Parmesan cheese
	Garlic salt, oregano and basil to taste

Beat cream cheese, cottage cheese and sour cream in mixer bowl until smooth. Spread thin layer of spaghetti sauce in 9x13-inch baking pan sprayed with nonstick cooking spray. Layer lasagna noodles, mashed beans, whole beans, spinach, cream cheese mixture and remaining spaghetti sauce 1/3 at a time in prepared baking pan, ending with spaghetti sauce. Sprinkle with remaining ingredients. Bake, covered, at 350 degrees for 45 to 60 minutes, removing cover 10 to 15 minutes before end of cooking time.

Approx Per Serving: Cal 348; Prot 18 g; Carbo 49 g; T Fat 10 g; 24% Calories from Fat; Chol 16 mg; Fiber 9 g; Sod 991 mg

Alyson Belatti, HFH NW Regional Center, Bend, OR

SKILLET LASAGNA

YIELD: 12 SERVINGS

2	pounds ground beef
2	(16-ounce) jars spaghetti sauce
2	teaspoons each oregano, salt, garlic powder and Italian seasoning
1	small onion, grated
1	large bay leaf
1 1/3	pounds cottage cheese
4	cups (1/2-inch) noodles
1 1/3	cups shredded mozzarella cheese

Brown ground beef in skillet, stirring until crumbly; drain. Stir in next 7 ingredients. Cook over low heat for 15 minutes, stirring frequently. Stir in cottage cheese. Add noodles, stirring until noodles are moistened and covered with sauce. Fill each spaghetti sauce jar 1/4 full of water and swirl. Stir into spaghetti sauce mixture. Cook, covered, over medium heat for 20 to 25 minutes, stirring every 5 minutes to prevent noodles from sticking. Remove from heat. Discard bay leaf. Sprinkle with cheese. Let stand, covered, until cheese melts.

Approx Per Serving: Cal 376; Prot 28 g; Carbo 21 g; T Fat 19 g; 47% Calories from Fat; Chol 84 mg; Fiber 3 g; Sod 1024 mg

Shirley Zanoni, North Oakland HFH, Clarkston, MI

STIR-FRY LASAGNA

YIELD: 6 SERVINGS

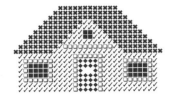

12	ounces lasagna noodles		1	red bell pepper, thinly sliced
3	carrots, cut into thin diagonal slices		1/4	cup corn oil
1/2	yam, julienned		1	(32-ounce) jar spaghetti sauce
1	onion, chopped		2	pounds Colby-Jack cheese, shredded
1/2	bunch broccoli, chopped			
2	ribs celery, thinly sliced			
1	yellow bell pepper, thinly sliced			

Cook noodles using package directions; drain. Stir-fry carrots, yam, onion, broccoli, celery, yellow pepper and red pepper in corn oil in skillet until tender-crisp; drain. Combine vegetable mixture and spaghetti sauce in bowl and mix well. Spread 1 cup spaghetti sauce mixture in 9x13-inch baking pan. Layer noodles, remaining spaghetti sauce mixture and cheese alternately in prepared baking pan until all ingredients are used, ending with spaghetti sauce mixture and cheese. Bake at 325 degrees for 15 minutes or until bubbly. Serve with tossed green salad and hot crusty garlic bread.

Approx Per Serving: Cal 1093; Prot 47 g; Carbo 77 g; T Fat 68 g; 55% Calories from Fat; Chol 151 mg; Fiber 10 g; Sod 1794 mg

Judy Colvard, Lincoln Co. HFH, Seal Rock, OR

MACARONI AND CHEESE

YIELD: 8 SERVINGS

4	cups water		2	cups milk
2	cups elbow macaroni		1	teaspoon salt
2	cups shredded sharp Cheddar cheese		1/2	teaspoon pepper
			1/4	teaspoon paprika

Bring water to a boil in saucepan. Stir in macaroni. Boil for 8 minutes; drain. Spoon pasta into greased 8x11-inch baking pan. Sprinkle with cheese. Pour milk over prepared layers; sprinkle with salt, pepper and paprika. Bake at 375 degrees for 50 minutes.

Approx Per Serving: Cal 249; Prot 12 g; Carbo 23 g; T Fat 12 g; 43% Calories from Fat; Chol 38 mg; Fiber 1 g; Sod 474 mg

Robert M. Kornowski, Wausau HFH, Wausau, WI

NOODLES ROMANOFF

YIELD: 4 SERVINGS

1	(7-ounce) package Noodles Romanoff		Salt and pepper to taste
1	pound ground beef	3	to 4 teaspoons butter or margarine
1	onion, chopped	4	or 5 butter crackers, crushed
1	(10-ounce) can cream of mushroom soup		

Cook Noodles Romanoff using package directions. Brown ground beef with onion in skillet, stirring until ground beef is crumbly; drain. Stir in soup. Add Noodles Romanoff, salt and pepper and mix well. Spoon into 2-quart baking dish. Bake at 350 degrees for 25 minutes. Dot with butter; sprinkle with crackers. Bake for 15 minutes longer. May subsitute Beef Stroganoff for Noodles Romanoff.

Approx Per Serving: Cal 589; Prot 34 g; Carbo 42 g; T Fat 32 g; 48% Calories from Fat; Chol 149 mg; Fiber 2 g; Sod 1452 mg

Nila Whitton, Grant County HFH, Marion, IN

SEAFOOD FETTUCCINI

YIELD: 4 SERVINGS

2	tablespoons chopped onion	4	teaspoons cornstarch
2	tablespoons chopped green bell pepper	2	(1-ounce) slices white American cheese, torn
1	tablespoon margarine	1/8	teaspoon basil
1 1/2	cups chicken broth	12	ounces imitation crab meat
1/2	cup skim milk	4	ounces fettuccini, cooked, drained
1/4	cup dry white wine		

Sauté onion and green pepper in margarine in skillet until tender. Add broth, skim milk, white wine and cornstarch. Cook for 2 minutes or until thickened, stirring constantly. Stir in cheese and basil. Add crab meat and mix well. Cook just until heated through, stirring constantly. Spoon over hot cooked fettuccini.

Approx Per Serving: Cal 312; Prot 20 g; Carbo 36 g; T Fat 9 g; 25% Calories from Fat; Chol 27 mg; Fiber 1 g; Sod 1227 mg

Sara Lynn Malte Squires, Orleans County HFH, Medina, NY

SPAGHETTI AND ITALIAN TUNA
Yield: 6 servings

PASTA

16	ounces spaghetti	1/4	cup olive oil
1	tablespoon butter	1	(14-ounce) can stewed
3	cloves of garlic, chopped		tomatoes
1	tablespoon parsley flakes	1	(6-ounce) can tuna,
1	teaspoon basil		drained, flaked

Cook spaghetti using package directions; drain. Toss with butter.
Cover to keep warm. Sauté garlic, parsley and basil in olive oil in
skillet over medium heat for 1 minute; do not allow garlic to brown.
Stir in undrained tomatoes. Cook over low heat for 20 minutes or
until olive oil separates, stirring occasionally. Stir in tuna. Simmer for
5 minutes, stirring occasionally. Spoon over hot cooked spaghetti on
serving platter.

Approx Per Serving: Cal 429; Prot 18 g; Carbo 61 g; T Fat 12 g;
26% Calories from Fat; Chol 14 mg; Fiber 3 g; Sod 289 mg

Anne-Marie Glynn, Case Western Reserve University HFH
Herndon, VA

SPAGHETTI AND VEGETABLES
Yield: 4 servings

1/3	cup chopped walnuts	1	clove of garlic, minced
2	tablespoons margarine	1/3	cup chicken broth
2	to 3 teaspoons olive oil	8	ounces thin spaghetti
1	cup cherry tomato halves	3	cups chopped broccoli
1/4	cup chopped fresh parsley	1/3	cup grated Parmesan
1/4	cup chopped fresh basil		cheese

Spread walnuts on baking sheet. Toast at 350 degrees for 5
minutes. Heat margarine and olive oil in skillet until margarine melts.
Stir in tomatoes, parsley, basil and garlic. Add broth and mix well.
Simmer for 2 to 3 minutes, stirring frequently. Combine spaghetti
with enough water to cover in saucepan. Bring to a boil. Boil for 5
minutes. Add broccoli. Cook for 5 to 6 minutes longer or until
spaghetti is tender and broccoli is tender-crisp; drain. Spoon
spaghetti mixture onto serving platter. Top with tomato mixture.
Sprinkle with walnuts and cheese.

Approx Per Serving: Cal 424; Prot 15 g; Carbo 50 g; T Fat 19 g;
40% Calories from Fat; Chol 7 mg; Fiber 4 g; Sod 314 mg

Nancy Broberg, Cape Cod HFH, Brewster, MA

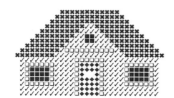

CHILI SPAGHETTI

YIELD: 4 SERVINGS

8	ounces spaghetti	1	(10-ounce) can tomato soup
1	pound ground beef	1	tablespoon sugar
1	large onion, chopped	1/2	teaspoon salt
1	large green bell pepper, chopped		Chili powder to taste
1	(16-ounce) can chili beans in chili gravy		

Cook spaghetti in boiling water in saucepan until al dente; drain. Brown ground beef with onion and green pepper in skillet, stirring until ground beef is crumbly; drain. Stir in undrained beans, soup, sugar, salt and chili powder. Add spaghetti and mix gently. Cook for 30 minutes, stirring occasionally.

Photo by Julie Lopez

Serve with grated Parmesan cheese. May omit green pepper.

Approx Per Serving: Cal 670; Prot 41 g; Carbo 74 g; T Fat 24 g; 32% Calories from Fat; Chol 103 mg; Fiber 8 g; Sod 1454 mg

Betsy Downey, Omaha HFH, Omaha, NE

CORN AND MACARONI

YIELD: 6 SERVINGS

1	(15-ounce) can whole kernel corn, drained	1	cup cubed Velveeta cheese
1	(15-ounce) can cream-style corn	1	cup uncooked elbow macaroni
		1/4	cup margarine

Combine whole kernel corn, cream-style corn, cheese, macaroni and margarine in bowl and mix well. Spoon into 3-quart baking dish. Bake at 350 degrees for 45 to 60 minutes or until brown and bubbly, stirring 3 or 4 times.

Approx Per Serving: Cal 326; Prot 10 g; Carbo 41 g; T Fat 14 g; 39% Calories from Fat; Chol 18 mg; Fiber 3 g; Sod 864 mg

Audrey Best, Webster County HFH, Fort Dodge, IA

FETTUCCINI WITH OLIVE SAUCE

Yield: 4 servings

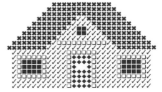

12	ounces fettuccini	1	small bunch parsley, finely chopped
2	cloves of garlic, minced	1	teaspoon oregano, crushed
1/4	cup olive oil	1/2	teaspoon red pepper, crushed
1	(6-ounce) can pitted black olives, drained, chopped	1/2	cup water
1	(3-ounce) jar pimento-stuffed green olives, drained, chopped	1/2	cup grated Parmesan cheese

Cook fettuccini using package directions; drain. Cover to keep warm. Sauté garlic in olive oil in 2-quart saucepan over medium heat just until garlic begins to brown. Stir in olives, parsley, oregano, red pepper and water. Bring just to a boil over high heat, stirring occasionally. Spoon over hot cooked fettuccini on serving platter. Sprinkle with cheese. May substitute vegetable oil for olive oil.

Approx Per Serving: Cal 569; Prot 17 g; Carbo 68 g; T Fat 26 g; 40% Calories from Fat; Chol 10 mg; Fiber 4 g; Sod 1055 mg

Billie Lombardo, East Polk County HFH, Winter Haven, FL

GREEN ONION NOODLES

Yield: 4 servings

8	ounces linguini	4	teaspoons soy sauce
	Salt to taste		Pepper to taste
1/4	cup peanut oil	1	cup thinly sliced green onions
2	tablespoons rice vinegar		

Cook linguini in boiling salted water in saucepan for 6 minutes or until al dente; drain. Whisk peanut oil, rice vinegar and soy sauce in bowl. Pour over pasta in bowl, tossing to coat. Season generously with pepper. Add green onions and mix well. May be prepared in advance.

Approx Per Serving: Cal 341; Prot 8 g; Carbo 45 g; T Fat 14 g; 38% Calories from Fat; Chol 0 mg; Fiber 2 g; Sod 351 mg

Judi Feniger, Greater Cleveland HFH, Chagrin Falls, OH

At the 1997 Anniversary Dinner, East Polk County affiliate raffled off a one hundred dollar gift certificate to a local supermarket. Two hundred dollars was brought in by ticket sales, and the winning ticket was bought by a homeowner.

Billie Lombardo
East Polk County HFH

PEANUT NOODLES

YIELD: *8 SERVINGS*

1	(16-ounce) package frozen peas	1	cup peanut butter
16	ounces spaghetti	1	cup water
1	cup soy sauce	½	cup vegetable oil
		2	tablespoons sugar

Place peas in colander. Cook spaghetti using package directions. Drain spaghetti over peas to thaw. Combine soy sauce, peanut butter, water, oil and sugar in saucepan. Cook until blended, stirring constantly. Pour over spaghetti and pea mixture in bowl, tossing to mix. Chill, covered, until serving time. May substitute peanut oil for vegetable oil. Convert this recipe to Japanese Sesame Noodles by substituting soba noodles for spaghetti, tahini for peanut butter and sesame oil for vegetable oil.

Approx Per Serving: Cal 594; Prot 20 g; Carbo 63 g; T Fat 31 g; 46% Calories from Fat; Chol 0 mg; Fiber 6 g; Sod 2278 mg

Heidi Baker, HFH of Colorado, Denver, CO

NOODLES NEWPORT

YIELD: *6 SERVINGS*

12	ounces Asian noodles	1	teaspoon finely chopped gingerroot, or to taste
8	ounces boneless skinless chicken breasts, cut into thin strips	2	teaspoons olive oil
1	cup thinly sliced peeled carrot	½	cup thinly sliced mushrooms
1	cup thinly sliced broccoli	½	cup bean sprouts
½	cup thinly sliced onion	½	cup thinly sliced green bell pepper
1	(or more) clove of garlic, chopped	1	tablespoon stir-fry sauce
		2	teaspoons soy sauce

Cook noodles until al dente using package directions; drain. Rinse chicken and pat dry. Stir-fry chicken, carrot, broccoli, onion, garlic, and gingerroot in olive oil in skillet or wok over medium-high heat or in 350-degree electric skillet. Add mushrooms, beans sprouts and green pepper. Stir-fry until chicken is cooked through and vegetables are tender-crisp. Add noodles, tossing to mix. Stir in stir-fry sauce and soy sauce. Stir-fry just until heated through.

Approx Per Serving: Cal 271; Prot 17 g; Carbo 39 g; T Fat 5 g; 16% Calories from Fat; Chol 71 mg; Fiber 3 g; Sod 199 mg

Catherine Ryan, Yaquina Bay HFH, Newport, OR

Photograph at right by Joe Matthews

VEGETABLES & SIDE DISHES

Then God said, "I give you every seed-bearing plant
on the face of the whole earth
and every tree that has fruit with seed in it.
They will be yours for food."

Genesis 1:29

EASY ELEGANT ASPARAGUS

YIELD: 4 SERVINGS

1 pound fresh asparagus, trimmed
1½ tablespoons pine nuts
2 tablespoons melted butter
1 tablespoon balsamic vinegar
Salt and pepper to taste

Rinse asparagus; discard tough ends. Steam or cook, covered, in a small amount of boiling water in steamer or saucepan for 3 to 6 minutes or until tender-crisp; drain. Spread pine nuts in single layer on baking sheet. Toast at 350 degrees for 5 minutes. Whisk butter and balsamic vinegar in bowl until blended. Arrange asparagus on serving platter. Drizzle with butter mixture; sprinkle with pine nuts. Serve immediately with salt and pepper.

Approx Per Serving: Cal 99; Prot 3 g; Carbo 7 g; T Fat 8 g; 65% Calories from Fat; Chol 16 mg; Fiber 3 g; Sod 64 mg

Donna Minich, HFHI, Americus, GA

BARBECUE BEANS

YIELD: 20 SERVINGS

16 ounces mild sausage
1 cup chopped celery
1 cup chopped onion
1 (15-ounce) can kidney beans
1 (15-ounce) can pork and beans
1 (15-ounce) can chili beans
1 (15-ounce) can butter beans
1 (15-ounce) can green beans, drained
1 (15-ounce) can wax beans, drained
1 (15-ounce) can lima beans, drained
1 (10-ounce) can tomato soup
1 cup packed brown sugar
1 (6-ounce) can tomato paste
1 tablespoon prepared mustard

Brown sausage with celery and onion in 10-inch skillet, stirring until sausage is crumbly; drain. Combine undrained kidney beans, undrained pork and beans, undrained chili beans and undrained butter beans in bowl and mix gently. Stir in green beans, wax beans and lima beans. Add soup, brown sugar, tomato paste and mustard and mix well. Stir in sausage mixture. Spoon into roasting pan. Bake at 350 degrees for 30 minutes; cover with lid. Bake for 30 minutes longer. May freeze baked beans for future use.

Approx Per Serving: Cal 209; Prot 9 g; Carbo 32 g; T Fat 6 g; 24% Calories from Fat; Chol 15 mg; Fiber 5 g; Sod 824 mg

Michelle Devine, Cambria County HFH, Johnstown, PA

Green Beans Supreme

Yield: 4 servings

1	pound fresh green beans, sliced
1	rib celery, sliced
¼	cup slivered almonds

2	tablespoons margarine
1	teaspoon salt
⅛	teaspoon pepper

Combine beans with enough water to cover in saucepan. Cook for 20 minutes or until tender; drain. Sauté celery and almonds in margarine in skillet over medium heat for 10 minutes or until celery is tender and almonds are light brown. Add beans, salt and pepper, tossing to mix. Cook just until heated through.

Approx Per Serving: Cal 138; Prot 4 g; Carbo 10 g; T Fat 10 g; 62% Calories from Fat; Chol 0 mg; Fiber 5 g; Sod 616 mg

Louella G. Dugger, Silver Valley HFH, Pinehurst, ID

Green and Navy Beans

Yield: 6 servings

½	cup dried navy beans
½	teaspoon baking soda
1	pound fresh green beans, trimmed

	Salt to taste
2	tablespoons bacon drippings

Sort and rinse navy beans. Combine with enough water to cover in saucepan. Bring to a boil. Stir in baking soda. Cook for 1 minute. Drain and rinse. Combine navy beans and green beans with enough water to cover in large saucepan. Bring to a boil; reduce heat. Simmer for 2 hours or until beans are tender; drain. Season with salt. Stir in bacon drippings.

Approx Per Serving: Cal 119; Prot 5 g; Carbo 15 g; T Fat 5 g; 35% Calories from Fat; Chol 5 mg; Fiber 6 g; Sod 135 mg

Meurial Stearns, Three Trails Neighbors HFH, Independence, MO

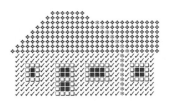

Recently I attended my first Habitat home dedication ceremony. It brought tears to my eyes as this family was so humble and appreciative of all that had been done to make it possible for them to own their own home. The four children were so grateful, and each expressed how thrilled they were to have a new home!

Louella G. Dugger, Silver Valley HFH

BROCCOLI WREATH

YIELD: 20 SERVINGS

Florets of 4 bunches
   broccoli
1   teaspoon salt

1/2   teaspoon pepper
1   cup cherry tomatoes
1/2   cup melted butter

Pour water into saucepan to depth of 1 inch. Bring to a boil. Add broccoli. Steam, covered, for 5 minutes; drain. Plunge into ice water in bowl; drain. Toss broccoli with salt and pepper in bowl. Arrange cherry tomatoes in ring mold or bundt pan. Pack broccoli around tomatoes. Drizzle with butter. Bake, covered with foil, at 350 degrees for 20 minutes. Invert onto serving platter. May be prepared 1 day in advance, stored in refrigerator and baked just before serving. Bring to room temperature before baking.

Approx Per Serving: Cal 47; Prot 1 g; Carbo 1 g; T Fat 5 g; 86% Calories from Fat; Chol 12 mg; Fiber 1 g; Sod 159 mg

Linda Thomas, Bay Area HFH, Houston, TX

GRANDMA'S RED CABBAGE

YIELD: 8 SERVINGS

1   small onion, shredded
1/4   teaspoon vegetable oil
1   medium head red cabbage, shredded
1/3   cup cider vinegar

1   (24-ounce) jar applesauce
2   tablespoons sugar
1   tablespoon caraway seeds
1   envelope gravy mix, prepared

Sauté onion in oil in heavy saucepan just until tender. Add cabbage and mix well. Stir in vinegar, applesauce, sugar and caraway seeds. Simmer for 30 minutes, stirring occasionally. Add gravy and mix well. Cook just until heated through, stirring constantly. Flavor is enhanced if prepared 1 day in advance.

Approx Per Serving: Cal 123; Prot 2 g; Carbo 30 g; T Fat 1 g; 6% Calories from Fat; Chol <1 mg; Fiber 4 g; Sod 158 mg

Evelyn M. Kaspar, Pinellas HFH, St. Petersburg, FL

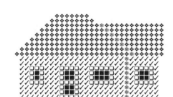

CARROT CASSEROLE

YIELD: 6 SERVINGS

4	cups chopped or sliced carrots	1/2	cup plus 2 tablespoons margarine
1/2	cup chopped onion	1/2	cup butter cracker crumbs
8	ounces Velveeta cheese, cubed	2	tablespoons melted butter or margarine

Combine carrots and onion with enough water to cover in saucepan. Cook until tender; drain. Combine cheese and margarine in microwave-safe dish. Microwave until blended, stirring frequently. Stir in carrot mixture. Spoon into 2-quart baking dish. Sprinkle with cracker crumbs. Drizzle with butter. Bake at 350 degrees for 20 to 30 minutes or until bubbly.

Approx Per Serving: Cal 396; Prot 10 g; Carbo 13 g; T Fat 34 g; 77% Calories from Fat; Chol 42 mg; Fiber 2 g; Sod 855 mg

Harriett E. Attanasio, Lewis County HFH, Weston, WV

DELUXE CARROTS

YIELD: 8 SERVINGS

2	pounds carrots, peeled	1/4	cup bread crumbs
	Salt to taste	2	tablespoons butter
1/2	cup mayonnaise	1	tablespoon chopped fresh parsley
1	tablespoon minced onion		
1	tablespoon horseradish	1/4	teaspoon paprika
	Pepper to taste		

Combine carrots and salt with enough water to cover in saucepan. Bring to a boil; reduce heat. Cook until tender. Drain, reserving 1/4 cup of the liquid. Slice carrots. Arrange in baking dish. Combine reserved liquid, mayonnaise, onion, horseradish, salt and pepper in bowl and mix well. Spoon over carrots. Sprinkle with bread crumbs; dot with butter. Sprinkle with parsley and paprika. Bake at 350 degrees for 20 minutes.

Approx Per Serving: Cal 188; Prot 2 g; Carbo 15 g; T Fat 14 g; 66% Calories from Fat; Chol 16 mg; Fiber 4 g; Sod 179 mg

Karen Fischer Fruth, Maumee Valley HFH, Toledo, OH

VEGETABLES

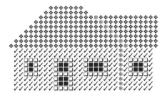

CORN CASSEROLE

YIELD: 6 SERVINGS

1	(16-ounce) can cream-style corn	1/2	cup chopped celery
1	cup cracker crumbs	1/4	cup chopped onion
1	cup milk	2	eggs, beaten
2/3	cup shredded Cheddar cheese	2	tablespoons melted margarine
		1/4	teaspoon paprika

Combine corn, cracker crumbs, milk, cheese, celery, onion, eggs, margarine and paprika in bowl and mix well. Spoon into 1 1/2-quart round baking dish. Bake at 350 degrees for 50 to 55 minutes or until brown and bubbly.

Approx Per Serving: Cal 259; Prot 9 g; Carbo 27 g; T Fat 13 g; 45% Calories from Fat; Chol 90 mg; Fiber 1 g; Sod 610 mg

Delma Brazle, Gallatin Valley HFH, Bozeman, MT

CORN PUDDING

YIELD: 6 SERVINGS

1/4   cup sugar
3   tablespoons cornstarch
2   eggs
1   (15-ounce) can cream-style corn
1   (12-ounce) can evaporated milk
2   to 3 tablespoons melted butter

Combine sugar, cornstarch and eggs in bowl and mix well. Stir in corn, evaporated milk and butter. Spoon into greased 8x8-inch baking pan. Bake at 350 degrees for 40 to 50 minutes or until brown and bubbly. Reduce oven temperature to 325 degrees if baking in glass baking dish.

Photo by Robert Baker

Approx Per Serving: Cal 255; Prot 7 g; Carbo 30 g; T Fat 12 g; 42% Calories from Fat; Chol 103 mg; Fiber 1 g; Sod 379 mg

Dorothy W. Ward, Salem County HFH, Woodstown, NJ

EGGPLANT AND SQUASH

Yield: 5 servings

Serve with yellow saffron rice and hot crisp sourdough bread.

½	cup canola oil	¼	teaspoon pepper
¼	cup light olive oil	1	large or 2 small eggplant, cut into ½-inch slices
¼	cup lemon juice		
2	tablespoons white wine	4	yellow squash, cut into ½-inch slices
1	teaspoon oregano		
1	teaspoon salt	4	zucchini, cut into ½-inch slices
½	teaspoon garlic powder		

Combine canola oil, olive oil, lemon juice, white wine, oregano, salt, garlic powder and pepper in bowl and mix well. Dip eggplant, squash and zucchini in oil mixture; drain slightly. Grill over medium-hot coals for 8 to 10 minutes per side or until brown. Serve immediately or cover to keep warm. May omit white wine.

Approx Per Serving: Cal 404; Prot 6 g; Carbo 25 g; T Fat 34 g; 70% Calories from Fat; Chol 0 mg; Fiber 10 g; Sod 441 mg

Linda Fuller, HFHI, Americus, GA

GOOSETONGUE GREENS

Yield: 2 servings

Goosetongue greens is the name given to marsh grass found growing along the Petitcodia River in New Brunswick. The greens are usually available in July or August. They were sometimes salted and preserved for eating in winter.

8	ounces beef, chopped	1	cup water
8	ounces pork, chopped	1½	to 2 quarts fresh goosetongue greens
2	to 3 tablespoons butter or margarine		

Sear beef and pork in butter in pressure cooker. Add water and mix well; seal cooker. Cook for 15 minutes. Cool cooker under cold water. Add greens; seal cooker. Cook for 10 minutes longer. Cool cooker under cold water. Serve with vinegar and/or lemon juice. May serve with potatoes cooked with greens or cooked separately.

Approx Per Serving: Cal 532; Prot 56 g; Carbo 11 g; T Fat 30 g; 50% Calories from Fat; Chol 192 mg; Fiber 4 g; Sod 324 mg

Claudia Tucker, Moncton Region HFH, Moncton, NB, Canada

A juvenile delinquent was required to do community service while he was waiting for his court date. When he appeared before the judge, the judge was the same man who had worked with him nailing shingles on the roof of a Habitat house.

Linda Fuller
HFHI

VEGETABLES

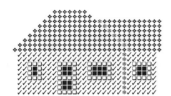

POTATO ONION CASSEROLE

YIELD: 6 SERVINGS

5	teaspoons vegetable oil	2	onions, sliced
6	medium potatoes, peeled, cut into 1/8-inch slices		Salt and pepper to taste

Coat bottom and sides of 10x10-inch baking dish with 2 teaspoons of the oil. Layer 1/3 of the potatoes and 1/2 of the onions in the prepared baking dish. Season with salt and pepper. Drizzle with 1 teaspoon of the oil. Repeat the layers. Top with the remaining potatoes, salt, pepper and remaining oil. Bake, covered, at 350 degrees for 1 hour.

Approx Per Serving: Cal 161; Prot 3 g; Carbo 30 g; T Fat 4 g; 22% Calories from Fat; Chol 0 mg; Fiber 2 g; Sod 7 mg

John Pelissier, Amherst County HFH, Amherst, VA

POTATO PANCAKES

YIELD: 6 SERVINGS

3	or 4 uncooked potatoes, grated	2	eggs, lightly beaten
1	onion, grated	1	teaspoon salt
1	cup flour		Vegetable oil for frying

Mix potatoes, onion, flour, eggs and salt in bowl. Shape into 3-inch patties. Fry in hot oil in skillet until brown on both sides; drain.

Approx Per Serving: Cal 183; Prot 6 g; Carbo 35 g; T Fat 2 g; 10% Calories from Fat; Chol 71 mg; Fiber 2 g; Sod 381 mg
Nutritional information does not include oil for frying.

Peg and David Picciano, Northeast Connecticut HFH, Putnam, CT

EASY CHEESE POTATOES

YIELD: 8 SERVINGS

1	(2-pound) package frozen cubed potatoes	1	(10-ounce) can cream of chicken soup
2	cups sour cream	1/2	small onion, chopped
2	cups shredded Cheddar cheese	2 1/2	cups crushed cornflakes
		1/2	cup melted butter

Combine potatoes, sour cream, cheese, soup and onion in bowl and mix well. Spoon into 9x13-inch baking pan. Sprinkle with mixture of cornflakes and butter. Bake at 350 degrees for 1 hour.

Approx Per Serving: Cal 550; Prot 15 g; Carbo 45 g; T Fat 35 g; 57% Calories from Fat; Chol 89 mg; Fiber 2 g; Sod 889 mg

Jane Foster, Gallatin Valley HFH, Bozeman, MT

POTATO CASSEROLE

YIELD: 8 SERVINGS

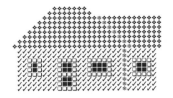

6	medium unpeeled potatoes	1/3	cup chives
3	cups sour cream	1	teaspoon salt
2	cups shredded Cheddar cheese	3/4	teaspoon white pepper
1/4	cup melted butter or margarine	2	tablespoons butter
			Paprika to taste

Combine potatoes with enough water to cover in saucepan. Bring to a boil. Boil until tender; drain. Chill in refrigerator. Peel potatoes and grate into baking dish. Combine sour cream, cheese, 1/4 cup butter, chives, salt and white pepper in bowl and mix well. Pour over potatoes, stirring slightly. Dot with 2 tablespoons butter; sprinkle with paprika. Bake at 350 degrees for 35 minutes. May be prepared 1 day in advance and stored, covered, in the refrigerator or frozen for future use.

Approx Per Serving: Cal 464; Prot 12 g; Carbo 25 g; T Fat 36 g; 69% Calories from Fat; Chol 91 mg; Fiber 2 g; Sod 604 mg

Dotty Albertson, Orange County HFH, Westminster, CA

HARVEST POTATOES

YIELD: 12 SERVINGS

1/2	cup melted butter or margarine	1	cup sour cream
1	(32-ounce) package frozen Southern-style hash brown potatoes, thawed	2	cups shredded Cheddar cheese
		1/2	cup chopped onion
		1 1/2	teaspoons salt
1	(10-ounce) can cream of chicken soup	1 1/2	cups crushed cornflakes

Pour butter over potatoes in bowl, stirring until mixed. Add soup, sour cream, cheese, onion and salt and mix well. Spoon into greased 9x13-inch baking dish. Sprinkle with cornflakes. Bake at 350 degrees for 1 1/2 hours or until brown and bubbly.

Approx Per Serving: Cal 359; Prot 9 g; Carbo 26 g; T Fat 25 g; 62% Calories from Fat; Chol 51 mg; Fiber 1 g; Sod 785 mg

Julia H. Lifer, Fairfield County HFH, Lancaster, OH

VEGETABLES

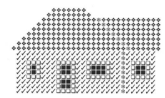

MASHED POTATO CASSEROLE
YIELD: 8 SERVINGS

8	to 10 medium potatoes, peeled, chopped	2	tablespoons flour
8	ounces cream cheese, softened	2	tablespoons minced fresh parsley
1/2	teaspoon salt	2	tablespoons minced chives or onion
1/2	teaspoon pepper	1	(4-ounce) can French-fried onions, lightly crushed
2	eggs, lightly beaten		

Combine potatoes with enough water to cover in saucepan. Bring to a boil. Boil until tender; drain. Beat in mixer bowl until smooth. Add cream cheese, salt and pepper. Beat until blended, scraping bowl occasionally. Stir in eggs, flour, parsley and chives, beating thoroughly. Spoon into buttered 2-quart baking dish. Sprinkle with French-fried onions. Bake at 325 degrees for 30 minutes or until golden brown. May be prepared in advance, stored in refrigerator and baked just before serving. Sprinkle with onions just before baking. May substitute an equivalent amount of egg substitute for eggs.

Approx Per Serving: Cal 358; Prot 8 g; Carbo 42 g; T Fat 18 g; 45% Calories from Fat; Chol 84 mg; Fiber 2 g; Sod 335 mg

Teresa Cook, Venice Area HFH, Inc., Venice, FL

SISTER'S POTATO PIE
YIELD: 8 SERVINGS

2	all ready pie pastries	1	teaspoon chopped fresh chives
4	medium Idaho potatoes, peeled, cut into 1/8-inch slices	1/2	teaspoon white pepper
1	medium onion, cut into 1/8-inch slices, separated into rings	1	cup whipping cream

Fit 1 of the pie pastries into 9-inch microwave-safe pie plate. Layer potatoes, onion and chives in prepared pie plate. Sprinkle with white pepper. Top with remaining pie pastry, crimping edge. Cut a slit in shape of cross in top of pie pastry. Bake at 350 degrees for 1 hour. Pour whipping cream gradually into pie through slit. Cool to room temperature. Chill for 3 1/2 hours or for up to 8 hours. Reheat in microwave for 5 minutes, turning once. May omit chives.

Approx Per Serving: Cal 405; Prot 3 g; Carbo 39 g; T Fat 26 g; 58% Calories from Fat; Chol 56 mg; Fiber 1 g; Sod 295 mg

Mindy Shannon Phelps, Kentucky HFH, Lexington, KY

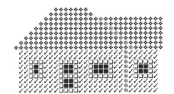

ZUCCHINI CASSEROLE

Yield: 6 servings

6	cups chopped zucchini	1	cup sour cream
1/4	cup chopped onion	1	cup shredded carrot
	Salt to taste	1	(8-ounce) package chicken
1	(10-ounce) can cream of		stove-top stuffing mix
	chicken soup	1/2	cup melted margarine

Cook zucchini and onion in boiling salted water in saucepan for 5 minutes; drain. Combine zucchini mixture, soup, sour cream and carrot in bowl and mix gently. Combine stuffing mix and margarine in bowl and mix well. Spread half the stuffing mixture over bottom of 2-quart baking dish. Spread with zucchini mixture. Top with remaining stuffing mixture. Bake at 350 degrees for 25 to 30 minutes or until bubbly. May substitute yellow squash or a combination of zucchini and yellow squash for zucchini.

Approx Per Serving: Cal 434; Prot 9 g; Carbo 41 g; T Fat 28 g; 56% Calories from Fat; Chol 21 mg; Fiber 2 g; Sod 1210 mg

Elizabeth Dunford, Southwest Volusia HFH, Orange City, FL

ZUCCHINI TOMATO CASSEROLE

Yield: 6 servings

1	large onion, thinly sliced	2	medium zucchini, thinly
1	clove of garlic, chopped		sliced
1	tablespoon olive oil	1	teaspoon basil
2	(15-ounce) cans stewed		
	tomatoes		

Cook onion and garlic in olive oil in skillet over low heat until tender, stirring frequently. Stir in undrained tomatoes, zucchini and basil. Spoon into 2-quart baking dish. Bake, covered, at 350 degrees for 30 minutes. Serve immediately. May delete basil.

Approx Per Serving: Cal 79; Prot 3 g; Carbo 14 g; T Fat 2 g; 26% Calories from Fat; Chol 0 mg; Fiber 4 g; Sod 364 mg

Carole Laughlin, Schuylkill County HFH, Orwigsburg, PA

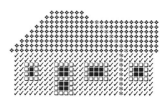

MIXED VEGGIE CASSEROLE

Yield: 10 servings

1   (32-ounce) package frozen mixed vegetables
8   ounces Velveeta cheese, cubed
1   (10-ounce) can cream of mushroom soup
1   (8-ounce) package corn bread stove-top stuffing mix with seasoning envelope
½   cup melted margarine

Cook mixed vegetables using package directions; drain. Combine cheese, soup and contents of seasoning envelope in bowl and mix well. Stir in mixed vegetables. Spoon into 9x13-inch baking dish. Top with stuffing mix; drizzle with margarine. Bake at 350 degrees for 30 minutes.

Approx Per Serving: Cal 341; Prot 11 g; Carbo 34 g; T Fat 19 g; 48% Calories from Fat; Chol 19 mg; Fiber 5 g; Sod 1003 mg

Sally Miller, Fayette County HFH, Vandalia, IL

While working on a Habitat house in Decatur, Illinois, I switched my hammer from one hand to another so as not to tire so quickly. My friend noticed and later reported that I could miss a nail with my left hand just as well as with my right!

Sally Miller
Fayette County HFH

CHEESE PUDDING

Yield: 8 servings

12 slices white bread, crusts trimmed, cubed
3   cups milk
3   eggs, beaten
1   teaspoon salt
¼   teaspoon dry mustard
16 ounces sharp Cheddar cheese, shredded

Arrange bread cubes in 9x13-inch baking dish sprayed with nonstick cooking spray. Whisk milk, eggs, salt and dry mustard in bowl until blended. Pour over bread; sprinkle with cheese. Bake at 325 degrees for 1 hour or until golden brown.

Approx Per Serving: Cal 392; Prot 22 g; Carbo 20 g; T Fat 25 g; 57% Calories from Fat; Chol 152 mg; Fiber 1 g; Sod 839 mg

Polky Parrish, Lexington HFH, Lexington, KY

Photo by Robert Baker

NEWT'S FRUIT

YIELD: 8 SERVINGS

While I have many favorite dishes, one which stands out in my mind is a wonderful dish which my mother-in-law, Mrs. Virginia Ginther, makes and which my nephews now refer to as "Newt's Fruit."

1	(16-ounce) can peaches	1	tablespoon butter or margarine
1	(15-ounce) can pears	1	teaspoon vanilla extract
1	(15-ounce) can chunk pineapple in light syrup	1/8	teaspoon salt
1/2	cup sugar	2	bananas, sliced
1	tablespoon cornstarch	1	(4-ounce) jar maraschino cherries, drained
1	tablespoon white vinegar		

Drain peaches, pears and pineapple, reserving 1 cup of the combined juices. Cut fruit into bite-size pieces and place in bowl. Mix reserved juice, sugar and cornstarch in saucepan. Cook until thickened, stirring constantly. Remove from heat. Stir in vinegar, butter, vanilla and salt. Pour over fruit and mix gently. Chill, covered, for 8 to 10 hours. Stir in bananas and maraschino cherries just before serving.

Approx Per Serving: Cal 213; Prot 1 g; Carbo 52 g; T Fat 2 g; 7% Calories from Fat; Chol 4 mg; Fiber 3 g; Sod 57 mg

Newt Gingrich, Speaker of the House of Representatives
Washington, DC

HOT FRUIT SALAD

YIELD: 12 SERVINGS

1	(29-ounce) can peaches	3	tablespoons cornstarch
1	or 2 (11-ounce) cans mandarin oranges	1/4	cup packed brown sugar
1	(20-ounce) can pineapple chunks	1	to 2 teaspoons almond extract
1	(16-ounce) can dark, sweet pitted cherries	1/2	to 1 teaspoon vanilla extract
1/2	cup margarine	1/8	teaspoon cinnamon

Drain fruit, reserving juices separately. Cut peaches into bite-size pieces. Place fruit in 2 1/2-quart baking dish and mix gently. Combine pineapple juice with any of the other reserved juices to measure 1 cup. Combine 1 cup juice, margarine, cornstarch and brown sugar in saucepan. Cook until thickened. Remove from heat. Stir in flavorings and cinnamon. Pour over fruit. Bake at 325 degrees for 45 minutes.

Approx Per Serving: Cal 217; Prot 1 g; Carbo 38 g; T Fat 8 g; 31% Calories from Fat; Chol 0 mg; Fiber 1 g; Sod 99 mg

Gail Ryan, Fort Worth Area HFH, Fort Worth, TX

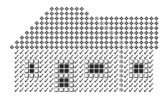

COMPANY HOT FRUIT SALAD

YIELD: 12 SERVINGS

Great to serve at breakfast or brunch.

1	(16-ounce) can sliced peaches	1	(4-ounce) jar maraschino cherries
1	(15-ounce) can pear halves	¼	cup packed brown sugar
1	(15-ounce) can pineapple chunks	2	tablespoons butter
1	(11-ounce) can mandarin oranges	¼	teaspoon nutmeg
1	(8-ounce) can apricot halves	¼	teaspoon cinnamon
		⅛	teaspoon ground cloves

Drain fruit, reserving ¾ cup of the combined juices. Arrange fruit in 2-quart baking dish. Combine reserved juices, brown sugar, butter, nutmeg, cinnamon and cloves in bowl and mix well. Pour over fruit. Bake at 350 degrees for 20 to 30 minutes. Serve warm.

Approx Per Serving: Cal 137; Prot 1 g; Carbo 32 g; T Fat 2 g; 12% Calories from Fat; Chol 5 mg; Fiber 2 g; Sod 29 mg

Kris Rash, Greater Black Hawk HFH, Denver, IA

LENTEJAS

YIELD: 6 SERVINGS

Lentejas was a comfort food for my Peruvian family as I grew up in the outskirts of Washington, D.C. We served this with roast pork to visiting family and embassy friends. We even took it on picnics. I guess you could say it is the equivalent of Boston Baked Beans.

1	cup wine vinegar	1	teaspoon salt
1	cup olive oil	1	teaspoon oregano
1	large onion, chopped	2	cloves of garlic, chopped
¼	cup chopped fresh cilantro	3	cups cooked rice
1	pound lentils		

Combine vinegar, olive oil, onion and cilantro in bowl and mix well. Marinate, covered, in refrigerator. Sort and rinse lentils. Place in slow cooker. Add water to measure 1 to 2 inches above lentils. Let stand for 8 to 10 hours. Stir in salt, oregano and garlic. Cook, covered, on Low for 6 to 8 hours or until of the consistency of baked beans, stirring occasionally. Ladle over hot cooked rice in bowls. Drizzle each serving with some of the olive oil marinade.

Approx Per Serving: Cal 732; Prot 24 g; Carbo 75 g; T Fat 37 g; 46% Calories from Fat; Chol 0 mg; Fiber 11 g; Sod 367 mg

Patricia Burk, Bryan/College Station HFH, College Station, TX

I have evolved in the "Habitat story" from a charter member of the local affiliate board to board president to organizer of our 1991 blitz build. I have been the executive director for the past two years. Lots of favorite stories mixed in there!

Patricia Burk
Bryan/College
Station HFH

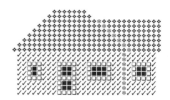

Scotch Oat Cakes

Yield: 12 servings

3	cups rolled oats	2	tablespoons butter
1	teaspoon salt	2	tablespoons vegetable oil

Combine oats and salt in bowl and mix well. Add water gradually, stirring until mixture adheres. Shape into 12 patties. Fry in mixture of butter and oil in skillet for 15 minutes or until brown on both sides; drain.

Approx Per Serving: Cal 115; Prot 3 g; Carbo 14 g; T Fat 5 g; 42% Calories from Fat; Chol 5 mg; Fiber 2 g; Sod 198 mg

Liz Patterson, Anderson County HFH, Oak Ridge, TN

Fried Dill Pickles

Yield: 15 servings

1	(32-ounce) jar dill pickles, drained	2	egg yolks
1	cup water	1½	cups flour
			Canola oil for frying

Trim ends from pickles. Cut into ¼-inch slices and pat dry. Beat water and egg yolks in bowl. Add flour gradually, beating until smooth; do not overbeat. Add canola oil to approximate depth of 1 inch in skillet. Heat to 375 degrees. Dip pickle slices in batter. Fry in single layer in hot oil until light brown on both sides; drain.

Approx Per Serving: Cal 64; Prot 2 g; Carbo 12 g; T Fat 1 g; 13% Calories from Fat; Chol 28 mg; Fiber 1 g; Sod 777 mg
Nutritional information does not include oil for frying.

June Frazier, Cumberland County HFH, Fairfield Glade, TN

Mexican Rice

Yield: 6 servings

1	cup rice	½	cup tomato juice
3	tablespoons vegetable shortening	2	chicken bouillon cubes
1½	cups water	½	teaspoon garlic powder
		½	teaspoon salt

Place rice in colander. Rinse with hot water until water runs clear; drain. Fry rice in shortening in skillet until golden brown. Combine remaining ingredients in saucepan. Bring to a boil and stir. Add rice; do not stir. Simmer for 30 minutes or until rice is tender.

Approx Per Serving: Cal 176; Prot 3 g; Carbo 26 g; T Fat 7 g; 35% Calories from Fat; Chol 0 mg; Fiber 0 g; Sod 637 mg

Carolyn Richardson, Ponca City Area HFH, Ponca City, OK

OLIVE RICE CASSEROLE

YIELD: 8 SERVINGS

3	cups water	1/2	cup margarine
1	cup rice	2	beef bouillon cubes
1	(7-ounce) jar pimento-stuffed green olives, drained, sliced	1	tablespoon chopped onion
1/2	(2-ounce) can mushroom stems and pieces, drained	1	tablespoon chopped green bell pepper

Combine water, rice, olives, mushrooms, margarine, bouillon cubes, onion and green pepper in bowl and mix well. Spoon into baking dish. Bake, covered, at 350 degrees for 30 minutes; remove cover and stir. Bake for 30 minutes longer. May add additional water if needed.

Approx Per Serving: Cal 215; Prot 2 g; Carbo 20 g; T Fat 14 g; 60% Calories from Fat; Chol <1 mg; Fiber 1 g; Sod 879 mg

Meurial Stearns, Three Trails Neighbors HFH, Independence, MO

TOMATO CHEESE RICE

YIELD: 4 SERVINGS

1	(16-ounce) can stewed tomatoes	1 1/3	cups instant rice
1/2	cup water	1/4	cup grated Parmesan cheese
2	tablespoons margarine		

Combine undrained tomatoes, water and margarine in saucepan. Bring to a boil. Stir in rice. Remove from heat. Let stand, covered, for 5 minutes. Stir in cheese. Serve immediately.

Approx Per Serving: Cal 229; Prot 6 g; Carbo 34 g; T Fat 8 g; 30% Calories from Fat; Chol 5 mg; Fiber 2 g; Sod 473 mg

Elizabeth F. (Betty) Clark, Greater Cleveland HFH
Cleveland Heights, OH

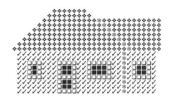

BAKED POTATO TOPPING

YIELD: 12 SERVINGS

1/2	ripe avocado, chopped
1	cup unsalted butter, softened
2	tablespoons lemon juice
1	tablespoon chopped fresh parsley
1/4	teaspoon oregano
1/4	teaspoon savory

Process avocado in blender until puréed. Add butter. Process until blended. Add lemon juice, parsley, oregano and savory gradually, processing constantly until light and fluffy. Serve with baked potatoes.

Approx Per Serving: Cal 150; Prot <1 g; Carbo 1 g; T Fat 17 g; 97% Calories from Fat; Chol 41 mg; Fiber <1 g; Sod 3 mg

Donna Coulson, Siskiyou County HFH, Weed, CA

DILL SAUCE

YIELD: 10 SERVINGS

1	cup sour cream
3	tablespoons brown sugar
1 1/2	tablespoons white vinegar
1 1/2	tablespoons Dijon mustard
2	teaspoons dillweed

Combine sour cream, brown sugar, vinegar, Dijon mustard and dillweed in bowl and mix well. Chill, covered, in refrigerator. Drizzle over your favorite vegetable. May substitute 2 tablespoons chopped fresh dillweed for dried dillweed.

Approx Per Serving: Cal 63; Prot 1 g; Carbo 4 g; T Fat 5 g; 70% Calories from Fat; Chol 10 mg; Fiber <1 g; Sod 70 mg

JoAnn Lyall, Fayetteville HFH, Fayetteville, AR

It was our pleasure to reach beyond our community to help a church in Mississippi that had been destroyed by fire. With good support from the public, we raised two thousand dollars at a garage sale. We were unexpectedly blessed ourselves by having new volunteers sign up, with two of the volunteers eventually becoming board members.

*Donna Coulson
Siskiyou County HFH*

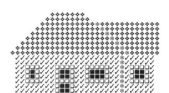

CRAN-PINEAPPLE RELISH

YIELD: 4 SERVINGS

1 (20-ounce) can crushed
pineapple, drained
1 (16-ounce) can whole
cranberry sauce

1 cup chunky applesauce
1/4 teaspoon cinnamon

Combine pineapple, cranberry sauce, applesauce and cinnamon in bowl and mix well. Chill, covered, until serving time. May top with crunchy nugget cereal or shredded coconut.

Approx Per Serving: Cal 293; Prot 1 g; Carbo 76 g; T Fat <1 g;
1% Calories from Fat; Chol 0 mg; Fiber 3 g; Sod 36 mg

Kathy Eckstam-Ames, Ashland County HFH, Ashland, OH

THREE-FRUIT MARMALADE

YIELD: VARIABLE

3 large organic oranges
2 organic grapefruit

2 organic lemons
Sugar

Wash oranges, grapefruit and lemons with soap and warm water and rinse. Slice fruit into halves, reserving seeds. Seeds may be tied in cheesecloth and added to fruit during cooking process for natural pectin. Chop peelings and pulp finely, reserving juice. Place fruit, peel and juice in bowl. Add just enough water to cover. Let stand, covered, at room temperature for 8 to 12 hours. Combine fruit mixture and cheesecloth filled with seeds if desired in saucepan. Bring to a boil; reduce heat. Simmer for 20 minutes, stirring occasionally. Let stand at room temperature for 8 to 12 hours. Add 1/2 cup sugar or to taste per cup of fruit and mix well; marmalade should be tart or even slightly bitter. Taste and adjust sugar according to taste. Bring to a rolling boil. Cook for 20 minutes or until thickened, stirring frequently with wooden spoon. Test by holding your wooden spoon over a saucer. When the drops run together along edge of spoon, and the drops in the saucer jell as they cool, it is ready. Spoon into hot sterilized jars, leaving 1/2-inch headspace; seal with 2-piece lids. Invert jars for 24 hours. Increase cooking time for thicker consistency. Commercial pectin will shorten cooking time, but it is not necessary. May substitute honey for some of sugar, but the flavor will be compromised.

Nutritional information for this recipe is not available.

Margot Olmstead, Lower Wisconsin River HFH, Inc., Dodgeville, WI

Photograph at right by John Curry

$\mathcal{B}$READS

Jesus answered, "It is written:
'Man does not live by bread alone.'"

Luke 4:4

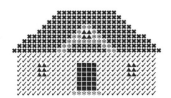

BROCCOLI CORN BREAD

YIELD: 15 SERVINGS

2   (9-ounce) packages corn
    bread mix
1   cup cottage cheese
1   (10-ounce) package frozen
    chopped broccoli

½   cup chopped onion
½   cup melted margarine
2   eggs, lightly beaten

Combine corn bread mix, cottage cheese, broccoli, onion, margarine and eggs in bowl and mix well. Spoon into greased 9x13-inch baking dish. Bake at 375 degrees for 25 minutes or until brown.

Approx Per Serving: Cal 220; Prot 5 g; Carbo 24 g; T Fat 11 g; 46% Calories from Fat; Chol 30 mg; Fiber 2 g; Sod 498 mg

Bettie Spiva, Smith County HFH, Carthage, TN

SPICY CORN BREAD

YIELD: 15 SERVINGS

1   cup cottage cheese
¼   cup melted margarine
4   eggs
⅛   teaspoon Tabasco sauce
1   medium onion, chopped

1   (10-ounce) package frozen
    chopped broccoli, thawed
2   (9-ounce) packages corn
    bread mix

Mix cottage cheese, margarine, eggs and Tabasco sauce in bowl. Stir in onion, broccoli and corn bread mix. Spoon into greased 9x13-inch baking pan. Bake at 375 degrees for 30 minutes or until brown.

Approx Per Serving: Cal 204; Prot 6 g; Carbo 24 g; T Fat 9 g; 40% Calories from Fat; Chol 59 mg; Fiber 2 g; Sod 481 mg

Ruth Craigo, Rapides HFH, Pineville, LA

JOHNNYCAKE

YIELD: 6 SERVINGS

1   cup cornmeal
1   cup flour
½   cup sugar
1   teaspoon baking soda

1   teaspoon salt
1   cup buttermilk
1   tablespoon melted
    vegetable shortening

Mix dry ingredients in bowl. Stir in buttermilk. Add shortening and mix well. Spoon into ungreased 9x9-inch baking pan. Bake at 350 degrees for 20 minutes. Cool slightly before serving.

Approx Per Serving: Cal 260; Prot 5 g; Carbo 52 g; T Fat 3 g; 11% Calories from Fat; Chol 1 mg; Fiber 2 g; Sod 609 mg

Nancy Ellis, York HFH, Felton, PA

BREAD...MADE EASY

YIELD: 12 SERVINGS

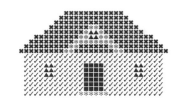

1	cup lukewarm water	1	egg
1	envelope dry yeast or	3	to 3½ cups flour
	1 tablespoon dry yeast	1	to 2 tablespoons butter,
2	tablespoons sugar		softened
2	teaspoons salt		
2	tablespoons butter,		
	margarine or vegetable		
	shortening		

Combine lukewarm water, yeast, sugar and salt in bowl, stirring until sugar and yeast dissolve. Test yeast by letting mixture stand for 5 minutes to see if heavy bubbles form on top. If there is no sign of bubbles, the yeast is not active, which may be due to age of the yeast or temperature of the water added. Add 2 tablespoons butter, egg and 3 cups of the flour, stirring until the dough is soft and sticky. Add remaining ½ cup flour if needed for desired consistency; dry firm dough will result in tough bread. Let stand, covered with tea towel, in warm place until doubled in bulk. Shape into loaf in greased 5x9-inch loaf pan or shape into rolls of choice. Bake at 350 degrees for 20 minutes. Coat top of loaf with 1 to 2 tablespoons butter. Remove from pan immediately. May substitute a mixture of 1½ cups whole wheat or rye flour and 1½ cups all-purpose flour for 3 cups all-purpose flour. Substitute molasses for sugar and reduce amount of water to allow for the added liquid if desired. Try these variations with the basic Bread . . . Made Easy recipe. For Caramel Cinnamon Rolls prepare the dough and let rise. Roll ⅔ inch thick on a lightly floured surface. Spread with softened butter or margarine; sprinkle with cinnamon and sugar. Roll as for jelly roll. Cut into 1- to 1½-inch slices. Spread 1 cup packed brown sugar in bottom of greased 9x12-inch baking pan.

Photo by Robert Baker

Drizzle with just enough milk to moisten brown sugar. Arrange slices in prepared pan. Bake at 350 degrees for 20 minutes. May freeze for future use and reheat in oven or microwave for 20 seconds just before serving.

Approx Per Serving: Cal 183; Prot 5 g; Carbo 30 g; T Fat 5 g; 23% Calories from Fat; Chol 28 mg; Fiber 1 g; Sod 401 mg
Nutritional information does not include variations.

Marcy E. Williams, Kootenai Valley Partners HFH, Libby, MT

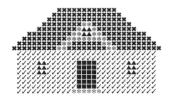

BEER BREAD

YIELD: 12 SERVINGS

3   cups self-rising flour
1   (12-ounce) can beer

3   tablespoons sugar

Combine self-rising flour, beer and sugar in bowl and mix well. Spoon into greased 5x9-inch loaf pan. Bake at 400 degrees for 40 minutes.

Approx Per Serving: Cal 134; Prot 3 g; Carbo 27 g; T Fat <1 g; 2% Calories from Fat; Chol 0 mg; Fiber 1 g; Sod 398 mg

Judy Yavello, South Oakland County HFH, Ferndale, MI

CORN OAT BREAD

YIELD: 36 SERVINGS

1   cup rolled oats
1/2   cup molasses
1/2   cup packed brown sugar
1/3   cup cornmeal
1   tablespoon shortening
2   teaspoons salt
2 1/2 cups boiling water
1/2   cup lukewarm water
1   teaspoon sugar
1   envelope dry yeast
6   to 6 1/2 cups sifted flour
3   tablespoons butter, softened

Combine oats, molasses, brown sugar, cornmeal, shortening and salt in bowl and mix well. Stir in boiling water. Let stand until lukewarm. Combine lukewarm water and sugar in bowl, stirring until sugar dissolves. Add yeast and mix well. Let stand for 10 minutes and stir. Add to oat mixture and mix well. Add flour gradually, mixing with a spoon and blending in the last addition with hands. Knead for 5 minutes. Let rise in warm place for 1 1/2 hours or until doubled in bulk. Divide dough into 3 equal portions. Let rest for 15 minutes. Shape each portion into a loaf in greased 5x9-inch loaf pan. Let rise in warm place for 1 hour or until doubled in bulk. Bake at 350 degrees for 50 to 60 minutes or until golden brown. Coat tops with butter.

Approx Per Serving: Cal 123; Prot 3 g; Carbo 24 g; T Fat 2 g; 12% Calories from Fat; Chol 3 mg; Fiber 1 g; Sod 132 mg

John and Carol Shears, Northeast Connecticut HFH, Putnam, CT

FRIENDSHIP BREAD

YIELD: 24 SERVINGS

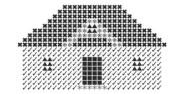

Friendship Bread is made from a cup of starter batter. Starter batter may be given to you by a friend or prepared by mixing one cup each of flour, sugar and water. Let stand outside, covered with a clean nylon stocking, in warm weather for 3 to 6 days. It takes ten days to complete the recipe. When you finish, you will have one or two loaves of Friendship Bread, a cup of starter for yourself and one or two cups of starter to give to friends. When the starter is given to others, friendship is nourished just as the finished bread provides nutritional nourishment. Kindness is catching! Sharing Friendship Bread batter is one way to pass kindness along to others.

Day One: Label the cup of starter with the date and mark "day one."
Day Two: Rest.
Day Three: Stir batter, using a nonmetal spoon.
Day Four: Rest.
Day Five: Rest.
Day Six: Pour batter into larger bowl. Stir in 1 cup flour, 1 cup sugar and 1 cup milk. May substitute sugar substitute for sugar.
Day Seven: Rest.
Day Eight: Stir batter.
Day Nine: Rest.
Day Ten: Pour batter into larger bowl. Stir in 1 cup flour, 1 cup sugar and 1 cup milk. Divide batter into 4 one-cup portions. Give 1 or 2 cups with this recipe to friends. Keep 1 cup for future use and use the remaining cup to bake Friendship Bread using the following directions.

Combine 1 cup Friendship Bread batter, 1 cup applesauce, 1/2 cup milk, 3 eggs or egg substitute equivalent, 2 tablespoons vegetable oil and 1 teaspoon vanilla extract in bowl and mix well. Combine 1 six-ounce package vanilla pudding and pie filling mix, 2 teaspoons cinnamon, 2 cups white, wheat or rye flour, 1 cup sugar or honey, 1/2 teaspoon baking soda, 1/2 teaspoon baking powder and 1/2 teaspoon salt in bowl and mix well. Stir in 1 cup chopped walnuts or nuts of choice if desired. Stir in applesauce mixture. Spoon into 2 greased loaf pans or large baking pan. Bake at 350 degrees for 50 minutes. May substitute 1 cup vegetable oil for mixture of 2 table-spoons vegetable oil and applesauce and chocolate or butterscotch pudding and pie filling mix for vanilla pudding and pie filling mix. Add cinnamon only if vanilla pudding and pie filling mix is used.

Nutritional information for this recipe is not available.

Marlin Languis, Greater Columbus HFH, Columbus, OH

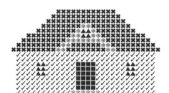

FLOATS

YIELD: 36 SERVINGS

Mrs. Guillory, a native of Trinidad, shares this breakfast bread of her native country with us. This bread is simple and inexpensive, but very filling. It provides a lot for a little...just like Habitat!

1	envelope dry yeast	2	cups lukewarm water
1	tablespoon sugar	8	cups flour
2	teaspoons salt		Vegetable oil for frying

Dissolve yeast, sugar and salt in lukewarm water in bowl and mix well. Add flour gradually and mix well; knead. Place in greased bowl, turning to coat surface. Let rise, covered with tea towel, in warm place for 2 hours or until doubled in bulk. Shape dough into small balls. Let rise in warm place for 30 minutes. Roll each ball very thin on a lightly floured surface. Fry in 400-degree oil in skillet until brown on both sides; drain. Serve immediately.

Approx Per Serving: Cal 103; Prot 3 g; Carbo 22 g; T Fat <1 g; 3% Calories from Fat; Chol 0 mg; Fiber 1 g; Sod 119 mg
Nutritional information does not include oil for frying.

Mrs. Wilmer S. "Frenchie" Guillory, Calcasieu Area HFH
Lake Charles, LA

OATMEAL BREAD

YIELD: 48 SERVINGS

2	cakes yeast	4	cups boiling water
1	cup lukewarm water	4	teaspoons salt
2	cups rolled oats	10	cups flour
¾	cup dark molasses		
5	tablespoons vegetable shortening		

Dissolve yeast in lukewarm water in bowl and mix well. Combine oats, molasses and shortening in bowl. Add boiling water, stirring until shortening melts. Cool slightly. Stir in yeast mixture and salt. Add flour gradually and mix well. Knead on lightly floured surface until smooth. Place dough in greased bowl, turning to coat surface. Let rise in warm place for 1 hour or until doubled in bulk. Divide dough into 4 equal portions. Shape each portion into loaf in greased 5x9-inch loaf pan. Let rise, covered with tea towel, in warm place until doubled in bulk. Bake at 350 degrees for 45 minutes.

Approx Per Serving: Cal 133; Prot 3 g; Carbo 26 g; T Fat 2 g; 12% Calories from Fat; Chol 0 mg; Fiber 1 g; Sod 181 mg

Mary Beth and Jim Irvine, HFHI Board of Directors, Boring, OR

ORANGE REFRIGERATOR ROLLS *Yield: 24 rolls*

2	envelopes dry yeast	1	egg, beaten
1/2	cup lukewarm water	4 1/2	cups sifted flour
1	teaspoon sugar	1/4	cup butter or margarine, softened
1	cup milk		
1/4	cup vegetable shortening	1/2	cup sugar
1/4	cup sugar	1/2	cup packed brown sugar
1 1/2	teaspoons salt		Grated peel of 2 oranges

Soften yeast in mixture of lukewarm water and 1 teaspoon sugar in bowl for 5 minutes. Scald milk with shortening, 1/4 cup sugar and salt in saucepan. Let cool. Mix milk mixture, yeast mixture and egg in bowl. Add flour gradually, stirring until blended. Place in greased bowl, turning to coat surface. Chill. Divide dough into 2 equal portions. Roll each into a 6x14-inch rectangle on lightly floured surface. Spread with butter. Sprinkle with mixture of 1/2 cup sugar, brown sugar and orange peel. Roll as for jelly roll. Cut each roll into 12 slices. Place in greased muffin cups. Let rise in warm place until doubled in bulk. Bake at 400 degrees for 15 minutes or until brown.

Approx Per Serving: Cal 165; Prot 3 g; Carbo 28 g; T Fat 5 g; 26% Calories from Fat; Chol 15 mg; Fiber 1 g; Sod 163 mg

Donna Ross, Kootenai Valley Partners HFH, Libby, MT

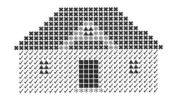

PILGRIM'S BREAD *Yield: 24 servings*

1/2	cup yellow cornmeal	2	tablespoons dry yeast
1/3	cup packed brown sugar	1/2	cup lukewarm water
1	tablespoon salt	3/4	cup whole wheat flour
2	cups boiling water	1/2	cup rye flour
1/4	cup vegetable oil	4	cups all-purpose flour

Mix cornmeal, brown sugar and salt in bowl. Stir in boiling water. Stir in oil. Cool to lukewarm. Dissolve yeast in lukewarm water. Stir into cornmeal mixture. Add whole wheat flour and rye flour and mix well. Add 3 cups of the all-purpose flour, mixing until easily handled. Knead in remaining 1 cup all-purpose flour on lightly floured surface until soft and pliable. Shape into ball. Place in greased bowl, turning to coat surface. Let rise, covered, in warm place until doubled in bulk. Punch dough down. Divide dough into 2 equal portions. Shape each portion into loaf in greased 5x9-inch loaf pan. Let rise, covered, in warm place until doubled in bulk. Bake at 350 degrees for 1 1/4 hours or until loaf sounds hollow when tapped. Invert onto wire rack to cool.

Approx Per Serving: Cal 138; Prot 3 g; Carbo 25 g; T Fat 3 g; 17% Calories from Fat; Chol 0 mg; Fiber 2 g; Sod 269 mg

Sister Joann Brodman, Huron River Valley HFH, Plymouth, OH

For "Monk," Habitat not only made possible a home for him and his family, but—as he witnessed, with tears in his eyes— working on a Habitat house gave him the skill and confidence to choose carpentry at the local vocational school for a career.

Sister Joann Brodman
Huron River Valley HFH

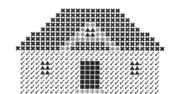

SWEDISH RYE BREAD

YIELD: 24 SERVINGS

1	envelope dry yeast	2	teaspoons salt
1/2	cup lukewarm water	2	cups boiling water
2	cups rye flour	6	to 6 1/2 cups all-purpose
3/4	cup dark molasses		flour
1/3	cup vegetable shortening		

Dissolve yeast in lukewarm water in bowl and mix well. Combine rye flour, molasses, shortening and salt in bowl. Add boiling water, stirring until shortening melts. Cool to lukewarm. Stir in yeast mixture. Add all-purpose flour and mix well. Let rise in warm place until doubled in bulk. Punch dough down. Let rest for 15 minutes. Divide dough into 2 equal portions. Shape each portion into a loaf in greased loaf pan or shape into 2 round loaves and place on greased baking sheet. Let rise in warm place until doubled in bulk. Bake at 350 degrees for 35 to 40 minutes or until brown and hollow sounding when tapped.

Approx Per Serving: Cal 204; Prot 4 g; Carbo 40 g; T Fat 3 g; 15% Calories from Fat; Chol 0 mg; Fiber 2 g; Sod 184 mg

Charlotte Jensen, McDonough County HFH, Macomb, IL

EASY WHITE BREAD

YIELD: 72 SERVINGS

1	cup margarine	3	cups cold water
1	cup sugar	2	envelopes dry yeast
1	cup nonfat dry milk powder	1	cup lukewarm water
2	cups boiling water	5	pounds flour

Combine margarine, sugar and milk powder in bowl. Add boiling water, stirring until blended. Let stand until cool. Stir in cold water. Dissolve yeast in lukewarm water in bowl and mix well. Stir into margarine mixture. Add flour gradually, mixing until blended. Knead on lightly floured surface until smooth and elastic. Place in greased bowl, turning to coat surface. Let rise in warm place until doubled in bulk. May let rise overnight in refrigerator. Divide dough into 6 equal portions. Shape each portion into loaf in greased 5x9-inch loaf pan. Let rise in warm place until doubled in bulk. Bake at 350 degrees for 30 to 45 minutes or until golden brown. Invert onto wire rack to cool. Cover with tea towels until cool. Recipe may be halved.

Approx Per Serving: Cal 152; Prot 4 g; Carbo 27 g; T Fat 3 g; 17% Calories from Fat; Chol 0 mg; Fiber 1 g; Sod 36 mg

Janet Johnson, Monroe County HFH, Tobyhanna, PA

ZUCCHINI PINEAPPLE BREAD

Yield: 24 servings

1	cup vegetable oil	3	cups flour
3	eggs	2	teaspoons baking soda
2	cups sugar	1½	teaspoons cinnamon
2	cups grated peeled zucchini	1	teaspoon salt
2	teaspoons vanilla extract	¾	teaspoon nutmeg
1	to 2 ounces canned drained crushed pineapple	½	teaspoon baking powder

Beat oil and eggs in mixer bowl until blended. Stir in sugar, zucchini and vanilla. Add pineapple and mix well. Combine flour, baking soda, cinnamon, salt, nutmeg and baking powder in bowl and mix well. Stir into zucchini mixture. Spoon into 2 greased and floured 5x9-inch loaf pans. Bake at 350 degrees for 50 to 60 minutes or until loaves test done.

Approx Per Serving: Cal 214; Prot 3 g; Carbo 29 g; T Fat 10 g; 41% Calories from Fat; Chol 27 mg; Fiber 1 g; Sod 221 mg

Theresa Moore, Androscoggin HFH, Auburn, ME

BIG SKY ZUCCHINI BREAD

Yield: 24 servings

3	cups flour	1	cup vegetable oil
1	tablespoon cinnamon	3	eggs
1	teaspoon baking soda	2	cups grated zucchini
1	teaspoon baking powder	1	cup chopped pecans
½	teaspoon salt	1	tablespoon vanilla extract
2½	cups sugar		

Sift flour, cinnamon, baking soda, baking powder and salt together. Beat sugar, oil and eggs in mixer bowl until creamy. Add dry ingredients and mix well. Stir in zucchini, pecans and vanilla. Spoon into two 5x9-inch loaf pans sprayed with nonstick cooking spray. Bake at 325 degrees for 1 hour.

Approx Per Serving: Cal 264; Prot 3 g; Carbo 34 g; T Fat 13 g; 44% Calories from Fat; Chol 27 mg; Fiber 1 g; Sod 130 mg

Dawn-Faye Phebus, Boise Valley HFH, Boise, ID

BREADS

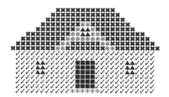

JUMBO BANANA MUFFINS

YIELD: 12 MUFFINS

1 1/2	cups sugar	1/2	cup buttermilk
1/2	cup butter, softened	1/2	teaspoon baking soda
3	medium bananas, mashed	1/2	teaspoon baking powder
3	eggs	1/4	teaspoon salt
2 1/2	cups cake flour	1/4	teaspoon cinnamon

Combine sugar, butter, bananas and eggs in mixer bowl. Beat at high speed until blended. Add cake flour, buttermilk, baking soda, baking powder, salt and cinnamon gradually, mixing just until moistened. Spoon into muffin cups sprayed with nonstick cooking spray. Bake at 350 degrees for 35 minutes.

Approx Per Serving: Cal 296; Prot 4 g; Carbo 50 g; T Fat 9 g; 28% Calories from Fat; Chol 74 mg; Fiber 1 g; Sod 223 mg

Mary Graczyk, Two Rivers-Manitowoc HFH, Manitowoc, WI

BLUEBERRY MUFFINS

YIELD: 18 MUFFINS

1	cup sugar	1	teaspoon salt
3/4	cup vegetable oil	1	cup milk
3	eggs	1	cup fresh or frozen
3	cups flour		blueberries
1	tablespoon baking powder	3	tablespoons sugar

Beat 1 cup sugar, oil and eggs in mixer bowl until blended. Stir in mixture of flour, baking powder and salt. Add milk, stirring just until moistened. Fold in blueberries. Spoon into muffins cups. Sprinkle with 3 tablespoons sugar. Bake at 375 degrees for 20 to 25 minutes. Do not thaw frozen blueberries before adding to batter.

Approx Per Serving: Cal 233; Prot 4 g; Carbo 31 g; T Fat 11 g; 41% Calories from Fat; Chol 37 mg; Fiber 1 g; Sod 218 mg

Kathleen Bonsaint, Franklin Regional High School HFH, Pittsburgh, PA

RAISIN BRAN MUFFINS

YIELD: 72 MUFFINS

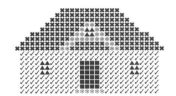

1	(15-ounce) package Raisin Bran	2	teaspoons salt
5	cups flour	4	cups buttermilk
2½	cups sugar	1	cup vegetable oil
5	teaspoons baking soda	4	eggs, beaten, or 1 cup egg substitute

Combine cereal, flour, sugar, baking soda and salt in bowl and mix well. Add buttermilk, oil and eggs, stirring until mixed. Spoon into muffins cups sprayed with nonstick cooking spray. Bake at 375 degrees for 20 minutes. Store leftover batter, covered, in refrigerator for up to 6 weeks. Do not stir batter after original mixing process. Just spoon desired amount into muffin cups. To avoid raw eggs that may carry salmonella, use an equivalent amount of pasteurized egg substitute.

Approx Per Serving: Cal 113; Prot 2 g; Carbo 19 g; T Fat 4 g; 28% Calories from Fat; Chol 12 mg; Fiber 1 g; Sod 197 mg

Joy Highnote, HFHI, Americus, GA

BRAN MUFFINS BY THE PAIL

YIELD: 72 MUFFINS

This recipe makes enough to fill a five-quart pail.

4	cups bran cereal	1	cup vegetable shortening
2	cups 100% bran	4	eggs or 1 cup egg substitute
1	teaspoon salt		
2	cups boiling water	5	cups flour
4	cups buttermilk	5	teaspoons baking soda
3	cups sugar		

Combine cereal, bran and salt in bowl and mix well. Stir in boiling water. Add buttermilk and mix well. Cool to lukewarm. Beat sugar and shortening in mixer bowl until creamy. Add eggs 1 at a time, beating well after each addition. Stir into bran mixture. Add mixture of flour and baking soda, stirring just until moistened. Spoon into muffin cups. Bake at 375 degrees for 20 to 25 minutes. Store leftover batter, covered, in refrigerator for up to 4 weeks. To avoid raw eggs that may carry salmonella, use an equivalent amount of pasteurized egg substitute.

Approx Per Serving: Cal 115; Prot 3 g; Carbo 21 g; T Fat 4 g; 25% Calories from Fat; Chol 12 mg; Fiber 3 g; Sod 202 mg

Mary Hanna, Marion County HFH, Knoxville, IA

BREADS

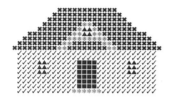

PEANUT BUTTER MUFFINS

YIELD: 12 MUFFINS

Spread with your favorite fruit jelly for a peanut butter and jelly muffin.

2	cups baking mix	1/2	cup honey
1	cup milk	1	tablespoon vanilla extract
3/4	cup peanut butter		

Combine baking mix, milk, peanut butter, honey and vanilla in bowl, stirring just until moistened. Spoon into muffin cups. Bake at 375 degrees for 10 to 12 minutes or until muffins pull from edges of pan.

Approx Per Serving: Cal 237; Prot 6 g; Carbo 29 g; T Fat 12 g; 43% Calories from Fat; Chol 3 mg; Fiber 2 g; Sod 342 mg

Patsy Kneller, San Angelo HFH, San Angelo, TX

CRANBERRY COFFEE CAKE

YIELD: 12 SERVINGS

2	cups baking mix	1/4	teaspoon cinnamon
2/3	cup water	2/3	cup whole cranberry sauce
2	tablespoons sugar	1	cup confectioners' sugar
1	egg	1	tablespoon water
1/2	cup chopped walnuts	1/2	teaspoon vanilla extract
1/4	cup packed brown sugar		

Combine baking mix, 2/3 cup water, sugar and egg in mixer bowl. Beat for 30 seconds. Spoon into greased 9x9-inch baking pan. Combine walnuts, brown sugar and cinnamon in bowl and mix well. Sprinkle over prepared layer. Spread with cranberry sauce. Bake at 400 degrees for 20 to 25 minutes. Spread warm coffee cake with mixture of confectioners' sugar, 1 tablespoon water and vanilla. May substitute milk for water in batter.

Approx Per Serving: Cal 208; Prot 3 g; Carbo 35 g; T Fat 7 g; 28% Calories from Fat; Chol 18 mg; Fiber 1 g; Sod 267 mg

Peg and David Picciano, Northeast Connecticut HFH, Putnam, CT

SUGAR SPICE COFFEE CAKE *Yield: 12 servings*

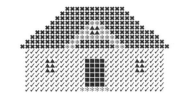

1/2	cup packed brown sugar	1	tablespoon baking powder
2	tablespoons flour	3/4	teaspoon salt
2	teaspoons cinnamon	6	tablespoons butter,
2	tablespoons melted butter		softened
1/2	cup chopped pecans	3/4	cup milk
2	cups flour	1	egg
3/4	cup sugar		

Photo by Robert Baker

Combine brown sugar, 2 tablespoons flour, cinnamon and 2 tablespoons butter in bowl and mix well. Stir in pecans. Sift 2 cups flour, sugar, baking powder and salt into bowl and mix well. Cut in 6 tablespoons butter until crumbly. Stir in mixture of milk and egg. Layer batter and brown sugar mixture 1/2 at a time in a greased 9x12-inch baking pan. Bake at 375 degrees for 35 minutes or until coffee cake tests done. May be prepared 1 day in advance, stored in refrigerator and baked just before serving.

Approx Per Serving: Cal 274; Prot 4 g; Carbo 39 g; T Fat 12 g; 39% Calories from Fat; Chol 40 mg; Fiber 1 g; Sod 350 mg

Berniece R. Roth, HFHI, Wayland, IA

BREAKFAST RING *Yield: 16 servings*

16	to 18 frozen yeast rolls, cut into halves or thirds	1	cup packed brown sugar
		1	tablespoon cinnamon
1/2	(4-ounce) package butterscotch pudding and pie filling mix	1/2	cup chopped pecans
		1/2	cup melted butter

Arrange rolls in greased bundt pan. Combine pudding mix, brown sugar and cinnamon in bowl and mix well. Stir in pecans. Sprinkle over rolls. Drizzle with butter. Let rise, covered, for 8 to 10 hours. Bake at 350 degrees for 30 minutes. Invert onto serving platter.

Approx Per Serving: Cal 225; Prot 3 g; Carbo 31 g; T Fat 11 g; 41% Calories from Fat; Chol 16 mg; Fiber 1 g; Sod 250 mg

William D. Powell, Knox County HFH, Wheatland, IN

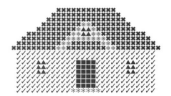

MONKEY BREAD

YIELD: 12 SERVINGS

3	(10-count) cans biscuits	1	tablespoon cinnamon
1	cup sugar	1/2	cup margarine

Cut each biscuit into 6 pieces. Combine sugar and cinnamon in bowl and mix well. Coat biscuit pieces with cinnamon and sugar mixture. Arrange in large bundt pan sprayed with nonstick cooking spray. Heat margarine in saucepan until melted. Stir in remaining sugar and cinnamon mixture. Bring to a boil, stirring occasionally. Pour over biscuits. Bake at 350 degrees for 30 minutes. Invert onto serving platter.

Approx Per Serving: Cal 368; Prot 5 g; Carbo 49 g; T Fat 18 g; 42% Calories from Fat; Chol 0 mg; Fiber 2 g; Sod 901 mg

Betty Warstler, Macon Co. HFH, Franklin, NC

PEPPERONI BREAD

YIELD: 18 SERVINGS

Great to take to potluck dinners and picnics. Make several loaves and freeze for future use. Reheat in the microwave.

1	loaf frozen bread dough, thawed	1 1/2	cups shredded Colby cheese
20	slices pepperoni	1 1/2	teaspoons oregano

Roll bread dough into 3/4-inch-thick rectangle on lightly floured surface. Arrange pepperoni slices over dough. Sprinkle with cheese and oregano. Roll into a 12-inch loaf. Seal edges with water; turn ends under. Arrange seam side down on greased baking sheet. Bake at 335 degrees for 40 minutes or until golden brown. Let stand until cool and slice. May substitute Cheddar cheese for Colby cheese.

Approx Per Serving: Cal 117; Prot 5 g; Carbo 13 g; T Fat 5 g; 39% Calories from Fat; Chol 11 mg; Fiber 1 g; Sod 238 mg

Cynthia L. Lamprecht, Fremont Area HFH, Fremont, NE

OVEN-BAKED FRENCH TOAST

YIELD: 8 SERVINGS

1/4	cup butter	3	eggs, lightly beaten
2	tablespoons sugar	8	slices French or Italian
1/4	teaspoon cinnamon		bread
3/4	cup orange juice		

Heat butter in 10x15-inch baking pan at 425 degrees until melted. Tilt pan to coat bottom. Sprinkle mixture of sugar and cinnamon over butter. Combine orange juice and eggs in bowl and mix well. Dip bread slices in orange juice mixture until saturated. Arrange in single layer in prepared pan. Bake at 425 degrees for 20 minutes or until set. Invert onto serving platter. Serve with syrup or whipped cream.

Approx Per Serving: Cal 197; Prot 6 g; Carbo 24 g; T Fat 9 g; 40% Calories from Fat; Chol 95 mg; Fiber 1 g; Sod 296 mg

Patricia Lemieux, Pinellas HFH, St. Petersburg, FL

EASY BREAKFAST PANCAKE

YIELD: 2 SERVINGS

1/4	cup butter or margarine	2	tablespoons confectioners'
1/2	cup flour		sugar
1/2	cup milk	2	tablespoons lemon juice
2	eggs, lightly beaten		

Heat butter in 9-inch ovenproof skillet at 425 degrees until melted. Combine flour, milk and eggs in bowl, stirring just until moistened. Pour into prepared skillet. Bake at 425 degrees for 20 minutes or until puffy and golden brown. Invert onto serving platter. Sprinkle with confectioners' sugar; drizzle with lemon juice. Serve immediately. For each additional serving add 1/4 cup flour, 1/4 cup milk and 1 egg. Increase skillet size and baking time proportionally. Bake a 10- to 12-egg recipe in a 12-inch skillet. As a variation for a lunch or brunch dish, add small amounts of finely chopped vegetables, omitting lemon juice and confectioners' sugar.

Approx Per Serving: Cal 462; Prot 12 g; Carbo 36 g; T Fat 30 g; 59% Calories from Fat; Chol 283 mg; Fiber 1 g; Sod 328 mg

Bernie Treichel, Dane County HFH, Oregon, WI

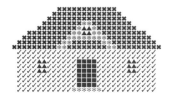

I found a niche of people bridging the gaps of prejudice and self service and working as one. I saw people putting aside "self" and overcoming personal ambitions for the further-ance of the common goal. I saw the spirit of frontiersmen and women, restless people seeking a better land, who chose to seek their adventure in their own back yard. I saw people being what our forefathers envisioned...I saw Americans!

Claudia Teeters
Statesville HFH

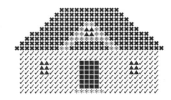

I arrived at my first West Chester-Mason Habitat for Humanity meeting seeking student volunteer information for my daughter. I departed with the desire to be a part of this group whose caring and genuine commitment to our community was inspiring.

Mona Phillips
West Chester-Mason HFH

WHOLE WHEAT PANCAKES

YIELD: 8 SERVINGS

1	cup whole wheat flour	2	teaspoons sugar
1	cup water	2	teaspoons baking powder
1/3	cup nonfat dry milk powder	1	or 2 eggs
1	to 2 tablespoons vegetable oil	1/8	teaspoon salt

Process whole wheat flour, water and milk powder in blender for 2 to 4 minutes while adding oil, sugar, baking powder, eggs and salt. Pour about 1/4 cup batter onto hot lightly greased griddle. Bake until brown on both sides, turning once. Repeat process with remaining batter. Serve with peanut butter, yogurt, jam or fruit.

Approx Per Serving: Cal 114; Prot 5 g; Carbo 14 g; T Fat 5 g; 38% Calories from Fat; Chol 54 mg; Fiber 2 g; Sod 187 mg

Lila Creager, Cottage Grove Area HFH, Cottage Grove, OR

WAFFLES FOR TWO

YIELD: 2 SERVINGS

1	tablespoon flour	1/4	teaspoon salt
1	tablespoon rolled oats	1	egg, lightly beaten
2	teaspoons baking powder	1/2	to 1/3 cup 1% milk
1	teaspoon sugar	1	tablespoon canola oil

Mix flour, oats, baking powder, sugar and salt in bowl. Whisk in egg, milk and oil. Bake in waffle iron using manufacturer's instructions.

Approx Per Serving: Cal 149; Prot 5 g; Carbo 10 g; T Fat 10 g; 59% Calories from Fat; Chol 108 mg; Fiber 0 g; Sod 806 mg

Nancy Broberg, Cape Cod HFH, Brewster, MA

FRUIT YOGURT SWEET BREAD *YIELD: 12 SERVINGS*

1/2	cup lukewarm water	2	cups white bread flour
1/3	cup low-fat yogurt	2	teaspoons dry yeast
2	tablespoons applesauce	3/4	teaspoon salt
2	teaspoons brown sugar	1/2	cup dried blueberries

Add all ingredients to bread machine pan in order recommended by manufacturer. May use any flavor yogurt and cranberries or cherries.

Approx Per Serving: Cal 108; Prot 3 g; Carbo 23 g; T Fat <1 g; 3% Calories from Fat; Chol 0 mg; Fiber 2 g; Sod 139 mg

Mona Phillips, West Chester-Mason HFH, West Chester, OH

Scandinavian Pastry

YIELD: 60 SERVINGS

Serve for breakfast or dessert or take to your next potluck dinner.

1/2	cup margarine	3	eggs
1	cup flour	1 1/2	cups confectioners' sugar
2	tablespoons water	2 2/3	tablespoons butter
1/2	cup margarine	1 1/2	tablespoons cream
1	cup water	1/2	egg yolk
1	teaspoon almond extract	1/2	teaspoon almond extract
1	cup flour	1/2	to 3/4 cup sliced pecans

Cut 1/2 cup margarine into 1 cup flour in bowl until crumbly. Sprinkle with 2 tablespoons water, stirring until mixture forms a ball. Pat into 6x10-inch rectangle on nonstick baking sheet. Bring 1/2 cup margarine and 1 cup water to a boil in saucepan. Stir in 1 teaspoon almond flavoring. Remove from heat. Add 1 cup flour, beating until smooth. Add eggs 1 at a time, beating well after each addition. Spread evenly over rectangle. Bake at 350 degrees for 45 to 60 minutes or until crisp and light brown. Let stand until cool. Beat confectioners' sugar, butter, cream, egg yolk and 1/2 teaspoon almond flavoring in mixer bowl until light and fluffy, scraping bowl occasionally. Spread over baked layer. Sprinkle pecans around outer edges of pastry. Cut into squares.

Approx Per Serving: Cal 74; Prot 1 g; Carbo 7 g; T Fat 5 g; 60% Calories from Fat; Chol 14 mg; Fiber 0 g; Sod 44 mg

Carol Thackray, Niles/Buchanan Area HFH, Niles, MI

Mustard Cheddar Rye

YIELD: 24 SERVINGS

1/2	cup lukewarm water	1	tablespoon gluten
1/2	cup lukewarm buttermilk	6	ounces nonfat Cheddar
1 1/2	teaspoons safflower oil		cheese, shredded
1 1/2	teaspoons brown sugar	2	cups bread flour
1	teaspoon salt	1 1/4	cups rye flour
1/4	cup Dijon mustard, at	2 1/4	teaspoons bread machine
	room temperature		yeast
1 1/4	tablespoons caraway seeds		

Add all ingredients to bread machine pan in order recommended by manufacturer. Set your machine for sweet large loaf with medium color setting.

Approx Per Serving: Cal 74; Prot 5 g; Carbo 12 g; T Fat 1 g; 10% Calories from Fat; Chol 1 mg; Fiber 1 g; Sod 212 mg

Laura J. Fye, Prince William Co., Manassas & Manassas Park Chantilly, VA

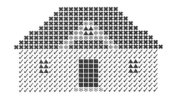

While finishing a Habitat house for a family with nine children, we asked the children if they were excited about the house. One of the younger children replied, "I am so glad to move into the house! Now I can have my own bed. I've always had to sleep on the couch because there was no room for a bed for me."

Veda Bafford
Statesville HFH

GLORIOUS GARLIC BREAD

YIELD: *12 SERVINGS*

Serve warm with your favorite Italian entrée.

³/₄	cup [1 cup plus 2 tablespoons]* water	¹/₂	teaspoon [³/₄ teaspoon] basil
2	cups plus 1 tablespoon [3 cups plus 2 tablespoons] bread flour	¹/₂	teaspoon [³/₄ teaspoon] crushed or finely chopped garlic
¹/₂	teaspoon [³/₄ teaspoon] salt	¹/₂	teaspoon [³/₄ teaspoon] butter
1	tablespoon [1¹/₂ tablespoons] sugar	¹/₂	teaspoon [³/₄ teaspoon] garlic powder
2	tablespoons [3 tablespoons] freshly grated Parmesan cheese	1¹/₂	teaspoons [2 teaspoons] dry yeast

Add water, bread flour, salt, sugar, cheese, basil, garlic, butter, garlic powder and yeast to bread machine pan in order recommended by manufacturer. Set your machine on regular or rapid bake cycle. May adjust garlic according to taste. *Use measurements in brackets to make a large loaf.

Approx Per Serving: Cal 79; Prot 3 g; Carbo 15 g; T Fat 1 g; 8% Calories from Fat; Chol 1 mg; Fiber 1 g; Sod 110 mg
Nutritional information does not include ingredients in brackets.

Veda Bafford, Statesville HFH, Statesville, NC

100% WHOLE WHEAT BREAD

YIELD: *12 SERVINGS*

3	cups whole wheat flour	3	tablespoons molasses
1¹/₂	tablespoons nonfat dry milk powder	1	egg
1	tablespoon gluten	1¹/₂	tablespoons vegetable oil
1	teaspoon salt		Water
¹/₂	teaspoon vitamin C crystals	1	teaspoon dry yeast

Combine whole wheat flour, milk powder, gluten, salt and vitamin C crystals in bowl and mix well. Combine molasses, egg and oil in 2-cup measuring cup. Add enough water to measure 1¹/₂ cups and beat lightly. Pour into bread machine pan. Stir in flour mixture. Sprinkle with yeast. Set your machine on light color setting.

Approx Per Serving: Cal 142; Prot 5 g; Carbo 26 g; T Fat 3 g; 16% Calories from Fat; Chol 18 mg; Fiber 4 g; Sod 189 mg

Dolores Eichler, Southern Portage Co. HFH, Atwater, OH

Photograph at right by Robert Baker

DESSERTS

"Surely goodness and mercy
shall follow me all the days of my life:
and I will dwell in the house of the LORD forever."

Psalms 23:6

DESSERTS

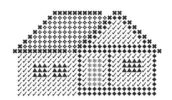

EASY APPLE PIE DESSERT

YIELD: 4 SERVINGS

1	large baking apple, peeled, sliced	1	all ready pie pastry, at room temperature
	Cinnamon to taste		Butter to taste
	Sugar to taste		

Rinse apple slices; do not dry. Coat liberally with mixture of cinnamon and sugar. Place in bowl. Let stand for 10 minutes. Place pastry in 9-inch pie plate. Drain apples. Arrange in center of pie pastry; dot with butter. Fold pastry to form square to enclose apples. Sprinkle with sugar. Bake at 350 degrees for 30 minutes or until brown.

Nutritional information for this recipe is not available.

Joel E. Richardson, Newnan-Coweta HFH, Newnan, GA

APPLE DUMPLINGS

YIELD: 15 SERVINGS

Serve warm with ice cream, or they're just as good cold.

3	apples, peeled, grated	1/2	cup milk
1/2	cup sugar	1/4	cup butter
2	teaspoons cinnamon	2	cups sugar
2	cups flour	2	cups water
2	teaspoons baking powder	1/4	cup butter
1	teaspoon salt	1/4	teaspoon cinnamon
3/4	cup vegetable shortening	1/4	teaspoon nutmeg

Combine apples, 1/2 cup sugar and 2 teaspoons cinnamon in bowl and mix well. Combine flour, baking powder and salt in bowl and mix well. Add shortening and milk, stirring until blended. Roll into 1/4-inch-thick rectangle on lightly floured surface. Spread with apple mixture; dot with 1/4 cup butter. Roll as for jelly roll. Cut into 1- to 1 1/2-inch slices. Arrange cut side up in 9x13-inch baking pan. Bring 2 cups sugar, water, 1/4 cup butter, 1/4 teaspoon cinnamon and nutmeg to a boil in saucepan. Boil for 5 minutes, stirring occasionally. Pour along sides of dumplings; do not pour directly on dumplings. Bake at 425 degrees for 25 minutes. May substitute 1 cup applesauce for apples or may substitute 1 cup apple butter, omitting 1/2 cup sugar and 2 teaspoons cinnamon.

Approx Per Serving: Cal 354; Prot 2 g; Carbo 50 g; T Fat 17 g; 42% Calories from Fat; Chol 18 mg; Fiber 1 g; Sod 274 mg

Debbie Hobson, Missoula HFH, Stevensville, MT

Apple Turnovers

Yield: 6 servings

2	cups dried apples	1	teaspoon cinnamon
2	cups apple cider or apple juice	1/2	teaspoon nutmeg
1/2	cup raisins	6	(6- or 8-inch) flour tortillas

Rehydrate apples in apple cider in microwave-safe bowl. Add raisins, cinnamon and nutmeg and mix well. Microwave on High for 15 to 20 minutes or until apples are tender. May add additional apple cider if needed. Spread 2 to 3 tablespoons of apple mixture on half of each tortilla; fold remaining half of each tortilla over filling to cover. Place tortillas in 12-inch nonstick skillet. Cook over medium heat until crisp and heated through, turning frequently. Serve plain or spread with yogurt. May add 2 teaspoons cornstarch to apple mixture if needed to thicken.

Approx Per Serving: Cal 257; Prot 4 g; Carbo 57 g; T Fat 3 g; 9% Calories from Fat; Chol 0 mg; Fiber 4 g; Sod 195 mg

Clarence E. Spier, Coachella Valley HFH, Indio, CA

Blueberry Dessert

Yield: 15 servings

8	ounces graham crackers, finely crushed	1	cup sugar
1/2	cup melted margarine	2	eggs
1/2	cup sugar	1	(21-ounce) can blueberry pie filling
16	ounces cream cheese, softened		

Combine graham cracker crumbs, margarine and 1/2 cup sugar in bowl and mix well. Pat over bottom and up sides of 9x12-inch baking dish. Combine cream cheese, 1 cup sugar and eggs in mixer bowl. Beat at high speed until smooth, scraping bowl occasionally. Spread over prepared layer. Bake at 350 degrees for 15 minutes. Let stand until cool. Spread with pie filling. Chill, covered, until serving time.

Approx Per Serving: Cal 353; Prot 4 g; Carbo 43 g; T Fat 19 g; 47% Calories from Fat; Chol 62 mg; Fiber 1 g; Sod 271 mg

Jeannine Severeid, Niles/Buchanan Area HFH, Niles, MI

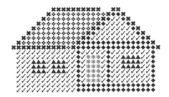

Our Coachella Valley affiliate has built four houses out of "flyash"—the residue of burning coal used for electricity. This reminds me of the fable of the Phoenix which, after a long life, threw itself into a fire and was resurrected from the ashes. This symbol of Hope and Renewal is appropriate, for the houses made of ashes bring hope to Partner families.

Clarence E. Spier
Coachella Valley HFH

CHERRY FLUFF

YIELD: 10 SERVINGS

1   (21-ounce) can cherry pie
     filling
12   ounces whipped topping

1   cup pecan halves
1/2 (10-ounce) package
     miniature marshmallows

Fold pie filling into whipped topping in bowl until mixture is pink. Fold in pecans and marshmallows. Chill, covered, until serving time.

Approx Per Serving: Cal 294; Prot 2 g; Carbo 39 g; T Fat 16 g; 47% Calories from Fat; Chol 0 mg; Fiber 1 g; Sod 21 mg

Pamela S. Chadbourne, Jefferson County HFH, Mt. Vernon, IL

CHOCOLATE CHERRY CAKE

YIELD: 12 SERVINGS

1   (2-layer) package chocolate
     cake mix
1   (12-ounce) can evaporated
     skim milk

1   (21-ounce) can cherry pie
     filling
1/2 cup chopped Georgia
     pecans

Stir cake mix and evaporated skim milk in bowl just until moistened. Spread in 9x13-inch baking pan sprayed with nonstick cooking spray. Top with pie filling. Bake at 350 degrees for 30 minutes. Sprinkle with pecans. Bake for 20 minutes longer or until pecans are toasted.

Approx Per Serving: Cal 294; Prot 5 g; Carbo 50 g; T Fat 10 g; 29% Calories from Fat; Chol 1 mg; Fiber 2 g; Sod 388 mg

Bonnie Wallace, Macon Co. HFH, Otto, NC

BAKED FUDGE

YIELD: 8 SERVINGS

1/2 cup sifted flour
1/2 cup baking cocoa
1/2 cup sugar
4   eggs, beaten

1   cup melted margarine
2   teaspoons vanilla extract
1   cup chopped pecans

Mix flour, baking cocoa and sugar in bowl. Add to eggs in bowl and mix well. Stir in margarine and vanilla. Add pecans and mix well. Spoon into 9x9-inch baking pan. Place in larger shallow baking pan with enough water to reach 1 inch up sides of smaller pan. Bake at 350 degrees for 1 hour or until set and crusty on top.

Approx Per Serving: Cal 430; Prot 6 g; Carbo 24 g; T Fat 36 g; 73% Calories from Fat; Chol 106 mg; Fiber 3 g; Sod 300 mg

Jean Leslie, Milwaukee HFH, Whitefish Bay, WI

Desserts

No-Bake Fruitcake

YIELD: *16 SERVINGS*

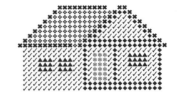

1	(16-ounce) package graham crackers, crushed	1	(16-ounce) package candied fruit, chopped
1	(16-ounce) package raisins	16	ounces pecans, chopped
1	(16-ounce) package candied red and green cherries	16	ounces walnuts, chopped
		2	cups evaporated milk
		1	(16-ounce) package marshmallows

Combine graham crackers, raisins, cherries, candied fruit, pecans and walnuts in order listed in bowl and mix well. Combine evaporated milk and marshmallows in double boiler. Cook until blended, stirring frequently. Add to graham cracker mixture and mix well. Press into angel food cake pan. Chill until serving time.

Approx Per Serving: Cal 893; Prot 012 g; Carbo 128 g; T Fat 42 g; 40% Calories from Fat; Chol 9 mg; Fiber 5 g; Sod 307 mg

Loretta M. Troyer, HFHI, Middlebury, IN

Peach Crisp

YIELD: *15 SERVINGS*

1	(29-ounce) can juice-pack sliced peaches	1/2	cup melted margarine
1	(2-layer) package any flavor cake mix	1	cup shredded coconut
		1	cup chopped pecans

Photo by Robert Baker

Pour peaches and juice into 9x13-inch baking pan. Sprinkle with cake mix; drizzle with margarine. Top with coconut and pecans. Bake at 325 degrees for 55 to 60 minutes or until bubbly and brown.

Approx Per Serving: Cal 310; Prot 3 g; Carbo 37 g; T Fat 18 g; 50% Calories from Fat; Chol 1 mg; Fiber 2 g; Sod 313 mg

Megan Foote, Denton HFH, Sanger, TX

DESSERTS

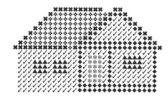

FRUIT CRISP

YIELD: 8 SERVINGS

6	to 8 cups sliced apples	1/2	cup packed brown sugar
2	tablespoons lemon juice	1/2	cup rolled oats
1/4	teaspoon cinnamon	1/3	cup margarine
2/3	cup flour		

Arrange apples in 2-quart baking dish. Drizzle with lemon juice; sprinkle with cinnamon. Combine flour, brown sugar and oats in bowl and mix well. Cut in margarine until crumbly. Sprinkle over apples. Bake at 375 degrees for 40 minutes. May substitute blueberries, peaches, cranberries or your favorite fruit for apples. If using cranberries increase amount of brown sugar. This recipe may be increased to serve larger groups.

Approx Per Serving: Cal 232; Prot 2 g; Carbo 39 g; T Fat 8 g; 31% Calories from Fat; Chol 0 mg; Fiber 3 g; Sod 94 mg

Susan L. Knack, Cornell HFH (CC), Ithaca, NY

LIME CHOCOLATE DELICIOUS

YIELD: 15 SERVINGS

2	cups chocolate wafer crumbs	1	cup sugar
1/3	cup melted butter	1/4	cup lime juice
1	(3-ounce) package lime gelatin	2	teaspoons lemon juice
1 3/4	cups hot water	1	(12-ounce) can evaporated milk, chilled

Combine wafer crumbs and butter in bowl and mix well. Pat over bottom of 9x12-inch dish. Dissolve gelatin in hot water in mixer bowl. Chill until partially set. Beat until fluffy. Add sugar, lime juice and lemon juice and mix well. Beat chilled evaporated milk in mixer bowl until fluffy. Fold into gelatin mixture. Spoon into prepared dish. Chill until set.

Approx Per Serving: Cal 216; Prot 3 g; Carbo 34 g; T Fat 8 g; 34% Calories from Fat; Chol 18 mg; Fiber 0 g; Sod 183 mg

Lynda Sneathen, Orange County HFH, Westminster, CA

MOM'S ICEBOX DESSERT

YIELD: 8 SERVINGS

1 (16-ounce) can juice-pack crushed pineapple
1 cup sugar
1 (3-ounce) package strawberry gelatin
1 cup whipped topping
1 (10-ounce) angel food cake

Combine undrained pineapple and sugar in saucepan. Cook until sugar dissolves, stirring frequently. Remove from heat. Add gelatin, stirring until dissolved. Chill until syrupy. Fold in whipped topping. Slice cake horizontally into 3 equal layers. Spread pineapple mixture between layers and over top and side of cake. Garnish with fresh strawberries. Chill for 3 hours. May substitute whipped cream for whipped topping and any flavor gelatin for strawberry gelatin.

Approx Per Serving: Cal 404; Prot 6 g; Carbo 91 g; T Fat 3 g; 7% Calories from Fat; Chol 0 mg; Fiber 2 g; Sod 623 mg

Jeanne Blasher, Mon County HFH, Morgantown, WV

TRIPLE-ORANGE DELIGHT

YIELD: 15 SERVINGS

2 (11-ounce) cans mandarin oranges
2 (3-ounce) packages orange gelatin
1 quart orange sherbet
12 ounces whipped topping
1 (10-ounce) angel food cake, cut into bite-size pieces

Drain mandarin oranges, reserving 1 cup juice. Bring reserved juice to a boil in saucepan. Add gelatin, stirring until dissolved. Pour into large bowl. Add sherbet, stirring until melted. Fold in whipped topping. Layer angel food cake, mandarin oranges and sherbet mixture 1/2 at a time in 9x13-inch dish. Chill, covered, for 8 to 10 hours. Garnish each serving with additional whipped topping and mint leaves.

Approx Per Serving: Cal 309; Prot 5 g; Carbo 59 g; T Fat 7 g; 20% Calories from Fat; Chol 3 mg; Fiber 1 g; Sod 375 mg

Carolyn Lehman, Flathead Valley HFH, Kalispell, MT

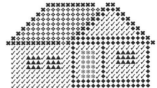

The following are comments after a week of building camp: "We are not the same . . . First I counted my blessings . . . It felt great knowing I was really needed . . . I was really impressed by the love and joy of a family who don't have much . . . I learned that God makes everyone equal, even though it doesn't always seem that way . . . I learned that God helps people in mysterious ways. He helped us as much as we helped the Snyder family . . ."

Jeanne Blasher
Mon County HFH

DESSERTS

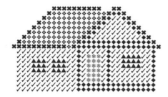

FANNIE'S BLANCMANGE

YIELD: 4 SERVINGS

2	to 3 tablespoons cold water	4	cinnamon sticks
2	cups skim milk	1/2	teaspoon vanilla extract
1	envelope unflavored gelatin	1/4	to 1/2 cup sugar

Soften gelatin in cold water in bowl. Heat skim milk in saucepan over low heat for 3 to 5 minutes. Add gelatin mixture, stirring until dissolved. Stir in cinnamon sticks and vanilla. Add sugar. Cook until dissolved, stirring constantly. Discard cinnamon sticks. Pour into 4 dessert dishes. Chill for 3 to 4 hours.

Approx Per Serving: Cal 146; Prot 6 g; Carbo 31 g; T Fat <1 g; 1% Calories from Fat; Chol 2 mg; Fiber 0 g; Sod 67 mg

Casey Lewis, Blue Spruce HFH, Denver, CO

BREAD PUDDING

YIELD: 8 SERVINGS

4	cups crumbled dry biscuits	3	eggs
3	cups milk, heated	1	teaspoon vanilla extract
1/4	teaspoon salt	1/2	teaspoon nutmeg
1/3	cup sugar		Caramel Sauce (page 169)

Soak biscuits in warm milk in bowl for 20 minutes. Stir in salt. Beat sugar, eggs, vanilla and nutmeg in mixer bowl until blended. Add to biscuit mixture and stir gently. Spoon into 7x11-inch baking pan; cover with foil. Place in larger shallow pan filled with hot water to reach halfway up sides of smaller pan. Steam at 350 degrees for 45 minutes. Serve warm with Caramel Sauce.

Approx Per Serving: Cal 494; Prot 7 g; Carbo 93 g; T Fat 11 g; 21% Calories from Fat; Chol 98 mg; Fiber 1 g; Sod 413

Charlene Toole, Somerset-Pulaski County HFH, Somerset, KY

CARAMEL SAUCE

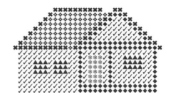

3	cups packed brown sugar	1	cup warm water
4	teaspoons sifted flour	1/4	teaspoon salt
4	teaspoons butter		

Mix brown sugar, flour and butter in saucepan. Stir in water and salt. Bring to a boil. Boil until thickened, stirring constantly.

Approx Per Serving: Cal 277; Prot 0 g; Carbo 67 g; T Fat 2 g; 6% Calories from Fat; Chol 5 mg; Fiber 0 g; Sod 113 mg

Charlene Toole, Somerset-Pulaski County HFH, Somerset, KY

CRAZY ORANGE PUDDING

YIELD: 8 SERVINGS

1 1/2	cups cottage cheese	3/4	cup chopped English walnuts
1	(11-ounce) can mandarin oranges, drained	1	(3-ounce) package orange gelatin
1	(8-ounce) can crushed pineapple	2	cups whipped topping

Combine cottage cheese, mandarin oranges, undrained pineapple, walnuts, gelatin and whipped topping in order listed in 2-quart bowl. Chill, covered, for 2 to 10 hours.

Approx Per Serving: Cal 257; Prot 8 g; Carbo 29 g; T Fat 14 g; 45% Calories from Fat; Chol 6 mg; Fiber 1 g; Sod 192 mg

Phyllis Will, Lancaster Area HFH, Lancaster, PA

HOT FUDGE PUDDING CAKE

YIELD: 6 SERVINGS

1	cup baking mix	1	teaspoon vanilla extract
1/2	cup sugar	1/2	cup sugar
3	tablespoons baking cocoa	1/3	cup baking cocoa
1/2	cup milk	1 2/3	cups hot water

Mix baking mix, 1/2 cup sugar and 3 tablespoons baking cocoa in bowl. Stir in milk and vanilla. Spoon into greased 8x8-inch baking dish. Sprinkle with mixture of 1/2 cup sugar and 1/3 cup baking cocoa. Pour hot water over top; do not stir. Bake at 350 degrees for 40 minutes or until top is firm. Sprinkle with confectioners' sugar.

Approx Per Serving: Cal 248; Prot 4 g; Carbo 51 g; T Fat 5 g; 16% Calories from Fat; Chol 3 mg; Fiber 3 g; Sod 265 mg

Judy Yavello, South Oakland County HFH, Ferndale, MI

While planning a dedication for six families, I was at a loss for a musical presentation. Our office secretary, Eidy, gathered all the families' children and with only a few days to rehearse we had a wonderful program.

Phyllis Will
Lancaster Area HFH

DESSERTS

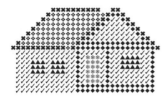

After four hard years of selling cookbooks I never dreamed of selling 552. The two cookbooks, From Our House to Yours and Home Sweet Habitat, have so many wonderful recipes. I sold my first one hundred in a month. I had no car and walked about one mile to get home from school. I asked Vernon Temple, the Habitat Board Chairman who ordered the cookbooks, if I could sell cookbooks as I walked home. The first day I sold ten, and the next day twenty. I sold a cookbook to every business owner in Sherman. At the first board meeting, Vernon told about the cookbooks he had ordered, and that I had sold the

(continued)

ON-THE-RUN PUDDING

YIELD: 4 SERVINGS

This recipe takes very little time and effort and thus allows more time for selling Habitat cookbooks or volunteering at a work site. Go to your nearest Kroger Grocery store to purchase the pudding mix and milk and make sure you don't forget your Kroger "Care Card." Using a Kroger "Care Card" means that 3 percent of your purchases are donated to HFH of Grayson County. In Grayson County the pudding mix is on aisle 20.

1	(4-ounce) package chocolate instant pudding mix	2	cups cold milk

Combine pudding mix and milk in mixer bowl. Beat for 2 minutes. Chill for 30 minutes before serving. May add vanilla wafers, sliced bananas or any other fruit if desired.

Approx Per Serving: Cal 163; Prot 5 g; Carbo 27 g; T Fat 5 g; 24% Calories from Fat; Chol 17 mg; Fiber 1 g; Sod 413 mg

Chris Johnson, Grayson County HFH, Sherman, TX

WOJOPI (INDIAN PUDDING)

YIELD: 6 SERVINGS

2	cups water	1	cup sugar
2	cups blueberries or blackberries	1	tablespoon cornstarch
		1	teaspoon (about) water

Combine 2 cups water, blueberries and sugar in saucepan. Bring to a boil. Combine cornstarch and 1 teaspoon water in bowl, stirring until of paste consistency. Stir into blueberry mixture. Simmer for 20 minutes, stirring occasionally. Let stand until cool. Pudding will thicken as it cools. Serve with Indian Fry Bread.

Approx Per Serving: Cal 161; Prot 0 g; Carbo 41 g; T Fat <1 g; 1% Calories from Fat; Chol 0 mg; Fiber 1 g; Sod 3 mg

Karen Jeffries, Okiciyapi Tipi HFH, Eagle Butte, SD

PINEAPPLE BREAD PUDDING

Yield: 10 servings

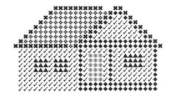

4	cups torn dry or lightly toasted bread
1/2	to 1 cup melted butter or margarine
2 1/2	cups sugar
1/2	teaspoon cinnamon
1	(20-ounce) can crushed pineapple

Combine bread and butter in bowl, tossing to coat. Combine sugar and cinnamon in bowl and mix well. Stir in undrained pineapple. Add bread mixture, stirring until bread is coated. Spoon into 7x11-inch or 9x13-inch baking dish. Bake at 350 degrees for 1 hour.

Approx Per Serving: Cal 438; Prot 2 g; Carbo 68 g; T Fat 19 g; 38% Calories from Fat; Chol 50 mg; Fiber 1 g; Sod 254 mg

Bev Snowden, Greater Bellevue HFH, Bellevue, NE

PUMPKIN TORTE

Yield: 15 servings

1	envelope unflavored gelatin
1/4	cup cold water
24	graham crackers, crushed
1/2	cup butter or vegetable shortening
1/3	cup sugar
8	ounces cream cheese, softened
3/4	cup sugar
2	eggs, beaten
2	cups canned or cooked pumpkin
3	egg yolks
1/2	cup sugar
1/2	cup milk
1	tablespoon cinnamon
1/2	teaspoon salt
3	egg whites
1/4	cup sugar
1	cup whipping cream, whipped

Soften gelatin in cold water in bowl and mix well. Combine graham cracker crumbs, butter and 1/3 cup sugar in bowl and mix well. Pat into 9x13-inch baking pan. Beat cream cheese, 3/4 cup sugar and eggs in mixer bowl until smooth. Spread over prepared layer. Bake at 350 degrees for 20 minutes. Combine pumpkin, egg yolks, 1/2 cup sugar, milk, cinnamon and salt in saucepan and mix well. Cook until thickened, stirring frequently. Remove from heat. Stir in gelatin mixture. Let stand until cool. Beat egg whites and 1/4 cup sugar in bowl until stiff peaks form. Fold into pumpkin mixture. Spoon over baked layers. Top with whipped cream.

Approx Per Serving: Cal 348; Prot 6 g; Carbo 37 g; T Fat 20 g; 52% Calories from Fat; Chol 127 mg; Fiber 2 g; Sod 280 mg

Mr. and Mrs. D. C. Myers, Kokomo Community HFH, Kokomo, IN

First hundred. People tell me how much they love the recipes, and they buy cookbooks for their families and friends. I have sold them at the county fair, the mall, the Sherman Arts Festival, and to the mayor of Sherman. I thank Linda Fuller, as well as the people who contributed recipes. James 2:17 states "Faith, if it has no works, is dead."

Chris Johnson
Grayson County HFH

Desserts

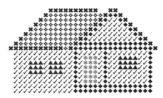

Strawberry Pizza

YIELD: 12 SERVINGS

2	cups flour	2	pints fresh strawberries
1	cup butter, softened	1	cup sugar
1/2	cup confectioners' sugar	1/4	cup cornstarch
8	ounces cream cheese, softened	1/4	cup water
1	cup confectioners' sugar	1	teaspoon vanilla extract
1	envelope whipped topping, prepared	3	or 4 drops of red food coloring
		8	ounces whipped topping

Combine flour, butter and 1/2 cup confectioners' sugar in bowl and mix well. Pat over bottom and up side of 12-inch pizza pan; flute edge. Bake at 350 degrees for 20 minutes. Let stand until cool. Beat cream cheese, 1 cup confectioners' sugar and prepared whipped topping in mixer bowl until smooth. Spread over baked layer. Mash 1 pint of the strawberries in saucepan. Stir in sugar. Bring to a boil. Stir in mixture of cornstarch and water. Cook until thickened, stirring constantly. Remove from heat. Stir in vanilla and food coloring. Let stand until cool. Slice 1/2 of the remaining strawberries. Add the sliced strawberries to the strawberry mixture and mix gently. Spoon over the prepared layers. Pipe 8 ounces whipped topping around outer edge of pizza. Arrange the remaining whole strawberries in decorative pattern in center of pizza.

Approx Per Serving: Cal 510; Prot 5 g; Carbo 60 g; T Fat 29 g; 50% Calories from Fat; Chol 64 mg; Fiber 1 g; Sod 227 mg

Marie Johnson, Towns-Union Counties HFH, Blairsville, GA

Slush

YIELD: 15 SERVINGS

1	(12-ounce) can frozen orange juice concentrate	3	bananas, sliced
1	(16-ounce) can crushed unsweetened pineapple	1	(12-ounce) can lemon-lime soda
		1	cup seedless grapes

Pour thawed orange juice concentrate into glass loaf pan. Stir in undrained pineapple and bananas. Add soda and mix gently. Taste and add artificial sweetener if needed. Freeze for 3 hours or until partially set. Stir in grapes gently. Freeze until firm. Let stand at room temperature for 45 minutes before serving. May store, covered with foil, in freezer for up to 1 month.

Approx Per Serving: Cal 92; Prot 1 g; Carbo 23 g; T Fat <1 g; 2% Calories from Fat; Chol 0 mg; Fiber 1 g; Sod 4 mg

Mary K. Warren, Maricopa HFH, Sun City, AZ

Moist Chocolate Cake

Yield: 15 servings

3	cups flour	2	cups cold water
2	cups sugar	2/3	cup corn oil
1/2	cup baking cocoa	2	teaspoons vinegar
2	teaspoons baking soda	2	teaspoons vanilla extract
1	teaspoon salt		Chocolate Frosting

Combine flour, sugar, baking cocoa, baking soda and salt in bowl and mix well. Add water, corn oil, vinegar and vanilla, stirring until blended. Spoon into ungreased 9x12-inch cake pan. Bake at 350 degrees for 30 minutes or until top bounces back when touched. Spread with Chocolate Frosting.

Approx Per Serving: Cal 476; Prot 4 g; Carbo 81 g; T Fat 17 g; 31% Calories from Fat; Chol 13 mg; Fiber 2 g; Sod 364 mg

Chocolate Frosting

Yield: 15 servings

2	ounces unsweetened chocolate, melted	1/4	cup (about) milk
6	tablespoons butter, softened	1	to 2 tablespoons corn syrup
1	(1-pound) package confectioners' sugar	1	teaspoon vanilla extract

Combine chocolate and butter in mixer bowl and mix well. Add confectioners' sugar, milk, corn syrup and vanilla, beating until of spreading consistency. May substitute evaporated milk for whole milk.

Approx Per Serving: Cal 188; Prot 1 g; Carbo 33 g; T Fat 7 g; 31% Calories from Fat; Chol 13 mg; Fiber 1 g; Sod 53 mg

Mrs. Jack Kemp, Washington, DC

Photo by Robert Baker

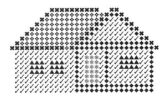

DATE NUT CAKES

YIELD: 36 SERVINGS

2	pounds walnut halves	1	teaspoon baking powder
2	pounds pitted dates	1 1/2	cups sugar
1	pound Brazil nuts, shelled	5	eggs
1 1/2	cups flour	1	teaspoon vanilla extract
1	teaspoon salt		

Combine walnuts, dates and Brazil nuts in bowl and mix well. Stir in mixture of flour, salt and baking powder. Add sugar and mix well. Beat eggs and vanilla in mixer bowl until blended. Add to walnut mixture and mix well. Spoon into 3 greased 5x9-inch loaf pans; press gently. Bake at 350 degrees for 1 hour.

Approx Per Serving: Cal 332; Prot 6 g; Carbo 36 g; T Fat 20 g; 52% Calories from Fat; Chol 30 mg; Fiber 4 g; Sod 85 mg

Emma Pelissier, Amherst County HFH, Amherst, VA

EGYPTIAN CAKE

YIELD: 15 SERVINGS

2	ounces unsweetened chocolate	1 1/2	cups sugar
5	tablespoons hot water	1	cup sour cream
1 1/2	cups sugar	1	egg
1/2	cup butter	1	tablespoon flour
4	egg yolks	1/4	teaspoon salt
1/2	cup milk	1	cup raisins
1 3/4	cups flour	1	cup chopped walnuts
2	teaspoons baking powder	1	ounce unsweetened chocolate
1	teaspoon vanilla extract	1	tablespoon butter
4	egg whites, beaten		

Combine 2 ounces chocolate and hot water in saucepan. Heat over low heat until blended. Beat 1 1/2 cups sugar and 1/2 cup butter in mixer bowl until light and fluffy. Add egg yolks, beating until blended. Mix in chocolate mixture. Beat in milk, 1 3/4 cups flour, baking powder and vanilla. Fold in egg whites. Spoon into 9x13-inch cake pan. Bake at 350 degrees for 30 to 40 minutes or until cake tests done. Mix 1 1/2 cups sugar, sour cream, 1 egg, 1 tablespoon flour and salt in saucepan. Bring to a boil, stirring frequently. Boil until thickened, stirring frequently. Remove from heat. Stir in raisins and walnuts. Let stand until cool. Spread over baked layer. Heat 1 ounce chocolate and 1 tablespoon butter in double boiler over low heat until blended, stirring frequently. Drizzle over top and swirl.

Approx Per Serving: Cal 448; Prot 7 g; Carbo 65 g; T Fat 20 g; 39% Calories from Fat; Chol 97 mg; Fiber 2 g; Sod 207 mg

John M. Nichols, Crow River HFH, Hutchinson, MN

GRAHAM STREUSEL CAKE

YIELD: 15 SERVINGS

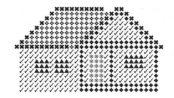
2	cups graham cracker crumbs	1	cup water
¾	cup packed brown sugar	¼	cup vegetable oil
¾	cup melted butter	3	eggs
1¼	teaspoons cinnamon	1	cup confectioners' sugar
1	(2-layer) package yellow cake mix	1	to 2 tablespoons water

Mix first 4 ingredients in bowl. Combine cake mix, 1 cup water, oil and eggs in bowl and mix well. Layer cake batter and crumb mixture ½ at a time in greased and floured 9x13-inch cake pan. Bake at 350 degrees for 45 minutes. Drizzle warm cake with mixture of confectioners' sugar and 1 to 2 tablespoons water.

Approx Per Serving: Cal 408; Prot 4 g; Carbo 56 g; T Fat 19 g; 42% Calories from Fat; Chol 68 mg; Fiber 1 g; Sod 430 mg

Sally Simpson, Oregon Trail HFH, Pendleton, OR

PUMPKIN SHEET CAKE

YIELD: 24 SERVINGS

1	(16-ounce) can pumpkin	3	ounces cream cheese, softened
2	cups sugar		
1	cup vegetable oil	5	tablespoons butter or margarine, softened
4	eggs, lightly beaten		
2	cups flour	1	teaspoon vanilla extract
2	teaspoons baking soda	1¾	cups confectioners' sugar
1	teaspoon cinnamon	3	to 4 teaspoons milk
½	teaspoon salt	½	to 1 cup chopped pecans

Beat pumpkin, sugar and oil in mixer bowl until blended. Add eggs and mix well. Beat in mixture of flour, baking soda, cinnamon and salt until blended. Spoon into greased 10x15-inch cake pan. Bake at 350 degrees for 25 to 30 minutes or until cake tests done. Let stand until cool. Beat cream cheese, butter and vanilla in mixer bowl until smooth. Add confectioners' sugar gradually and mix well. Add milk, beating until of spreading consistency. Spread over cake; sprinkle with pecans.

Approx Per Serving: Cal 303; Prot 3 g; Carbo 36 g; T Fat 17 g; 50% Calories from Fat; Chol 46 mg; Fiber 1 g; Sod 196 mg

Lou Ann Derham, Knox HFH (CC), E. Galesburg, IL

DESSERTS

SIMPLE SHEET CAKE
YIELD: 16 SERVINGS

1	cup margarine	1	teaspoon baking soda
1	cup water	1	teaspoon salt
1/4	cup baking cocoa	1/2	cup sour cream
2	cups flour	2	eggs
2	cups sugar		Chocolate Walnut Frosting

Bring margarine, water and baking cocoa to a boil in saucepan. Remove from heat. Stir in mixture of flour, sugar, baking soda and salt. Add sour cream and eggs and mix well. Spoon into greased and floured jelly roll pan. Bake at 375 degrees for 20 minutes. Spread warm cake with Chocolate Walnut Frosting. Cool before serving. May bake in two 9-inch cake pans.

Approx Per Serving: Cal 501; Prot 5 g; Carbo 69 g; T Fat 25 g; 43% Calories from Fat; Chol 31 mg; Fiber 2 g; Sod 429 mg

CHOCOLATE WALNUT FROSTING
YIELD: 16 SERVINGS

1/2	cup margarine	1	(1-pound) package
6	tablespoons milk		confectioners' sugar
1/4	cup baking cocoa	1	cup chopped walnuts

Bring margarine, milk and baking cocoa to a boil in saucepan, stirring frequently. Remove from heat. Add confectioners' sugar, stirring until blended. Stir in walnuts.

Approx Per Serving: Cal 217; Prot 2 g; Carbo 31 g; T Fat 11 g; 43% Calories from Fat; Chol 1 mg; Fiber 1 g; Sod 71 mg

Wilma Wood, Middletown HFH, Middletown, OH

CRUSTLESS APPLE PIE
YIELD: 6 SERVINGS

3/4	cup sugar	1	egg, lightly beaten
1/2	cup flour	1	teaspoon vanilla extract
1	teaspoon baking powder	2	cups sliced tart apples
1/4	teaspoon salt	1/2	cup chopped pecans

Combine sugar, flour, baking powder and salt in bowl and mix well. Stir in egg and vanilla. Add apples and pecans, stirring until mixed. Spoon into buttered 9x9-inch baking pan. Bake at 350 degrees for 30 minutes. Serve with whipped topping or ice cream.

Approx Per Serving: Cal 235; Prot 3 g; Carbo 40 g; T Fat 8 g; 29% Calories from Fat; Chol 35 mg; Fiber 1 g; Sod 181 mg

Jimmie H. Powers, Texarkana HFH, Texarkana, AR

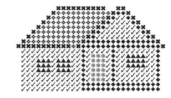

CHOCOLATE ALMOND PIE

YIELD: 6 SERVINGS

16	ounces milk chocolate with almonds	1	(9-inch) graham cracker pie shell
2	cups whipping cream, whipped		

Heat chocolate in double boiler over low heat until melted. Let stand until cool. Fold whipped cream into chocolate in bowl. Spoon into pie shell. Chill until serving time.

Approx Per Serving: Cal 939; Prot 11 g; Carbo 78 g; T Fat 69 g; 64% Calories from Fat; Chol 123 mg; Fiber 6 g; Sod 395 mg

Virginia Henke, Menominee River HFH, Iron Mountain, MI

COCONUT LAYERED PIES

YIELD: 16 SERVINGS

8	ounces cream cheese, softened	2	cups shredded coconut
1	cup milk	3	(4-ounce) packages vanilla instant pudding mix
2	envelopes whipped topping mix	6	cups half-and-half
1/2	cup sugar	2 1/2	teaspoons vanilla extract
2	teaspoons vanilla extract	8	ounces whipped topping
2	baked (9-inch) pie shells	1	cup shredded coconut, toasted

Beat cream cheese, milk, whipped topping mix, sugar and 2 teaspoons vanilla in mixer bowl until fluffy, scraping bowl occasionally. Spoon into pie shells. Sprinkle with 2 cups shredded coconut. Chill for several hours. Beat pudding mix, half-and-half and 2 1/2 teaspoons vanilla in mixer bowl until smooth and slightly thickened. Spoon over chilled layers. Chill until set. Spread with whipped topping; sprinkle with 1 cup toasted coconut. Chill until serving time.

Approx Per Serving: Cal 584; Prot 7 g; Carbo 56 g; T Fat 38 g; 57% Calories from Fat; Chol 51 mg; Fiber 1 g; Sod 538 mg

University of Maryland College Park (CC), College Park, MD

DESSERTS

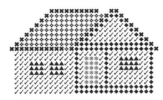

KEY LIME PIE

YIELD: 8 SERVINGS

1	(14-ounce) can sweetened condensed milk	3	drops of green food coloring
3	egg yolks	8	ounces whipped topping
1/3	cup Key lime juice	3	egg whites, stiffly beaten
1½	teaspoons grated lime peel	1	baked (9-inch) pie shell

Combine condensed milk and egg yolks in bowl and mix well. Stir in lime juice, lime peel and food coloring. Fold in whipped topping. Fold in beaten egg whites. Spoon into pie shell. Bake at 250 degrees for 10 minutes or until set. Chill until serving time.

Approx Per Serving: Cal 399; Prot 8 g; Carbo 45 g; T Fat 21 g; 47% Calories from Fat; Chol 97 mg; Fiber 0 g; Sod 215 mg

Mary Fleming, Pensacola HFH, Pensacola, FL

MILLION-DOLLAR PIES

YIELD: 16 SERVINGS

1	(14-ounce) can sweetened condensed milk	1	cup chopped pecans
1/4	cup lemon juice	12	ounces whipped topping
1	(15-ounce) can crushed pineapple, drained	2	(9-inch) graham cracker pie shells

Mix first 4 ingredients in bowl. Fold in whipped topping. Spoon into pie shells. Chill, covered, for 8 to 10 hours.

Approx Per Serving: Cal 412; Prot 5 g; Carbo 50 g; T Fat 23 g; 48% Calories from Fat; Chol 8 mg; Fiber 2 g; Sod 269 mg

Sue Ramsey, Claiborne County HFH, New Tazewell, TN

AUNT FRANCES' PEACH PIE

YIELD: 6 SERVINGS

7	peaches, peeled, sliced	1/3	cup flour
1	unbaked (9-inch) pie shell	1	egg
1	cup sugar	1/4	teaspoon vanilla extract
1/3	cup butter		

Arrange peaches in pie shell. Cream sugar and butter in mixer bowl. Beat in flour. Add egg and vanilla and mix well. Spoon into prepared pie shell. Bake at 300 to 325 degrees for 1 hour or until brown.

Approx Per Serving: Cal 459; Prot 4 g; Carbo 64 g; T Fat 22 g; 41% Calories from Fat; Chol 63 mg; Fiber 3 g; Sod 278 mg

Claudia Ricci, Northeast Connecticut HFH, Putnam, CT

PECAN PIE

YIELD: 6 SERVINGS

1	all ready pie pastry	3	eggs
1	cup corn syrup	1/3	teaspoon salt
2/3	cup sugar	1	cup pecan halves or broken
1/3	cup melted margarine		pecans

Fit pastry into 9-inch pie plate. Trim and flute edge. Beat corn syrup, sugar, margarine, eggs and salt in mixer bowl until blended. Stir in pecans. Spoon into prepared pie plate. Bake at 375 degrees for 40 to 50 minutes or until set. Cool slightly before serving. Serve warm or chilled.

Approx Per Serving: Cal 648; Prot 5 g; Carbo 84 g; T Fat 35 g; 47% Calories from Fat; Chol 116 mg; Fiber 1 g; Sod 522 mg

Tammy Smith, Wilmington College HFH (CC), Wilmington, OH

SWEET POTATO PIE

YIELD: 6 SERVINGS

1 1/2	cups canned mashed sweet potatoes	1	tablespoon butter
1	cup whole milk	1/4	teaspoon salt
1	cup sugar	1/4	teaspoon nutmeg
2	eggs, lightly beaten	1/4	teaspoon cinnamon
		1	unbaked (9-inch) pie shell

Combine sweet potatoes, milk, sugar, eggs, butter, salt, nutmeg and cinnamon in bowl and mix well. Spoon into pie shell. Bake at 425 degrees for 45 minutes or until knife inserted in center comes out clean. May substitute freshly cooked sweet potatoes for canned sweet potatoes.

Approx Per Serving: Cal 406; Prot 6 g; Carbo 62 g; T Fat 15 g; 34% Calories from Fat; Chol 82 mg; Fiber 2 g; Sod 319 mg

Dorothy Gilliam, Pinellas HFH, St. Petersburg, FL

DESSERTS

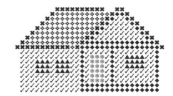

In January 1995, a group of seventeen college students spent a week of their Christmas vacation renovating a church building into a dormitory for Farrell-Sherard HFH in Mississippi. We will never forget the pecans we were given from the nearby pecan plantation. Willie, a friend in Coahoma, Mississippi, taught us how to make a pecan pie the southern way.
The pie was "mm, mm, good."

Tammy Smith
Wilmington College
HFH (CC)

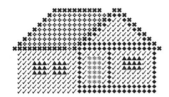

EDNA'S SWEET POTATO PIE

YIELD: 6 SERVINGS

2	cups mashed cooked sweet potatoes	2	eggs, lightly beaten
1	cup sugar	1	teaspoon vanilla extract
1	cup milk	1	teaspoon lemon extract
1/2	cup melted margarine	1/2	teaspoon salt
		1	unbaked (9-inch) pie shell

Combine sweet potatoes, sugar, milk, margarine, eggs, flavorings and salt in bowl and mix well. Spoon into pie shell. Bake at 400 degrees for 45 minutes or until knife inserted in center comes out clean.

Approx Per Serving: Cal 543; Prot 7 g; Carbo 66 g; T Fat 29 g; 47% Calories from Fat; Chol 76 mg; Fiber 2 g; Sod 569 mg

Joyce Spear, Rockingham HFH, Eden, NC

RANGE-TOP PUMPKIN PIE

YIELD: 6 SERVINGS

3/4 cup sugar
2 teaspoons cornstarch
1 teaspoon cinnamon
1/4 teaspoon nutmeg
1/4 teaspoon ginger
1/4 teaspoon ground cloves
1 (16-ounce) can pumpkin
2 eggs, lightly beaten
1 cup whipped topping
1 baked (9-inch) pie shell

Photo by Robert Baker

Combine sugar, cornstarch, cinnamon, nutmeg, ginger and cloves in 2-quart saucepan and mix well. Stir in pumpkin and eggs. Add whipped topping gradually and mix well. Bring to a boil over medium heat, stirring constantly. Boil for 2 minutes, stirring constantly. Cool to room temperature. Spoon into pie shell. Chill for 2 hours or longer. Garnish each serving with additional whipped topping.

Approx Per Serving: Cal 348; Prot 5 g; Carbo 49 g; T Fat 15 g; 39% Calories from Fat; Chol 71 mg; Fiber 4 g; Sod 190 mg

Shirley Schultz, Jefferson County HFH, Mt. Vernon, IL

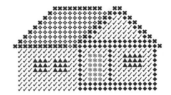

RED RASPBERRY TARTS

YIELD: 24 SERVINGS

1	recipe (2-crust) pie pastry	1	teaspoon vanilla extract
1/2	cup raspberry preserves	1	cup flaked coconut
2	eggs, beaten	1/3	cup milk
1/2	cup sugar		
1/4	cup melted butter or margarine, cooled		

Roll pie pastry on lightly floured surface. Cut pastry with round cutter large enough to fit muffin cups. Line 24 muffin cups with pastry rounds. Spoon 1 teaspoon of preserves into each muffin cup. Combine eggs, sugar, butter and vanilla in bowl and mix well. Stir in coconut and milk. Spoon 1 tablespoon of coconut mixture into each muffin cup. Bake at 375 degrees for 10 to 15 minutes.

Approx Per Serving: Cal 143; Prot 2 g; Carbo 16 g; T Fat 8 g; 50% Calories from Fat; Chol 23 mg; Fiber 0 g; Sod 103 mg

Richard Duro, Alliance HFH, Alliance, OH

NEVER-FAIL PIE PASTRY

YIELD: 5 PIE PASTRIES

4	cups flour	1/2	cup water
1 3/4	cups vegetable shortening	1	tablespoon vinegar
1	tablespoon sugar	1	egg
2	teaspoons salt		

Mix flour, shortening, sugar and salt in bowl with fork. Combine water, vinegar and egg in bowl and mix well. Add to flour mixture, stirring with fork until moistened. Shape into ball. Chill, covered, for 1 hour or longer. Divide into 5 equal portions. Roll into individual pie pastries or freeze, wrapped, for future use.

Approx Per Pastry: Cal 1023; Prot 12 g; Carbo 79 g; T Fat 74 g; 65% Calories from Fat; Chol 43 mg; Fiber 3 g; Sod 867 mg

Marian Tidd, Cabarrus County HFH, Concord, NC

This recipe for
life is free;
The ingredients,
just five.
But if you follow
faithfully
You'll truly be alive!

The prime
ingredient is love,
So use abundantly.
Add some faith in
God above—
'Twill bring
consistency.

Now stir in hope,
ingredient three
For when you're
feeling blue.
Compassion next,
that you may see
And help the needy
through.

Forgiving others,
that's the last,
Though surely not
the least;
For if you can't
forgive the past,
You bake without
the yeast!

Richard Duro
Alliance HFH

DESSERTS

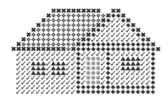

FUDGE FROM ABOVE

YIELD: 64 (1-OUNCE) SERVINGS

18	ounces peanut butter	7	tablespoons baking cocoa
1½	cups margarine	2	(1-pound) packages
3	tablespoons vanilla extract		confectioners' sugar

Combine peanut butter and margarine in saucepan. Cook until blended. Stir in vanilla and baking cocoa. Fold in confectioners' sugar. Pour into waxed-paper-lined 9x13-inch dish. Chill until set.

Approx Per Serving: Cal 143; Prot 2 g; Carbo 16 g; T Fat 8 g; 51% Calories from Fat; Chol 0 mg; Fiber 1 g; Sod 88 mg

Marsha C. Critchfield, Cambria County HFH, Johnstown, PA

TWO-MINUTE FUDGE

YIELD: 16 (1-OUNCE) SERVINGS

1	(1-pound) package confectioners' sugar	⅓	cup evaporated milk
½	cup baking cocoa	1	cup chopped pecans
½	cup margarine	1	teaspoon vanilla extract

Combine confectioners' sugar and baking cocoa in microwave-safe 2-quart bowl. Make well in center of mixture. Place margarine in well; pour evaporated milk around margarine. Microwave on High for 2½ minutes; stir. Add pecans and vanilla and mix well. Pour into buttered 5x9-inch dish. Chill for 30 minutes.

Approx Per Serving: Cal 225; Prot 1 g; Carbo 32 g; T Fat 11 g; 44% Calories from Fat; Chol 2 mg; Fiber 1 g; Sod 73 mg

Louise W. Lawson, Fort Worth Area HFH, Fort Worth, TX

EASY FUDGE

YIELD: 32 (1-OUNCE) SERVINGS

3	cups sugar	½	cup margarine
1¼	cups milk	1½	teaspoons vanilla extract
¾	cup baking cocoa	1	cup chopped pecans

Combine sugar, milk, baking cocoa and margarine in saucepan. Bring to a boil over medium heat. Cook to 234 to 240 degrees on candy thermometer, soft-ball stage. Stir in vanilla. Beat until thickened and mixture loses luster. Stir in pecans. Pour into buttered 8x8-inch dish. Cool slightly. Cut into squares. Let stand until completely cool.

Approx Per Serving: Cal 134; Prot 1 g; Carbo 21 g; T Fat 6 g; 38% Calories from Fat; Chol 1 mg; Fiber 1 g; Sod 38 mg

Kathleen Jones, Somerset-Pulaski County HFH, Somerset, KY

Peanut Butter Cups

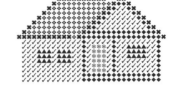

Desserts

1   cup margarine
2⅓ cups confectioners' sugar
1⅓ cups graham cracker
        crumbs
1½ cups peanut butter
2   cups chocolate chips,
        melted

Heat margarine in saucepan until melted. Remove from heat. Stir in next 3 ingredients. Spread in 9x9-inch dish. Chill in freezer for 15 minutes. Spread with chocolate. Let stand until set.

Approx Per Serving: Cal 303; Prot 5 g; Carbo 29 g; T Fat 21 g; 57% Calories from Fat; Chol 0 mg; Fiber 2 g; Sod 208 mg

Don Humason, Westfield HFH, Westfield, MA

Easy Brownies

¾   cup baking cocoa
¾   cup vegetable oil
2   cups sugar
3   eggs
1   teaspoon vanilla extract
1   cup flour
1   cup chopped pecans

Mix baking cocoa and oil in bowl. Stir in sugar, eggs, vanilla, flour and pecans in order listed. Spread in greased 9x13-inch baking pan. Bake at 350 degrees for 40 minutes. Cut into squares when cool.

Approx Per Serving: Cal 194; Prot 2 g; Carbo 23 g; T Fat 11 g; 50% Calories from Fat; Chol 27 mg; Fiber 1 g; Sod 8 mg

Elizabeth Copeland, Satilla HFH, Waycross, GA

Mincemeat Brownies

1   cup sugar
2   eggs
½   cup prepared mincemeat
½   cup butter, softened
1   teaspoon vanilla extract
1½ ounces unsweetened
        chocolate, melted
¾   cup flour
¼   teaspoon salt

Cream sugar and eggs in mixer bowl. Stir in mincemeat, butter, vanilla and chocolate. Add flour and salt, stirring until mixed. Spoon into greased 9x9-inch baking pan. Bake at 350 degrees for 30 minutes. Cut into squares when cool.

Approx Per Serving: Cal 206; Prot 2 g; Carbo 27 g; T Fat 11 g; 46% Calories from Fat; Chol 56 mg; Fiber 1 g; Sod 142 mg

Kathleen R. Walton, HFHI, Americus, GA

DESSERTS

CHOCOLATE CHIP COOKIES

YIELD: *48 SERVINGS*

These cookies are a favorite of First Lady Hillary Clinton.

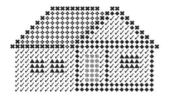

1½	cups flour	½	cup sugar
1	teaspoon salt	1	teaspoon vanilla extract
1	teaspoon baking soda	2	eggs
1	cup vegetable shortening	2	cups rolled oats
1	cup packed light brown sugar	2	cups semisweet chocolate chips

Combine flour, salt and baking soda and mix well. Beat shortening, brown sugar, sugar and vanilla in mixer bowl until creamy. Add eggs, beating until light and fluffy. Add flour mixture and oats gradually, beating until mixed. Stir in chocolate chips. Drop by rounded teaspoonfuls onto greased cookie sheet. Bake at 350 degrees for 8 to 10 minutes or until golden brown. Cool on cookie sheet on wire rack for 2 minutes. Remove to wire rack to cool completely.

Photo by Robert Baker

Approx Per Serving: Cal 124; Prot 2 g; Carbo 16 g; T Fat 7 g; 47% Calories from Fat; Chol 9 mg; Fiber 1 g; Sod 76 mg

Hillary Rodham Clinton, The White House, Washington, DC

CHOCOLATE OATMEAL COOKIES

YIELD: *72 SERVINGS*

1	cup vegetable shortening	2	cups rolled oats
½	cup sugar	1½	cups flour
½	cup packed brown sugar	1	teaspoon baking soda
¼	cup peanut butter	½	teaspoon salt
2	eggs	1	to 2 cups chocolate chips
1	teaspoon vanilla extract	1	cup chopped pecans

Cream shortening, sugar, brown sugar, peanut butter, eggs and vanilla in mixer bowl. Add oats, flour, baking soda and salt and mix well. Stir in chocolate chips and pecans. Drop by teaspoonfuls onto greased cookie sheet. Bake at 375 degrees for 10 minutes. Cool on cookie sheet for 2 minutes. Remove to wire rack to cool completely.

Approx Per Serving: Cal 94; Prot 1 g; Carbo 10 g; T Fat 6 g; 56% Calories from Fat; Chol 6 mg; Fiber 1 g; Sod 39 mg

Janice K. Rinne, San Joaquin HFH, Stockton, CA

CHOCOLATE ROCKS

4	cups flour	1/2	cup margarine
5	tablespoons baking cocoa	1	cup sugar
1 1/4	tablespoons baking powder	2	eggs
5	teaspoons cinnamon	1/2	cup milk
1	teaspoon allspice	1	cup chocolate chips
3/4	teaspoon salt	4	cups confectioners' sugar
1/2	cup vegetable shortening	10	tablespoons milk, heated

Sift flour, baking cocoa, baking powder, cinnamon, allspice and salt together. Beat shortening and margarine in mixer bowl until creamy. Add sugar, beating until light and fluffy. Add eggs 1 at a time, beating well after each addition. Add 1/2 of the flour mixture and 1/4 cup of the milk and mix well. Add remaining flour mixture and remaining milk, beating until blended. Stir in chocolate chips. Shape by teaspoonfuls into balls. Place on nonstick cookie sheet. Bake at 350 degrees for 8 to 10 minutes or until light brown. Roll cookies in mixture of confectioners' sugar and milk. Cool on waxed paper.

Approx Per Serving: Cal 93; Prot 1 g; Carbo 15 g; T Fat 3 g; 32% Calories from Fat; Chol 6 mg; Fiber 1 g; Sod 60 mg

Janet Gummett, Blue Spruce HFH, Evergreen, CO

OATMEAL CRISPS

3	cups quick-cooking oats	1/2	to 3/4 cup shredded coconut
1	cup vegetable shortening		
1	cup sugar	1/2	to 3/4 cup chopped walnuts
1	cup packed light brown sugar	1 1/2	cups flour
2	eggs	1	teaspoon baking soda
1	teaspoon vanilla extract	1/2	teaspoon salt

Spread oats in ungreased 9x13-inch baking pan. Toast at 350 degrees for 10 minutes, stirring every 5 minutes; do not brown. Cool. Beat shortening, sugar and brown sugar in mixer bowl until creamy. Beat in eggs 1 at a time. Stir in vanilla. Add oats and mix well. Stir in coconut and walnuts. Add sifted mixture of flour, baking soda and salt, stirring with wooden spoon just until moistened. Drop by spoonfuls onto greased cookie sheet. Bake at 350 degrees for 10 to 12 minutes or until golden brown. Cool on cookie sheet for 2 minutes. Remove to wire rack to cool completely.

Approx Per Serving: Cal 124; Prot 2 g; Carbo 15 g; T Fat 7 g; 46% Calories from Fat; Chol 9 mg; Fiber 1 g; Sod 57 mg

Margaret "Pat" Walkley, Castile, NY

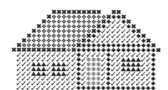

SHORTBREAD COOKIES

YIELD: 36 SERVINGS

This is an old recipe from our cook on the Lawton Plantation located on James Island in South Carolina. Store these cookies safely under lock and key.

2	cups sugar	3	cups flour
1	cup butter	1	cup (or more) chopped
3	eggs		pecans
4	teaspoons vanilla extract		

Beat sugar and butter in mixer bowl until creamy. Add eggs and vanilla and mix well. Stir in flour until blended. Add pecans and mix well. Drop by teaspoonfuls onto nonstick cookie sheet. Bake at 350 to 400 degrees until light brown. Cool on cookie sheet for 2 minutes. Remove to wire rack to cool completely.

Approx Per Serving: Cal 155; Prot 2 g; Carbo 20 g; T Fat 8 g; 45% Calories from Fat; Chol 32 mg; Fiber 0 g; Sod 58 mg

Clyde W. Bresee, Penn-York Valley HFH, Athens, PA

SUGAR COOKIES

YIELD: 24 SERVINGS

2¼	cups flour	½	cup butter, softened
1	teaspoon baking powder	1	egg
½	teaspoon baking soda	1	teaspoon vanilla extract
½	teaspoon salt	⅓	cup sour cream
1	cup sugar		

Mix flour, baking powder, baking soda and salt together. Beat sugar and butter in mixer bowl until creamy. Add egg and vanilla, beating until blended. Add flour mixture alternately with sour cream, beating well after each addition. Chill, covered, for 12 hours. Divide dough into small portions. Roll dough 1 portion at a time on floured pastry sheet; cut with cookie cutter. Arrange on cookie sheet. Bake at 350 degrees for 8 minutes. Cool on cookie sheet for 2 minutes. Remove to wire rack to cool completely. May triple recipe and freeze for future use.

Approx Per Serving: Cal 119; Prot 2 g; Carbo 17 g; T Fat 5 g; 36% Calories from Fat; Chol 21 mg; Fiber 0 g; Sod 135 mg

Sandy Foster, Ponca City Area HFH, Ponca City, OK

MOLASSES SUGAR COOKIES
YIELD: 48 SERVINGS

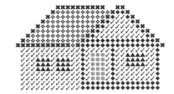

2 cups sugar	2 teaspoons cinnamon
1½ cups melted vegetable shortening, cooled	1 teaspoon ginger
½ cup light molasses	1 teaspoon salt
2 eggs	¼ teaspoon ground cloves
4 cups flour	1 cup sugar
1 tablespoon plus 1 teaspoon baking soda	

Combine 2 cups sugar, shortening and molasses in bowl and mix well. Add eggs and mix well. Stir in mixture of flour, baking soda, cinnamon, ginger, salt and cloves. Shape into 1-inch balls. Roll in 1 cup sugar. Arrange on ungreased cookie sheet. Bake at 375 degrees for 8 to 10 minutes or until light brown. Cool on cookie sheet for 2 minutes. Remove to wire rack to cool completely.

Approx Per Serving: Cal 156; Prot 1 g; Carbo 23 g; T Fat 7 g; 38% Calories from Fat; Chol 9 mg; Fiber 0 g; Sod 154 mg

Marilyn Y. Miller, Sheboygan County HFH, Sheboygan Falls, WI

SNACK MOLASSES COOKIES
YIELD: 36 SERVINGS

1½ cups sifted flour	¼ cup molasses
¾ teaspoon baking soda	1 egg
½ teaspoon salt	½ cup shredded coconut
¾ cup sugar	½ cup chopped pecans
½ cup vegetable shortening	

Sift flour, baking soda and salt together. Beat sugar and shortening in mixer bowl until creamy. Add molasses and egg, beating until blended. Add dry ingredients gradually and mix well. Stir in coconut and pecans. Drop by rounded teaspoonfuls 2 inches apart onto greased cookie sheet. Bake at 375 degrees for 10 minutes. Cool on cookie sheet for 2 minutes. Remove to wire rack to cool completely. May substitute walnuts for pecans.

Approx Per Serving: Cal 85; Prot 1 g; Carbo 10 g; T Fat 5 g; 53% Calories from Fat; Chol 6 mg; Fiber 0 g; Sod 62 mg

Betty Woods, Jefferson County HFH, Mt.Vernon, IL

PEANUT BUTTER COOKIES

YIELD: 24 SERVINGS

1 cup peanut butter
1 cup sugar

1 egg

Combine peanut butter, sugar and egg in bowl and mix well. Drop by teaspoonfuls onto greased cookie sheet. Bake at 375 degrees for 10 to 12 minutes. Cool on cookie sheet for 2 minutes. Remove to wire rack to cool completely.

Approx Per Serving: Cal 98; Prot 3 g; Carbo 11 g; T Fat 6 g; 48% Calories from Fat; Chol 9 mg; Fiber 1 g; Sod 54 mg

Julie Gray, Indianapolis HFH, Indianapolis, IN

SPICE COOKIES

YIELD: 36 SERVINGS

$1/2$ cup buttermilk
1 teaspoon baking soda
1 cup sugar
$1/2$ cup butter
1 egg

$1/2$ cup molasses
3 cups flour
1 teaspoon cinnamon
1 teaspoon ground cloves
1 cup raisins

Combine buttermilk and baking soda in bowl and mix well. Beat sugar and butter in mixer bowl until creamy. Add egg, molasses and buttermilk mixture and mix well. Stir in flour, cinnamon and cloves. Add raisins and mix well. Drop by teaspoonfuls onto buttered cookie sheet. Bake at 375 degrees until light brown. Cool on cookie sheet for 2 minutes. Remove to wire rack to cool completely.

Approx Per Serving: Cal 111; Prot 2 g; Carbo 20 g; T Fat 3 g; 23% Calories from Fat; Chol 13 mg; Fiber 0 g; Sod 69 mg

Emily Diamond, St. Tammany West HFH, Covington, LA

Photograph at right by Robert Baker

LIGHT FARE

If you lend money to one of my people
among you who is needy, do not be like a
moneylender; charge him no interest.

Exodus 22:25

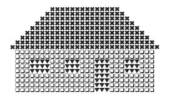

LIGHT FARE

BLACK WHITE BEAN SOUP
YIELD: 6 SERVINGS

1	cup chopped onion	1	(14-ounce) can low-fat chicken broth
1	clove of garlic, minced		
1/3	cup flour	1	(4-ounce) can chopped green chiles
1	teaspoon chili powder		
1/2	teaspoon cumin	2	tablespoons chopped fresh cilantro
2	cups skim milk		
2	(10-ounce) packages frozen white corn		Salt and pepper to taste
		2	tablespoons chopped red bell pepper
1	(16-ounce) can white beans		
1	(16-ounce) can black beans		

Heat saucepan sprayed with nonstick cooking spray over medium-high heat until hot. Add onion and garlic. Cook until tender, stirring constantly. Stir in flour, chili powder and cumin. Stir in skim milk gradually. Mix in corn, undrained white beans, undrained black beans, broth and green chiles. Bring to a boil, stirring constantly; reduce heat. Simmer until thickened, stirring occasionally. Stir in cilantro, salt and pepper. Ladle into soup bowls. Top with red pepper.

Approx Per Serving: Cal 296; Prot 17 g; Carbo 58 g; T Fat 2 g; 4% Calories from Fat; Chol 1 mg; Fiber 11 g; Sod 757 mg

Wanda Kay Dirks, Lincoln County HFH, Sprague, WA

MANHATTAN CLAM CHOWDER
YIELD: 18 SERVINGS

Double or triple this recipe if serving a larger crew.

5	(7-ounce) cans chopped or minced clams	2	cups finely chopped cabbage
1	(28-ounce) can crushed tomatoes	1/2	cup catsup
3	cups water	1	tablespoon chopped fresh parsley, or 1 1/2 teaspoons parsley flakes
2	cups finely chopped potatoes		
2	cups finely chopped onions	1	to 2 teaspoons salt
2	cups finely chopped carrots	1/2	teaspoon thyme
2	cups finely chopped celery	1/4	to 1/2 teaspoon pepper
		1	bay leaf

Combine all ingredients in stockpot and mix well. Bring to a boil, stirring frequently; reduce heat. Simmer over low heat for 1 to 2 hours or until of the desired consistency, stirring occasionally. Discard bay leaf. Ladle into soup bowls. May freeze for future use.

Approx Per Serving: Cal 87; Prot 9 g; Carbo 12 g; T Fat 1 g; 8% Calories from Fat; Chol 20 mg; Fiber 2 g; Sod 495 mg

Dr. Arthur J. Florack, York County HFH, Tega Cay, SC

ONION SOUP

YIELD: 6 SERVINGS

1½	cups dry white wine	2	tablespoons Beau Monde seasoning
3	or 4 medium to large onions, thinly sliced	1	to 3 teaspoons Tabasco sauce
3	beef bouillon cubes		Freshly ground pepper to taste
4	teaspoons minced garlic		
2	(15-ounce) cans fat-free chicken broth	6	slices French bread, toasted
2	cups water	6	slices low-fat Swiss cheese
2	tablespoons sugar		

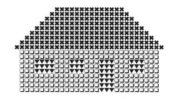

Bring white wine to a boil in 4-quart saucepan. Add onions, bouillon cubes and garlic; reduce heat. Cook, covered, over low heat for 15 to 20 minutes or until onions and garlic are tender. Stir in broth, water, sugar, Beau Monde seasoning, Tabasco sauce and pepper. Simmer for 1 to 3 hours, stirring occasionally; flavor is enhanced if simmered for 3 hours. Arrange 6 ovenproof soup bowls on baking sheet. Ladle soup into bowls. Top each serving with 1 slice of bread and 1 slice of cheese. Broil for 3 minutes or until cheese is light brown and bubbly. Serve immediately.

Approx Per Serving: Cal 236; Prot 13 g; Carbo 32 g; T Fat 2 g; 9% Calories from Fat; Chol 7 mg; Fiber 2 g; Sod 1777 mg

Mary Diane Hanna, Marion County HFH, Lexington, KY

CHICKEN CHILI OVER RICE

YIELD: 4 SERVINGS

2	whole chicken breasts, split	¼	to ⅓ cup salsa
1	(22-ounce) can chili beans	3	cups hot cooked rice
1	onion, chopped		

Rinse chicken. Place in slow cooker. Cook on Medium-High for 3 hours or until tender. Let stand until cool. Chop chicken, discarding skin, bones and broth. Return chicken to slow cooker. Add chili beans, onion and salsa and mix well. Cook on Medium for 1 hour, stirring occasionally. Spoon over hot cooked rice. May omit salsa. May substitute 4 chicken legs or thighs for chicken breasts.

Approx Per Serving: Cal 534; Prot 40 g; Carbo 66 g; T Fat 12 g; 21% Calories from Fat; Chol 100 mg; Fiber 8 g; Sod 973 mg

Cynthia Solomon, West Chester-Mason HFH, West Chester, OH

I wore my Habitat tee shirt to work on a casual dress day. Several people inquired about my interest and involvement and asked how they could become involved.

Cynthia Solomon
West Chester-Mason
HFH

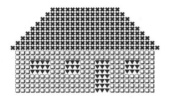

BAKED CHICKEN BREASTS

YIELD: 6 SERVINGS

6	boneless skinless chicken breast halves	2	teaspoons celery salt
2	cups nonfat sour cream	2	teaspoons paprika
1/4	cup lemon juice	1	teaspoon salt
1	tablespoon Worcestershire sauce	1/2	teaspoon pepper
1	tablespoon chopped garlic	1	cup finely crushed bread crumbs

Rinse chicken and pat dry. Cut each chicken breast half into halves. Arrange in single layer in 9x13-inch baking dish. Combine sour cream, lemon juice, Worcestershire sauce, garlic, celery salt, paprika, salt and pepper in bowl and mix well. Spread over chicken. Marinate, covered, in refrigerator for 8 to 10 hours. Drain, reserving marinade. Coat chicken with bread crumbs. Arrange in same baking dish. Spread with reserved marinade. Bake at 350 degrees for 45 minutes or until cooked through.

Approx Per Serving: Cal 298; Prot 34 g; Carbo 28 g; T Fat 4 g; 13% Calories from Fat; Chol 73 mg; Fiber 1 g; Sod 1150 mg

Ermal Byam, Halifax HFH, Daytona Beach, FL

OVEN-FRIED CHICKEN

YIELD: 6 SERVINGS

3	whole medium chicken breasts, split, skinned	1/2	cup fine dry bread crumbs
3	tablespoons skim milk	1	teaspoon basil, crushed
			Salt and pepper to taste

Rinse chicken and pat dry. Dip in skim milk; coat with mixture of bread crumbs and basil. Arrange in single layer in 9x13-inch baking pan; do not allow pieces to touch. Sprinkle with salt and pepper. Bake at 375 degrees for 45 minutes or until cooked through. May substitute oregano or Italian seasoning for basil

Approx Per Serving: Cal 177; Prot 28 g; Carbo 6 g; T Fat 4 g; 19% Calories from Fat; Chol 73 mg; Fiber 0 g; Sod 139 mg

Loretta Risser, Lancaster Area HFH, Leola, PA

EGGPLANT PEPPER

YIELD: *3 SERVINGS*

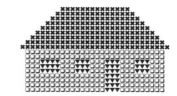

Eggplant is inexpensive, low in calories and filling, with a mild flavor that blends well with other foods. Pick eggplant that are unblemished and firm but not hard. The entire eggplant can be used...peeling is optional. If you are concerned that the eggplant is bitter, salt slices before cutting into cubes, drain for 30 minutes, rinse and pat dry. This dish is quick to make, low in fat and highly nutritious. Serve as a main entrée or as a side dish. All of the ingredient measurements are estimates and can be adjusted according to personal taste and size of crowd serving.

1	large eggplant, peeled, sliced
1	large onion, chopped
1	tablespoon olive oil
8	ounces green beans, snapped into 2-inch pieces
1	small to medium green bell pepper, chopped
1	jalapeño, finely chopped
1	cup tomato sauce
1	(7- or 15-ounce) can garbanzo beans
2	to 3 teaspoons oregano, or 1 to 1½ tablespoons chopped fresh oregano
½	teaspoon salt
	Freshly ground pepper to taste
	Hot pepper sauce to taste
¼	cup grated Parmesan cheese

Photo by Robert Baker

Cut eggplant into 1-inch pieces. Sauté eggplant and onion in olive oil in skillet for 10 minutes or until eggplant is light brown and tender. Stir in green beans, green pepper and jalapeño. Sauté for 5 to 10 minutes longer or until green beans and green pepper are tender-crisp. Add tomato sauce, garbanzo beans and oregano and mix well. Cook until heated through, stirring frequently. Season with salt, liberal amounts of pepper and hot pepper sauce. Sprinkle with cheese. May omit jalapeño, hot pepper sauce and Parmesan cheese. May substitute spaghetti sauce or a mixture of ½ cup tomato or spaghetti sauce and 2 chopped tomatoes for 1 cup tomato sauce.

Approx Per Serving: Cal 390; Prot 16 g; Carbo 66 g; T Fat 10 g; 21% Calories from Fat; Chol 7 mg; Fiber 17 g; Sod 1442 mg

Alice Alexander, Loudoun HFH, Leesburg, VA

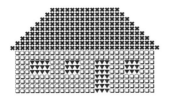

BAKED APPLES

YIELD: 7 SERVINGS

7	McIntosh apples, peeled	1	teaspoon cinnamon
3	teaspoons artificial sweetener	1	teaspoon cornstarch
		½	cup orange juice

Cut apples into thick slices. Arrange in microwave-safe 8x12-inch dish. Sprinkle with mixture of artificial sweetener, cinnamon and cornstarch. Pour orange juice over top. Microwave on High for 11 minutes or until apples are tender; stir. Serve warm or cold. May substitute apple juice for orange juice.

Approx Per Serving: Cal 83; Prot 0 g; Carbo 21 g; T Fat <1 g; 4% Calories from Fat; Chol 0 mg; Fiber 2 g; Sod 0 mg

Sara Janice Shaffer, Lehigh Valley HFH, Allentown, PA

APPLE PANCAKES

YIELD: 12 SERVINGS

2	cups pancake mix	1	cup chopped peeled apple
1	cup unsweetened applesauce	1	teaspoon cinnamon
1	cup skim milk	⅛	teaspoon nutmeg
			Yogurt Sauce

Combine pancake mix, applesauce, skim milk, apple, cinnamon and nutmeg in bowl and mix well. Heat griddle sprayed with nonstick cooking spray over medium heat until hot. Pour 2 tablespoons batter onto griddle. Bake until bubbles appear on surface and underside is golden brown. Turn pancake over. Bake until golden brown. Repeat process with remaining batter. Serve with Yogurt Sauce. May substitute any fruit for apple.

Approx Per Serving: Cal 163; Prot 6 g; Carbo 31 g; T Fat 2 g; 11% Calories from Fat; Chol 8 mg; Fiber 1 g; Sod 360 mg

YOGURT SAUCE

YIELD: 12 SERVINGS

2	cups vanilla or plain low-fat yogurt	1	cup fresh, frozen or canned blueberries
	Cinnamon to taste		

Combine yogurt, cinnamon and blueberries in bowl and mix gently. May substitute any fruit for blueberries.

Approx Per Serving: Cal 42; Prot 2 g; Carbo 7 g; T Fat 1 g; 12% Calories from Fat; Chol 2 mg; Fiber 0 g; Sod 28 mg

Henrietta Shader, Washington County HFH, McMurray, PA

FULL OF BEANS

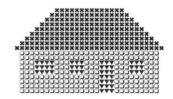

1	onion, chopped
2	large cloves of garlic, minced
2	tablespoons vegetable oil
3	tablespoons flour
1	(14-ounce) can stewed tomatoes
2	tablespoons tomato purée
1	teaspoon chili powder
1	(15-ounce) can kidney beans, rinsed, drained
1	(15-ounce) can whole kernel corn, rinsed, drained
1	(16-ounce) can beef stock
1	(15-ounce) can garbanzo beans, rinsed, drained
2	zucchini, sliced
1/2	green bell pepper, chopped
1	teaspoon salt
1	teaspoon pepper

Sauté onion and garlic in oil in saucepan until tender. Stir in flour. Cook for 1 minute, stirring constantly. Add undrained tomatoes, tomato purée and chili powder and mix well. Stir in kidney beans, corn, stock, garbanzo beans, zucchini, green pepper and salt. Simmer for 20 minutes, stirring occasionally. Stir in pepper. Serve with hot cooked rice and crusty French bread. Add mixture of cornstarch and water for thicker consistency. May substitute vegetable stock for beef stock and omit green pepper.

Approx Per Serving: Cal 313; Prot 14 g; Carbo 53 g; T Fat 7 g; 20% Calories from Fat; Chol 2 mg; Fiber 14 g; Sod 1482 mg

Christine Sayell, HFHI, Americus, GA

RICE AND CORN CASSEROLE

2	cups frozen corn, thawed
2	cups cooked brown rice
2	large tomatoes, chopped
1/3	cup chopped green bell pepper
1/3	cup chopped onion
1/4	cup chopped fresh cilantro
1	(4-ounce) can chopped black olives, drained
1	teaspoon curry powder
3	tablespoons Dijon mustard
3	tablespoons balsamic vinegar
3	tablespoons honey

Combine corn, brown rice, tomatoes, green pepper, onion, cilantro, black olives and curry powder in bowl and mix gently. Combine Dijon mustard, balsamic vinegar and honey in bowl and mix well. Pour over corn mixture, tossing to mix. Spoon into 9x12-inch baking pan. Bake at moderate temperature just until heated through. May serve cold. May omit curry powder.

Approx Per Serving: Cal 123; Prot 3 g; Carbo 26 g; T Fat 2 g; 14% Calories from Fat; Chol 0 mg; Fiber 2 g; Sod 221 mg

Cora Cockrum, Foothills HFH, Penrym, CA

One thing have I desired of the LORD, that will I seek after; that I may dwell in the house of the LORD all the days of my life, to behold the beauty of the LORD, and to inquire in his temple.

Psalms 27:4

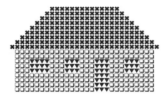

$\mathcal{L}$IGHT FARE

Habitat not only builds houses but changes lives, as I found out while working in our young affiliate. We had just completed framing in a house when a young man named Michael noticed it. He was experienced in construction, especially roofing. While he was in the neighborhood working on another project, he noticed the half-finished house, which was a Habitat project, and decided to go over and talk to the people working on it. He had lots of questions and finally said that he wanted to help because he had been given help in the past, and now he was ready to give back to the

(Continued)

LOW-CALORIE ITALIAN ZUCCHINI   YIELD: 6 SERVINGS

1½	medium zucchini, cut into ½-inch slices	1	clove of garlic, minced
2	cups chopped peeled fresh tomatoes	½	teaspoon salt
½	cup minced onion	¼	teaspoon pepper
1	tablespoon chopped fresh parsley	⅛	teaspoon thyme
		⅛	teaspoon basil
		1	bay leaf

Combine zucchini, tomatoes, onion, parsley, garlic, salt, pepper, thyme, basil and bay leaf in saucepan and mix gently. Simmer until zucchini and onion are tender, stirring occasionally. Discard bay leaf.

Approx Per Serving: Cal 28; Prot 1 g; Carbo 6 g; T Fat <1 g; 9% Calories from Fat; Chop 0 mg; Fiber 2 g; Sod 186 mg

Carolyn McCombs, St. Joseph HFH, St. Joseph, MO

GRILLED ZUCCHINI WITH DILL   YIELD: 8 SERVINGS

4	medium zucchini	3	tablespoons olive oil
	Salt to taste		Dillweed to taste

Cut ends from zucchini; cut lengthwise into halves. Combine zucchini and salt with enough water to cover in saucepan. Boil for 2 minutes; drain. Brush cut side with olive oil; sprinkle with dillweed. Grill over hot coals for 6 minutes or until tender.

Approx Per Serving: Cal 63; Prot 2 g; Carbo 4 g; T Fat 5 g; 69% Calories from Fat; Chol 0 mg; Fiber 2 g; Sod 4 mg

Terri Burnett, Monroe County HFH, E. Stroudsburg, PA

CHILI SALSA   YIELD: 10 SERVINGS

2	cups finely chopped tomatoes	¼	cup finely chopped fresh parsley
⅓	cup finely chopped green onions	1	to 2 tablespoons chopped seeded chiles
1	clove of garlic, minced	¼	teaspoon oregano

Combine tomatoes, green onions, garlic, parsley, chiles and oregano in bowl and mix well. Chill, covered, for several hours.

Approx Per Serving: Cal 10; Prot 0 g; Carbo 2 g; T Fat <1 g; 10% Calories from Fat; Chol 0 mg; Fiber 1 g; Sod 5 mg

Jane S. Oleksak, Cambria County HFH, Johnstown, PA

FAT-FREE CHOCOLATE TRIFLE

YIELD: 10 SERVINGS

2	envelopes whipped topping mix	1	(10-ounce) package frozen raspberries in syrup, thawed
2¾	cups skim milk		
1	teaspoon vanilla extract	1	fat-free chocolate loaf cake, cubed
2	(4-ounce) packages chocolate instant pudding mix	4	cups nonfat whipped topping
1	(16-ounce) package frozen sliced peaches, thawed		

Beat topping mix, 1 cup of the skim milk and vanilla in mixer bowl for 6 minutes, scraping bowl occasionally. Add remaining skim milk and pudding mix. Beat at low speed until blended. Beat at high speed for 2 minutes, scraping bowl occasionally. Combine undrained peaches and undrained raspberries in bowl and mix gently. Alternate layers of cake cubes, peach mixture and pudding mixture in trifle bowl until all ingredients are used. Spread with whipped topping. Chill for 4 to 10 hours. Spoon into bowls. May top with additional whipped topping. For Strawberry Shortcake Trifle, substitute angel food cake for chocolate cake, sweetened fresh or frozen strawberries for peaches and raspberries and vanilla pudding mix for chocolate pudding mix.

Approx Per Serving: Cal 404; Prot 6 g; Carbo 79 g; T Fat 7 g; 16% Calories from Fat; Chol 1 mg; Fiber 3 g; Sod 534 mg

Suzy Dobie, Greater Cleveland HFH, Cleveland, OH

CRANBERRY DESSERT

YIELD: 15 SERVINGS

2	cups cranberry juice cocktail	1½	cups Cranberry Relish (page 198)
2	(3-ounce) packages cranberry or raspberry gelatin	1	(10-ounce) angel food cake, torn
2	cups cranberry juice cocktail, chilled	1	cup nonfat whipped topping

Heat 2 cups cranberry juice cocktail in saucepan until hot. Add gelatin, stirring until dissolved. Stir in 2 cups chilled cranberry juice cocktail. Chill until partially set. Beat gelatin mixture in mixer bowl at high speed until light and fluffy. Fold in Cranberry Relish and angel food cake. Pour into 9x13-inch dish; press lightly. Chill for 2 hours or until set. Serve with whipped topping.

Approx Per Serving: Cal 182; Prot 2 g; Carbo 44 g; T Fat <1 g; 1% Calories from Fat; Chol 0 mg; Fiber 1 g; Sod 172 mg

Marjorie L.C. Burgan, Missoula HFH, Missoula, MT

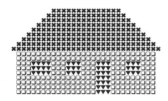

LIGHT FARE

CRANBERRY RELISH

YIELD: 16 (1/4-CUP) SERVINGS

1   (12-ounce) package
       cranberries
2   small unpeeled red apples,
       cored

1¾ cups sugar
1   (8-ounce) can crushed
       pineapple

Process cranberries and apples in food processor until finely chopped. Combine cranberry mixture, sugar and undrained pineapple in glass bowl and mix well. Chill, covered, for 24 hours. May store in refrigerator for 1 to 2 months or freeze for future use.

Approx Per Serving: Cal 114; Prot 0 g; Carbo 29 g; T Fat 0 g; 0% Calories from Fat; Chol 0 mg; Fiber 1 g; Sod 1 mg

Marjorie L.C. Burgan, Missoula HFH, Missoula, MT

FRUIT SORBET

YIELD: 5 SERVINGS

2   cups fresh or frozen
       strawberries
¾   cup unsweetened pineapple
       juice

1   cup orange juice
1   banana, peeled, frozen
5   ice cubes

Process all ingredients in blender on High for 1 minute or until thick and icy. Spoon into festive glassware and serve with spoons.

Approx Per Serving: Cal 82; Prot 1 g; Carbo 20 g; T Fat <1 g; 5% Calories from Fat; Chol 0 mg; Fiber 1 g; Sod 2 mg

Deb Edson, South Atlantic Regional Center, Easley, SC

PINEAPPLE DELIGHT

YIELD: 8 SERVINGS

2   small packages sugar-free
       vanilla instant pudding mix
1⅔ cups unsweetened
       pineapple juice
1   (20-ounce) can juice-pack
       crushed pineapple

8   ounces light whipped
       topping
1   (10-ounce) angel food
       cake, torn

Mix pudding mix and pineapple juice in bowl. Stir in undrained pineapple. Fold in whipped topping. Layer cake and pineapple mixture ½ at a time in glass bowl. Chill, covered, for 8 to 10 hours.

Approx Per Serving: Cal 246; Prot 3 g; Carbo 49 g; T Fat 4 g; 15% Calories from Fat; Chol 0 mg; Fiber 1 g; Sod 400 mg

Claudia B. Holcombe, South Atlantic Regional Center, Easley, SC

Healthy Cake

Yield: 15 servings

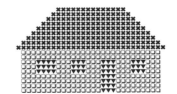

1	(2-layer) package light white cake mix	8	ounces light whipped topping
2½	cups diet lemon-lime soda	1	small package sugar-free pistachio instant pudding mix
1	small package sugar-free pistachio instant pudding mix	1	cup diet lemon-lime soda
3	egg whites		

Combine cake mix, 2½ cups diet soda, 1 package pudding mix and egg whites in bowl and mix well. Spoon into 9x13-inch cake pan sprayed with nonstick cooking spray. Bake at 350 degrees for 30 to 35 minutes or until cake tests done. Let stand until cool. Combine whipped topping, pudding mix and 1 cup diet soda in bowl and mix gently. Spread over cake.

Approx Per Serving: Cal 199; Prot 2 g; Carbo 35 g; T Fat 4 g; 21% Calories from Fat; Chol 0 mg; Fiber 1 g; Sod 437 mg

Jean Sommer, Michigan City, Indiana HFH, Michigan City, IN

Sour Cream Pound Cake

Yield: 16 servings

2¼	cups flour	1	cup nonfat sour cream
2	cups sugar	1	cup melted light margarine
1	(3-ounce) package any flavor gelatin	3	eggs
1	teaspoon baking powder	1	teaspoon vanilla extract
½	teaspoon baking soda	1	cup confectioners' sugar
½	teaspoon light salt	2	to 3 tablespoons lemon juice

Combine flour, sugar, gelatin, baking powder, baking soda and light salt in bowl and mix well. Stir in sour cream, margarine, eggs and vanilla. Spoon into greased bundt pan. Bake at 325 degrees for 60 to 70 minutes or until cake tests done. Cool in pan on wire rack for 30 minutes. Invert onto cake plate. Drizzle with mixture of confectioners' sugar and lemon juice. May substitute lime juice or orange juice for lemon juice depending on flavor of gelatin used. May omit gelatin, but use lemon juice in icing. May use egg substitute.

Approx Per Serving: Cal 306; Prot 4 g; Carbo 54 g; T Fat 8 g; 25% Calories from Fat; Chol 40 mg; Fiber 1 g; Sod 213 mg

Christy Strickland, Denton HFH, Denton, TX

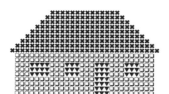

ROCKY ROAD BROWNIES

YIELD: 18 SERVINGS

4	egg whites	1/2	teaspoon salt
1/2	cup sugar	1/2	teaspoon baking powder
1	tablespoon vanilla extract	1/2	cup flour
1/2	cup baking cocoa	1	cup marshmallow creme

Add egg whites, sugar, vanilla, baking cocoa, salt, baking powder and flour in order listed to mixer bowl, beating well after each addition. Add marshmallow creme, stirring just until brown and white swirls are created. Spoon into 7x11-inch or 9x13-inch baking pan sprayed with nonstick cooking spray. Bake at 325 degrees for 18 minutes.

Approx Per Serving: Cal 98; Prot 2 g; Carbo 23 g; T Fat <1 g; 3% Calories from Fat; Chol 0 mg; Fiber 1 g; Sod 93 mg

Millie M. Rinker, Lincoln County HFH, Reardan, WA

LOW-FAT BROWNIE COOKIES

YIELD: 24 SERVINGS

2	cups reduced-fat semisweet chocolate chips	2	teaspoons margarine
		1	cup flour
1	(14-ounce) can low-fat sweetened condensed milk		

Photo by John Curry

Combine chocolate chips, condensed milk and margarine in microwave-safe dish. Microwave for 5 to 8 minutes or until blended, stirring every 2 minutes. Stir in flour. Drop by teaspoonfuls onto nonstick cookie sheet. Bake at 350 degrees for 5 to 8 minutes. Cool on cookie sheet for 2 minutes. Remove to wire rack to cool completely. May add chopped nuts.

Approx Per Serving: Cal 71; Prot 2 g; Carbo 14 g; T Fat 1 g; 13% Calories from Fat; Chol 3 mg; Fiber 0 g; Sod 20 mg

Joanna and Emily Branson, Habitat Southwest, Waco, TX

SALT SUBSTITUTES

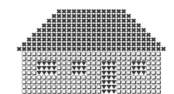

SPICE BLEND I

YIELD: 16 (1-TEASPOON) SERVINGS

2	tablespoons savory, crushed	1¼	teaspoons ground white pepper
1	tablespoon dry mustard		
2½	teaspoons onion powder	1¼	teaspoons cumin
1¾	teaspoons curry powder	½	teaspoon garlic powder

Mix all ingredients in bowl. Spoon into jar with tightfitting lid. Add a few grains of raw rice to mixture to prevent caking.

Approx Per Serving: Cal 8; Prot 0 g; Carbo 1 g; T Fat <1 g; 30% Calories from Fat; Chol 0 mg; Fiber 0 g; Sod 1 mg

SPICE BLEND II

YIELD: 11 (1-TEASPOON) SERVINGS

2	tablespoons dillweed or basil	1	teaspoon celery seeds
2	tablespoons onion powder	¼	teaspoon dried grated lemon peel
1	teaspoon oregano, crushed	¹⁄₁₆	teaspoon ground pepper

Mix all ingredients in bowl. Spoon into jar with tightfitting lid. Add a few grains of raw rice to mixture to prevent caking.

Approx Per Serving: Cal 7; Prot 0 g; Carbo 1 g; T Fat <1 g; 11% Calories from Fat; Chol 0 mg; Fiber 0 g; Sod 2 mg

SPICE BLEND III

YIELD: 24 (1-TEASPOON) SERVINGS

3	tablespoons each parsley flakes, marjoram, basil and thyme	4½	teaspoons chives
		2½	teaspoons each rosemary, paprika and onion powder

Mix all ingredients in bowl. Spoon into jar with tightfitting lid. Add a few grains of raw rice to mixture to prevent caking.

Approx Per Serving: Cal 5; Prot 0 g; Carbo 1 g; T Fat <1 g; 17% Calories from Fat; Chol 0 mg; Fiber 0 g; Sod 1 mg

Henrietta Shader, Washington County HFH, McMurray, PA

INDEX

ORDER FORM Habitat for Humanity's *Partners in the Kitchen* Cookbooks

Please send me _____ copies of **From Our House To Yours**.
  _____ $12.95 each (5 or fewer)   (Item #1410)
  _____ $10.95 each (6 or more – up to a case)
  _____ $6.50 per book by case (24 per case)

Please send me _____ copies of **Home Sweet Habitat**.
  _____ $12.95 each (5 or fewer)   (Item #1414)
  _____ $10.95 each (6 or more – up to a case)
  _____ $6.50 per book by case (18 per case)

Please send me _____ copies of **Simple, Decent Cooking**.
  _____ $12.95 each (5 or fewer)   (Item #1442)
  _____ $10.95 each (6 or more – up to a case)
  _____ $6.50 per book by case (24 per case)

Subtotal $ _____
Shipping/Handling $ _____
Total Amount $ _____

Shipping & Handling (USA Only)	
Under $10.00	$2.00
$10.00–$19.99	$3.00
$20.00–$49.99	$5.00
$50.00–$99.99	$7.00
$100 and over	$11.00

Method of payment:
☐ Check   ☐ Money Order   ☐ VISA   ☐ MasterCard

Account # _____

Expires _____ / _____   Phone Number (   )

Signature _____

Bill order to:

Name _____

Affiliate Name _____

Address _____

City _____

State _____   Zip _____

Ship order to:

Name _____

Street Address _____

City _____

State _____   Zip _____

Mail form to: *Order Entry, Habitat for Humanity International*
121 Habitat Street
Americus, GA 31709-3498

Or call *1-800-422-5914* **or fax** *912-924-5730*

ORDER FORM Habitat for Humanity's *Partners in the Kitchen* Cookbooks

Please send me _____ copies of **From Our House To Yours**.
  _____ $12.95 each (5 or fewer)   (Item #1410)
  _____ $10.95 each (6 or more – up to a case)
  _____ $6.50 per book by case (24 per case)

Please send me _____ copies of **Home Sweet Habitat**.
  _____ $12.95 each (5 or fewer)   (Item #1414)
  _____ $10.95 each (6 or more – up to a case)
  _____ $6.50 per book by case (18 per case)

Please send me _____ copies of **Simple, Decent Cooking**.
  _____ $12.95 each (5 or fewer)   (Item #1442)
  _____ $10.95 each (6 or more – up to a case)
  _____ $6.50 per book by case (24 per case)

Subtotal $ _____
Shipping/Handling $ _____
Total Amount $ _____

Shipping & Handling (USA Only)	
Under $10.00	$2.00
$10.00–$19.99	$3.00
$20.00–$49.99	$5.00
$50.00–$99.99	$7.00
$100 and over	$11.00

Method of payment:
☐ Check   ☐ Money Order   ☐ VISA   ☐ MasterCard

Account # _____

Expires _____ / _____   Phone Number (   )

Signature _____

Bill order to:

Name _____

Affiliate Name _____

Address _____

City _____

State _____   Zip _____

Ship order to:

Name _____

Street Address _____

City _____

State _____   Zip _____

Mail form to: *Order Entry, Habitat for Humanity International*
121 Habitat Street
Americus, GA 31709-3498

Or call *1-800-422-5914* **or fax** *912-924-5730*